HOW SMART IS YOUR BABY?

HOW SMART IS YOUR BABY?

DEVELOP AND NURTURE YOUR NEWBORN'S FULL POTENTIAL

GLENN DOMAN
JANET DOMAN

SQUAREONE
PUBLISHERS

The information and advice contained in this book are based upon the research and the personal and professional experiences of the authors. They are not intended as a substitute for consulting with a health care professional. The publisher and authors are not responsible for any adverse effects or consequences resulting from the use of any of the suggestions, preparations, or procedures discussed in this book. All matters pertaining to the physical health of you or your child should be supervised by a health care professional. It is advisable to secure more than one opinion in considering any course of treatment or other healthcare related decisions.

Editor: Janet Gauger • Cover Designer: Jeannie Tudor • Typesetter: Gary A. Rosenberg

Cover photography: Sherman Hines • Photography: Alicia Ahumada, Sherman Hines, Jim Kaliss, Kerper Studio, Inc. • Artwork: Jim Kaliss

Square One Publishers
115 Herricks Road • Garden City Park, NY 11040
(516) 535-2010 • (877) 900-BOOK • www.squareonepublishers.com

Library of Congress Cataloging-in-Publication Data

Doman, Glenn J.
   How smart is your baby? : develop and nurture your newborn's full potential /
Glenn Doman, Janet Doman.
     p. cm.
   Includes bibliographical references and index.
   ISBN 0-7570-0194-7 — ISBN 0-7570-0195-5
  1. Infants—Development. 2. Infants—Intelligence levels. 3. Cognition in infants.
4. Child rearing. 5. Parent and infant. I. Doman, Janet. II. Title.

HQ774.D65   2005
649'.122—dc22

                                    2005026764

The Institutes for the Achievement of Human Potential, The Institutes, Dot Cards, Bit of Intelligence, What To Do About Your Brain-Injured Child, How To Multiply Your Baby's Intelligence, The Gentle Revolution, Better Baby, and the *"Boy on Hand"* logo are registered trademarks of The Institutes for the Achievement of Human Potential and Registered in the U.S. Patent and Trademark Office.

How To Teach Your Baby To Read, How To Teach Your Baby Math, How To Give Your Baby Encyclopedic Knowledge, How To Teach Your Baby To Be Physically Superb, the Developmental Profile, and *IAHP* are trademarks of The Institutes for the Achievement of Human Potential.

Glenn Doman is a registered trademark and service mark of Glenn Doman (Registered in the U.S. Patent and Trademark Office) and is used with his permission.

Printed in Singapore

10   9   8   7   6   5   4   3   2   1

Contents

For my wife, Katie Massingham Doman,
who has lovingly taught thousands of mothers
the world over how to teach their babies —
and will continue to do so, through this book,
for as long as there are mothers who want to teach
and babies who want to learn.

There are no chauvinists at The Institutes, either male or female. We love and respect mothers and fathers, baby boys and baby girls.

To solve the maddening problem of referring to all human beings as "grown-up male persons" or "tiny female persons," we have referred most often throughout this text to all parents as mothers, and to all children as boys.

Seems fair.

Acknowledgments

This book has been many years in the making. It is the product of the search and discovery of many courageous, thoughtful, and determined people over the past half-century. Many of these people are still hard at work today; some are here no longer. Some have made lasting and gigantic contributions; others may have offered a critical insight at the perfect moment.

First we must acknowledge a host of mothers who were keen observers of their babies and who knew that babies are much, much smarter than we were raised to think they are. Their certainty and their persistence helped us to keep climbing higher and looking further. Their insights were our inspiration and their frustrations spurred us on.

Secondly, a host of babies, both brain-injured and well, who patiently helped us to learn who they really were and who forgave us our mistakes along the way. We especially thank Maria, Olivia, Isolda, and Caleb for their patience and their sparkle.

The great ones whose own love of learning made them superb teachers:

Temple Fay, a dean of neurosurgeons, who had a monumental curiosity and a unique ability to question whether accepted "truths" were true or not, and who first set us on fire.

Shinichi Suzuki, one of the greatest teachers of all time, who not only loved mothers and babies but, what is equally important, he respected them. His contribution is beyond measure or description.

William Johntz, the founder of Project SEED, who took Socratic teaching and transformed it into the more civilized and elegant and effective Discovery Teaching. He did for the teaching of mathematics what Dr. Suzuki did for the teaching of music, and he did it equally well.

The pioneers of Child Brain Development:

Katie Doman, who began this adventure by teaching mothers of brain-injured children and proving that brain-injured children are highly intelligent, frequently brighter than their well peers.

Douglas and Rosalind Doman, who are really co-authors of this book. Every word on mobility is theirs. They know more about babies and mobility development than anyone on earth. Also, the staff members of The Institute for the Achievement of Physical Excellence: Leia Coelho Reilly, Rumiko Ion Doman, Jennifer Myers Canepa, Nati Tenacio Myers, and Rogelio Marty.

Susan Aisen, one of the editors of this book, whose knowledge of mothers and babies and The Institutes Developmental Profile has helped make this book a reality. Miki Nakayachi, whose insights on language and communication in babies have influenced us greatly. Teruki Uemura, a superb evaluator, who has taught a generation of parents and staff how to evaluate their babies. Also, the staff members of The Institute for the Achievement of Intellectual Excellence: Olivia Fernandes Pelligra, Kathy Myers, Yoshiko Kumagai, Mitsue Noguchi, Eliane Hollanda, and Susanna Horn.

Ann Ball and the entire staff of The Institute for the Achievement of Physiological Excellence, whose knowledge and experience in physiology and especially the development of respiration and nutrition has been vital to the well-being of our babies: our medical director Dr. Coralee Thompson, Dr. Leland Green, Dr. Ernesto Vasquez, Dr. Li Wang, Yukie Kamino, and Dawn Price.

The board of directors of The Institutes for the Achievement of Human Potential: Dr. Ralph Pelligra, Dr. Roselise Wilkinson, Dr. Richard Klich, Stewart Graham, and Philip Bond, in addition to the members named elsewhere.

Dr. Mihai Dimancescu, outstanding neurosurgeon, father, and board member, who has spent his life making certain that coma arousal is the order of the day.

Dr. Denise Malkowicz, highly skilled neurologist and experienced mother, who did a careful critique of the book and initially alarmed us by not changing a word. We are grateful for the additional information she provided.

Sherman Hines, world-famous photographer, father, and board member, who has devoted a significant part of his life to photographing the mothers, fathers, and children of The Institutes. His beautiful images will endure not only on these pages but in our hearts.

This book had a prolonged labor before it was delivered. Those who helped make it happen cannot be thanked enough. The first editor of the book, J. Michael Armentrout, who spent many hours getting the first manuscript into shape. The primary editor, Janet Gauger, who has meticulously poured over the book so many times that she can probably recite it. Donald Barnhouse, superb teacher and equally superb writer, who edited the book and kindly made many invaluable suggestions. We are very grateful for the illustrations done by our artist, Jim Kaliss, whose legendary patience and kind-heartedness must have been stretched to the limit by our requests.

Our assistants—Nest Holvey, Cathy Ruhling, and Tammy Cadden—who helped by keeping us organized and holding down the fort so well that we could find the time to write, edit, and rewrite the book.

Our administrator, Linda Maletta, and our director of finance, Robert Derr, who do their jobs so well that we could steal the time needed to complete the book. This is no small accomplishment for a small non-profit organization.

Our publisher, Rudy Shur, president of Square One Publishers, who loves books and makes sure that venerable and important works stay in print, so that each new mother has the opportunity to teach her baby.

Foreword

Children are the greatest gift that we will ever receive. The world over, we cherish our children. Mothers have performed heroic acts and displayed incredible physical strength to protect their children from physical harm. Universally, parents want their children to accomplish more in life than they ever accomplished.

The suffering of children evokes greater emotion in each and every one of us than any other of mankind's misfortunes.

From the earliest days of humankind, parents have taught their children the skills that they know will help them become better hunters of food and better in turn at nurturing and protecting their children.

The battle from the beginning has always been for the survival of the fittest. In prehistoric times that meant having the physical fitness to run fast and the strength to carry heavy loads; it also required the skills to build shelter and to find food, and the ability to fend off animal or other human predators.

In the overpopulated, rapidly changing, highly technological world of the twenty-first century, survival of the fittest demands that each individual be physically fit, have a sound physiological constitution, and develop the intellectual and emotional capacity to succeed in an economically, geopolitically, and biochemically threatening environment. If we can give our children a solid educational foundation today, they will become the leaders of a better and safer world tomorrow.

How to best prepare our children to survive and to excel in the modern world has been the subject of scores of volumes of writings by educators, pediatricians, politicians, child psychologists, and psychiatrists. Notably, the list of well-meaning advisors and authors does not include "mothers"!

The expectations upon reading erudite proclamations about the right way to educate your child usually start with the child as school age or kindergarten age, arbitrarily set at about five years old. Any exploration of what to do with the child before that time tends to deal with "what kind of diapers to put on your child" or "for how long you should breastfeed your baby" or "what store-bought prepared formulas give your baby the best nutrition"!

The developmental strides of the newborn from birth through the first years of childhood were first described in detail by Dr. Arnold Gesell, cited in Chapter 2. His work led to the widespread use of the "time-clock" notion of *developmental readiness for certain activities.* The authors of this book underscore the fallacies and the pitfalls of the "time-clock" developmental timeline. If the notion were true, then why are some children reading well before they even start school, and why are some children speaking in full sentences or expressing themselves fluently in more than one language before the time-clock says that they should be? Why do babies enjoy listening to Mozart just as much as they do to "Twinkle, Twinkle, Little Star" and why do they take in stories of volcanic eruptions and of the movement of earth's tectal plates as easily as they take in Big Bird's adventures on "Sesame Street"?

In a comprehensive and exhaustive study of thousands of babies in all kinds of cultures and societies, and through a half-century of experience in their Institutes, the authors have derived a compelling story of why babies soak up information like sponges, and how they develop the way they do. The authors then proceed to explain how to take advantage of the newborn's remarkable abilities to begin teaching your baby from birth onward in a loving and enjoyable setting. Teaching your baby when he or she is the most receptive to learning, able to acquire knowledge without effort, and enjoying every moment of learning gives your baby the very best opportunity to develop the physiological constitution, the fitness, and the intellectual skills to excel in our highly complex world. Never again in life will your baby's brain have the learning capacity that it enjoys in its first three years after birth.

—Mihai Dimancescu, M.D.

Introduction

The majestic organ that is the brain starts developing in utero. Although learning continues throughout life, there is a special window of opportunity for permanent brain growth and special learning that occurs in the first year of life.

The newborn period, or first few weeks, is a remarkable time and incredible things are occurring. This is not just a passive beginning; it is the explosive start to learning and brain growth.

During the first year the baby's amazing growth and learning continues. The baby's brain is rapidly growing, which is reflected in the astonishing changes in head circumference.

This period is vitally important for brain development. Doctors, scientists, and educators now acknowledge that the first several years of life is a critical time for the acquisition of skills—and that appropriate stimulation and experience is critical to optimizing a child's growth and development.

These early years are extremely important. It is now recognized that the sooner the baby receives sensory stimulation and opportunity for mobility and language expression, the more likely that brain growth, development, and skills will be optimized.

It is important to understand how this occurs in order to maximize your understanding of the programs in this book. The baby in utero is creating billions and billions of brain cells prior to birth. Those brain cells only await *stimulation* to create networks of function that will allow the child to see, hear, feel, taste, and smell, and the *experience* that develops mobility, language, and manual ability.

The normal newborn will have some basic functions at birth, but must incorporate sensory stimulation and motor experience in order to grow or enhance these functions and learn or make associations. When an object is perceived by the five sensory pathways and gains meaning for the baby, a type of learning has taken place.

The newborn must also learn to integrate sensory information in order to produce coordinated mobility, sounds, and manual competence. Sensory pathways must supply information to association areas, to primary sensory decoding areas, and to memory and planning areas of the brain in order to produce proper output (such as motor action). The motor pathways (mobility, language, and manual competence) must be monitored by the sensory pathways to refine output.

In the healthy "normal" newborn, this is a wonderful cycle that reinforces learning. In the brain-injured newborn, this may be a vicious cycle in which poor sensory input will result in poor or inappropriate output.

A premature newborn has earlier access to sensory stimulation than the term infant who is still in utero. For example, the premature baby has the advantage of seeing light-dark contrast while the baby in utero does not have access to such stimulation. Visual maturation begins immediately for the premature infant.

In the newborn, the brain is undergoing three natural but important processes that we can call *pruning, learning,* and *myelination. Pruning* is an interesting and basic brain phenomenon. In the young baby, billions and billions of brain cells are in place at birth. However, only those brain cells that are used and properly stimulated with sufficient frequency, intensity, and duration early on will be reinforced and become permanent neurological connections functioning as important circuits or networks. Those that are not sufficiently used are "pruned." That is, if they are not used they die away.

Unfortunately, there have been cases of children who were born with essentially "normal" or uninjured brains who have been placed in environments of sensory deprivation and lost the opportunity to develop significant abilities. Some have been in overcrowded orphanages. Others have been in caring homes, but due to a lack of knowledge on the part of the parents or caretakers these babies have been placed in bland, uninteresting, quiet, unstimulating environments and received little sensory stimulation or motor opportunity. They may have been confined to baby carriers, cribs, walkers, or other restrictive devices that do not permit free movement and appropriate sensory-motor stimulation and integration.

Studies have shown that children placed in walkers can be developmentally delayed compared to children who are allowed to crawl, creep, and walk in a safe environment. In addition, devices like walkers are a leading cause of injury in young children. To the degree that a newborn is deprived of sensory stimulation or motor experience and opportunity for expression, the baby will lose the opportunity for some function.

While the pruning of brain cells may appear to be a harsh or unproductive phenomenon, it represents the realities of brain-body economy. The brain requires a constant, high-quality source of energy and nutrients, and an astonishing twenty percent of all incoming oxygen. Those areas that are not used are shut down to send these resources elsewhere as needed.

At the same time pruning is occurring, its opposite, *learning,* occurs. This reinforcement of brain neural circuits allows the permanent acquisition of neural networks if proper stimulation is given.

Myelination is also occurring. This process, in which neurons develop the insulated covering on their processes, helps establish connections and speeds up information exchange. Simply put, the brain grows by use and one must "use it or lose it."

But how does the brain work?

Can it be influenced for the better?

Why are the newborn and infancy periods so special?

How does the brain and nervous system develop?

What does the brain and nervous system do?

How does it function?

What can a mother do to help the process of sensory and motor development?

Could mother unknowingly do something that might inhibit or stop optimal development of the brain?

Is your child well?

Is your child normal?

What is normal?

If your child has an injury to the brain, how can you recognize this?

How can you help your baby if he does have a problem?

These and dozens of other questions run through the minds of concerned parents. The Institutes for the Achievement of Human

Potential, founded in 1955 by Glenn Doman, has been posing these questions and finding the answers for a half-century.

This book explains exactly how to evaluate the sensory and motor pathways of the baby and exactly how to design a program that will enhance the growth and development of these pathways. It is an inspired guided tour of the first twelve months of brain growth and development.

All of the information in this book is presented so that any mother and father, without a medical background, can benefit from it. In it we gain a sense of what the world may look like and feel like to our newborns. We acquire a better understanding of the challenges and frustrations the newborn experiences. Armed with this knowledge, we know what our baby needs and wants and we can have the great joy of creating an ideal environment for him.

Every day is precious, and your baby is hungry for knowledge about the world around him, starting from the moment of birth. To feed your child's brain is as important as feeding his stomach.

The goal of this book is to help parents understand the brain and nervous system. Parents may then follow a clear pathway to enhance the abilities of their child. This is not only an extremely important process—it is also a very joyous one for mother and baby.

—Denise Malkowicz, M.D.

1

What Mothers Know

From the moment a baby is born, a struggle begins. Mother does her best to keep her baby close to her, and the world does its best to separate mother from baby.

This is a mistake because mothers are the best teachers in the world for their babies.

It starts with the well-meaning hospital staff who often whisk the baby away to a nursery far from mother. Later, there are the professionals who are certain that a two-year-old is better off in a day care center than home with mother. On their heels comes the school system where the child will spend the better part of his life to age 18. Educators now say they want the child at the age of five, four, or even three.

There are strong forces at work to separate mother from child, and most people have come to regard each of these encroachments on mother's domain as normal. It is as if that is the way it has always been.

But hospital nurseries, day care centers, and even compulsory education are *not* the way it has always been for mothers and babies. They are newfangled notions, and a radical departure from the age-old human tradition of children being with their mothers until they are ready, willing, and able to handle life on their own.

In contrast to these patterns of modern society, all mothers know intuitively that the first six years of a child's life are the most important.

In this they are absolutely correct.

Most mothers know that the first few months of life are vital to the life-long well-being of their children.

Most mothers know that the first six years of life are the most important.

Again they are correct in this belief.

Unfortunately the vast majority of mothers are not equipped with the information they need to use these first few months to their child's best advantage, and to make the first six years of life as stimulating and rewarding as they could be—and should be.

New cars come with owner's manuals—new babies do not—and yet we all know that babies are a great deal more important than cars. To be sure, there are manuals for the feeding and changing of babies. There are books about the general stages of development that can be observed in average, healthy children.

But these aids are based on two main underlying assumptions. The first is that baby's needs are primarily physiological and emotional. The second is that baby's development is triggered by the ringing of a series of genetically preset alarm clocks that go off on schedule regardless of what does or does not happen to him.

These assumptions are false.

It is perhaps because of these false assumptions that modern babies are being raised by accident instead of on purpose. That is a great shame because the growth and development of the human child is much too important to be left to chance.

It is also because of these false assumptions that mothers have increasingly been persuaded, against their better judgment, to let their babies be cared for by others.

A baby's natural, inborn human potential is enormous.

If it were true that babies simply need to be fed and changed and cuddled a bit, and nothing more, then society could safely put babies together like so many little sheep with one caretaker for many babies. This model was in fact established and used by the Soviets.

But babies are not little sheep. It is true that they have physiological and emotional needs, but beyond these they have enormous *neurological* needs as well. This neurological need is the need of the brain for stimulation and opportunity.

When these neurological needs are fully met, the child's physical and intellectual abilities are enhanced.

If, on the other hand, the baby's neurological needs are not met, and if barriers that may stop or slow brain growth and development are not noticed and eliminated, the child will not achieve that enormous natural human potential.

Every baby arrives equipped with a mother—there is good reason for that. Every mother, whether she is new to the job or highly

> Modern babies are being raised by accident instead of on purpose.

experienced, has a marvelous ability and opportunity to observe her baby, and then to act intuitively based on her observations.

On her *worst* day she will do this better with her own baby than most others would do on their *best* days.

This helps to explain why mothers have always been suspicious of the *preset alarm clock theory* of development. They have seen their babies defy its supposedly unalterable schedule.

Mothers have been equally skeptical of the notion that human ability is predetermined by one's genetic make-up. From time immemorial, mothers and fathers have helped their children develop abilities that neither father nor mother nor grandparents ever had.

Mothers have known more about babies than anyone else since the world began.

It is mothers who have successfully brought us from prehistoric caves to the present.

However, the modern mother faces a very large problem: her own possible extinction.

She has the same powers of observation, the same intuition, the same instincts, and the same love for her baby that mothers have had throughout human history. But she is threatened by a world in which it is no longer safe to be a mother. In this world she must battle to keep her baby by her side from the instant he is born. In this world she is often told that her baby is better off in a nursery than in her arms.

It is a world in which it is no longer considered fashionable or useful to be a mother.

Mothers know that there is something very wrong with a society that no longer respects mothers and has little time or interest in the development of its youngest and most vulnerable members.

When a new mother does win that first battle, and finally gets her hands on her own newborn baby with everyone else out of the room, she does what all mothers have always done. She starts counting: ten fingers, ten toes, two ears, one mouth.

She begins an inventory to evaluate her own baby. She makes certain that he has arrived with everything he should have and that he is functioning as he should function.

Since she knows how to count she does not need any help with her first inventory. But once that is completed, she is on her own. She looks into the eyes of her baby and to her utter astonishment and amazement she sees an intelligence for which no one has prepared her.

> Mothers have known more about babies than anyone else since the world began.

New parents are
amazed at how
intelligent their
baby really is.

Father sees it too. For a moment they are stunned. They are overwhelmed by the potential they sense in the baby, and by the responsibility they have undertaken. They make a thousand unspoken promises to their new baby.

They will more than likely keep the majority of those promises. Sadly, the most important promise, the one about helping the baby to become the best he can be, may elude them, simply because mother and father do not know how to help bring this about.

They have been told about how to provide for the physical growth and health of the baby, and something about his emotional needs, but the world has little awareness and hardly any respect for the real potential of the baby.

"Feed 'em and love 'em," a better-than-average doctor may have told them, but probably no one told them about helping the baby learn. They have been told that there is plenty of time to think about that when the child goes to school. Some have even told them they are damaging the baby if they help him to learn too soon, before the baby is "ready."

The truth is that such delay wastes his six most important years. Sadly, many mothers and fathers have been intimidated by the world around them. Our goal is to help parents provide for the growth and development of their babies in the fullest sense. Parents need to know what is important and what is not important.

Armed with this knowledge, mother and father can combine it with their unique knowledge of their baby to create an environment that addresses both the baby's basic survival needs and the needs of his developing brain.

This book is the story of how to give a baby a running start at achieving his full potential. Its aim is to help parents *understand* the process of brain growth and development in the newborn baby, so that parents are able to *create* an environment that enhances and enriches that growth and development.

2

The Search for Wellness

When we began treating brain-injured children, most of our children were unable to walk or to talk. Many lacked both of these abilities. Our first focus, therefore, was on understanding the development of walking and talking.

Our study began as most studies do, with a search through the medical literature to learn what had been recorded up to that time on the subject. We were astonished. We were dumbfounded to discover that virtually nothing had been written about the development of the young child. Arnold Gesell, a pioneer in the study of child development, was all there was. It appeared that Gesell was perhaps the first man in all of recorded medicine to make his life's work the study of the healthy child.

We wanted to know how the baby learned and why he learned the way he did.

Gesell had certainly studied the well child on a broad scale, not only a child's movement and speech but his social growth as well. He had not, however, attempted to *explain* the child's growth; he had devoted himself to being a careful *observer* of the child and how he grew.

We had a much broader interest. Where Gesell recorded *when* the child learned to move and speak, we wanted to know *how* he did it, and *why* he did it. We wanted to identify those factors significant to the child's growth. Clearly we had to seek these answers on our own.

At first we went to those people who might be expected to know. "*How* does a child grow?" we asked the experts. "What are the factors necessary to his growth?" We asked pediatricians, therapists, nurses, obstetricians, and all the other specialists that were concerned with the growth of the well child. We were surprised and distressed by the lack of knowledge we encountered.

Gradually we came to understand the reason: the people we consulted seldom saw a well child! The reason for taking a child to the doctor, nurse, or therapist, obviously, is that the child is not well. So the people we were asking saw primarily sick children. We found, therefore, both in the literature and in our interviews with other professionals, that though much information existed about the unwell child, very little existed about the well child and why he grows as he does.

Finally we realized that those who knew most about the growth of healthy children were mothers. But though mothers had a great deal to tell us they were naturally a bit vague as to the exact times that a child did what he did, and what was significant in what he did. For a scientific inquiry we needed more precision, and so we decided to go to the source—the infants themselves.

The world became our laboratory and babies our most precious clinical material.

The world became our laboratory and babies our most precious clinical material. We asked permission to study every baby we could find. We focused first on walking. We followed the child carefully from the moment he was born until he learned to walk.

What, we asked ourselves, were the things that would prevent walking if they were denied to a child or removed from his environment? What were the things that, if given to the child in abundance, would speed his walking? We studied many, many newborn well children.

After several fascinating years of study, we knew we had discovered the pathway that each of us had individually trod as babies. We also came to feel that we understood this pathway. In a dark and formerly unpromising tunnel, we were beginning to see the light.

Four Stages of Movement

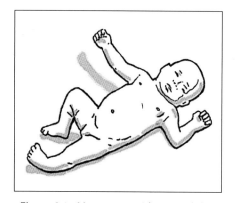

Figure 2.1. Movement without mobility

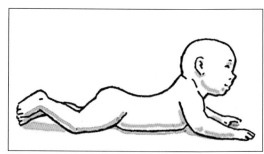

Figure 2.2. Crawling

It was particularly evident that this road of growth that the baby followed to become a human being in the full sense of the term was both a very ancient road and a very well-defined one. This road, it was interesting to note, permitted not the slightest variance. There were no detours, no crossroads, no intersections, nothing that changed along the way. It was an unvarying road, which every well child followed in the process of growing up. Anyone who could observe carefully could learn how a well baby learned to walk.

When all extraneous factors not vital to walking were removed, it became clear that along the road to walking there were four vitally important stages.

The first stage began at birth, when the baby was able to move his limbs and body but was not able to use these motions to move his body from place to place. This we called "movement without mobility" (see Figure 2.1).

The second stage occurred when the baby learned, sometimes within hours, that by moving his arms and legs in a certain manner with his stomach pressed to the floor, he could move from Point A to Point B. This we called "crawling" (see Figure 2.2).

Quite a bit later, stage three occurred, when the baby learned to defy gravity for the first time and to get up on his hands and knees and move across the floor in this more effective and more skillful manner. This we called "creeping" (see Figure 2.3).

The last significant stage occurred when the baby learned to stand up on his feet and walk, the stage we all know as "walking" (see Figure 2.4).

The pathway we discovered was a very ancient road and a very well-defined one.

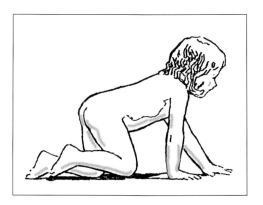

Figure 2.3. Creeping

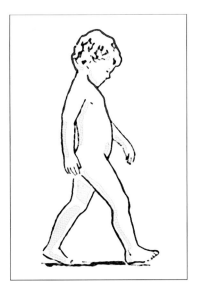

Figure 2.4. Walking

It is vital to understand the significance of these four stages. We can see their importance if we view them as schools. Think of stage one, that of moving arms and legs and body without mobility, as kindergarten; think of stage two, crawling, as grammar school; think of stage three, creeping, as high school; and then think of stage four, that of walking, as college. No child ever misses an entire school. No child completes college before he completes high school.

There is an ancient saying that you have to creep before you can walk.

There is an ancient saying that you have to creep before you can walk. We now feel safe in saying that you have to move your arms and legs before you can crawl, and you have to crawl on your belly before you can creep on hands and knees.

We became convinced that no well child ever missed a stage along this road, and we became convinced of this despite the fact that mothers sometimes reported that their children did not crawl. However, when such a mother was asked, "Do you mean that your child simply lay in his crib until the day he started to creep on hands and knees or stand up and walk?" Mother generally reconsidered and allowed as how the child had crawled for a short period of time.

While there was no way to travel this road without passing each and every milepost, there was indeed a difference in the time factors. Some children would spend ten months in the crawling stage and two months in the creeping stage, while other children spent two months in the crawling stage and ten months in the creeping stage. However, these four significant stages always occurred in the same sequence.

Along the ancient road there were no detours for the well child. So convinced did we become of this that we also became convinced of two other factors.

First, we became convinced that if an otherwise well child were to miss, for any reason, any stage along this road, that child would not be normal and would not learn to walk until given the opportunity to complete the missed stage.

We were persuaded, and we still are, that if one took a well child and suspended him by some sort of sling device in midair when he was born and fed him and cared for him until he was twelve months of age and *then* placed this child on the floor and said, "Walk, because you're twelve months of age and this is the stage at which well children walk," that the child would, in fact, not walk. He would instead first move arms, legs, and body; second, crawl; third, creep; and fourth and last, walk. This was not a mere chronology of events but instead was a planned road in which each step was necessary to the subsequent step.

Second, we became convinced that if any of these basic stages were merely slighted, rather than wholly skipped, as for example in the case of the child who had begun to walk before he had crept enough, there would be adverse consequences such as poor coordination, poor concentration, hyperactivity, difficulty in becoming totally right-handed or left-handed, and learning problems—particularly in the areas of reading and writing.

Crawling and creeping, it began to appear, were essential stages not only in learning to walk but also in the overall programming of the brain, stages in which the two hemispheres of the brain learned how to work together.

After years of observing thousands of children in many parts of the world, we are more convinced than ever that when we see a child who did not go through each of these major stages in order, we are looking at a child who later on will show evidence of having a neurological problem.

Now we had our first set of facts. We knew what was normal, at least so far as mobility went. This helped to define the next two tasks: 1) To learn how this knowledge could be used to benefit a brain-injured child, and 2) To learn what was normal in all the *other* areas of function that are important to human beings.

After two decades of work it became clear that what we were studying was not just therapy, or mobility, but child brain development.

To this day we have not exhausted the thousands of ways to stimulate the brain and enrich the environment. As a result, more brain-injured children are seeing, hearing, walking, and talking than have ever done so before. In some cases, they have become totally well.

Crawling and creeping are essential not only to walking but in the overall programming of the brain.

3

A New Kind of Kid

The search for better and better ways to improve the mobility of our brain-injured children led us naturally to examine their over-all intellectual development, and in the early 1960s we began to teach very young brain-injured children how to read.

Many of our children had problems in understanding, and we reasoned that the earlier they got started learning to read the better would be their chance of success.

We were also treating many children who had no problems whatever with understanding. They were injured in the midbrain and subcortical areas of the brain. They had huge problems in mobility, language, and manual competence, but they understood very well. In fact, these children, who are frequently hurt in utero, are extraordinarily intelligent.

While their well brothers and sisters and next-door neighbors are crawling and creeping and walking and jumping all over the house, they are forced, by their injury, to watch and listen. They quickly develop very sharp powers of observation and comprehension. As a result they are highly tuned in to everything and everyone around them.

Since they move poorly or not at all, they have a great need to charm adults into getting them whatever they need or want. The result is that by the time these children are two or three years old they have the understanding of children several years older, and they will maintain this intellectual edge throughout life.

We saw our challenge as learning how to fix these children so that they could walk and talk and use their hands like all children do. Since they had very high understanding, we reasoned that they also could benefit from an early reading program. So we began to teach parents how to teach their severely brain-injured two- and three-year-olds to read.

The results were immediate and astounding.

The children injured in the midbrain and early subcortical areas who did not have understanding problems also learned to read with astonishing ease.

Even more astounding, children with understanding problems also learned to read quickly and easily. Still more important, we were surprised to see that their comprehension improved substantially as a result of this new stimulation.

The children were thrilled with this new program, their parents were elated, and, of course, so were we.

We did not realize at the time that we were entering a whole new field of knowledge in which we would gain understanding of the process of *intellectual* growth and vital new insights into the development of the well baby.

> We began to ask ourselves what was wrong—not with the brain-injured child, but the well child who could *not* do what the brain-injured child *could* do.

By this point, brain-injured children were coming regularly to The Institutes to be evaluated by the staff. New programs were designed for each child based on the progress he or she had achieved, and parents would return home to do their new program on a daily basis for approximately six months.

Their home program had been a balance between a mobility program and a physiological program to insure good health and function. Now we added an intellectual program of early reading.

As a result of this program, we began to see children who— although they were still severely brain-injured—were able to read and comprehend whatever they read years before well children of the same age. These four-year-olds were not yet able to walk or talk, but they could read at a third- or fourth-grade level, and occasionally higher.

What did it mean?

Was it possible to be severely brain-injured from the waist down and intellectually superior from the waist up? Was it an advantage to be severely brain-injured? Nobody thought that. What did it mean?

We began, reluctantly at first, to ask ourselves what was wrong—not with the brain-injured child on the road to recovery, but with his healthy peers who could not do things that this severely brain-injured child could do.

It seemed clear that well kids were not as well as they ought to be.

At just about the time when this uncomfortable thought was haunting us, we began to see a new kind of kid.

We should have predicted that he would start arriving on our doorstep, but we did not. Instead, he took us totally by surprise.

He came into our offices with his mother and father and his brain-injured brother or sister. He usually sat in on all the adult talk, the long history, the evaluation, and the lengthy programming sessions. He frequently asked very incisive questions and often volunteered answers to the questions that came up. He was articulate, extremely well-coordinated, very well-behaved, and totally and completely involved with the treatment program of his hurt brother or sister.

However, this child was not the older brother or sister of the brain-injured child. This was the *younger* brother or sister of the brain-injured child. This was the baby of the family.

He was not like any other child we had ever met.

He was a bit like a dehydrated adult, only more charming and likeable than most adults tend to be. All the characteristics for which children are loved he had in abundance. All the characteristics for which children are sometimes considered a pain in the neck were absent in him.

We should have expected him, but we did not.

When his brain-injured older brother or sister began on a daily neurological program he had been a newborn baby. Mother had very wisely made sure that he was with her and his hurt brother or sister at all times. The baby was always included in whatever mother and hurt child were doing on their neurological program.

If older brother was crawling on his belly, then that was a good opportunity for baby to crawl with him. And so the baby had the maximum opportunity to be on his belly on the floor to explore and to crawl.

If older brother was doing log rolls to improve his balance and vestibular development, then baby got to do the same log rolls side by side with big brother. And so the baby's brain had more stimulation to the balance and vestibular areas than it would have otherwise received on a hit-or-miss basis.

When mother started to teach older brother how to read, the baby sat by his side. Every word that older brother saw, baby saw. Because older brother had visual problems, the reading words were written very large. The baby could see these large words easily, and

This new kid had all the characteristics for which we admire children and none of the characteristics which annoy and irritate us.

as a result his visual pathways were given the opportunity to develop faster and better. These words were chosen from the household environment, so the baby could easily understand them as well. By the time the baby was less than a year old, he could actually differentiate many single reading words from each other.

In short, mother and father had taken great pains to provide their brain-injured child with an excellent neurological environment so that they could grow those pathways that had been injured and close the break in the circuit created by the brain injury. The environment was rich in that it provided abundant sensory stimulation to the pathways that go *into* the brain and ample motor opportunity to use the pathways that go *out of* the brain.

We had theorized that if such an environment provided brain-injured children with the stimulation that they needed to become well, would it not also be beneficial for a well baby? After all, the well newborn baby must face the same challenges that confront the brain-injured child. Like the brain-injured child, the newborn is neurologically immature. In truth, the well newborn and the brain-injured child, although very different in some ways, are neurologically very similar indeed.

Our work with brain-injured children provided the answers to create a superb environment for the newborn baby.

If we now knew how to get blind brain-injured children to see, deaf brain-injured children to hear, and paralyzed brain-injured children to move, did we not also have the answers to create a superb environment for the newborn baby?

A well-designed program would provide the newborn with an environment that encourages his development *on purpose*. In addition, it would act as a kind of insurance plan by handling any neurological problems he might have if we left his growth and development *to chance*.

This was a wonderfully exciting prospect for the staff. It made for many debates and discussions at three o'clock in the morning. These usually ended when someone observed that we had an army of hurt kids who were depending on us to find the answers that would help them to get well.

Our team was dedicated but it was small. We knew we could not afford to think about making well kids better while hurt kids still struggled to survive in a world in which they were regularly warehoused and forgotten.

And so our dream of newborn babies having the benefit of this precious knowledge remained only a dream for a while. In time, however, those highly articulate, very well-coordinated, and absolutely charming tiny children started appearing in our offices with predictable regularity. They were not a dream. They were no longer a theory. They were very real and very, very impressive.

Now we had no choice. These children had real names and real faces. We were hooked. We knew that no matter how long it took and no matter how little funds there were to go around, we were going to have to *do* something about well kids.

4

About the Brain

The human brain is an organ superb beyond imagination. Oddly enough, it is commonly believed that there is little known about this mysterious organ except that it weighs three to four pounds and is responsible for virtually everything that we do.

In truth, the brain is not a mysterious organ at all. A great deal has been known and understood about the brain for thousands of years. Of all the organs of the body it is the most capable of change. In fact, it is constantly changing, in a physical *and* functional way, either for better or for worse.

It is very important to remember that when we speak of the human brain we are speaking of that physical organ that occupies the skull and the spinal column and weighs three to four pounds.

We are not speaking of that nebulous thing called "the mind." The confusion between the organ called "the brain" and the idea called "the mind" has created problems in the past.

The mind has defied any agreed upon definition of what it is or what it is not. The brain, however, is material. It is easier to study. We can see it, feel it, and smell it. We can even taste it if we are inclined to do so.

The brain is a nice, clean orderly organ whose job is to take in data and process that data in such a way that its owner can relate to his environment appropriately at all times.

This is a tall order, and the brain handles it on a twenty-four-hour-a-day basis for the entire life of the individual.

The brain continues to grow from conception throughout life, but the pattern of that growth is not even. The brain grows explosively from conception to six years of age. After that growth contin-

> The brain grows explosively from conception to six years of age.

ues, but compared to that initial period, growth after age six is slight by comparison.

The growth of the head reveals this clearly. From conception to birth the head grows from zero to thirty-five centimeters in circumference. From birth to age two-and-a-half years, it grows another fifteen centimeters. From the age of two-and-a-half years to adulthood, the head will only grow another five centimeters, and most of that will take place before six years of age.

From the moment of birth, the rate of growth of the brain is on a descending curve. Each day the brain grows a little less than it did the day before.

During the period of greatest growth, the baby is able to take in raw information at a rate that is truly astounding. But this process will be a little bit slower each day.

Some people are interested in providing stimulation to the baby in utero, but this has not been our area of search and discovery. While there may be much to learn about the baby in utero, we will confine ourselves to the time following birth, when we are able to observe and evaluate the baby and see what he needs and how he reacts to the things we are doing with him.

Since the critical period of brain growth is between birth and six years, it is clear that the earlier we provide baby with stimulation and opportunity, the more he will be able to take in the stimulation and use the opportunity to its fullest.

Sadly, the world has tended to look at brain growth and development as if it were predestined and unchangeable. The truth is that brain growth and development is a dynamic and ever-changing process.

It is a process that can be stopped, as it is by profound brain injury.

It is a process that can be slowed, as it is by an environment that inhibits the opportunity of the child to explore and discover his environment through seeing, hearing, feeling, tasting, and smelling, and through inhibiting the opportunity to move, speak, and use his hands.

But most important, it is a process that can be accelerated and enhanced.

All that we need to do to speed development is to provide visual, auditory, and tactile stimulation—with increased frequency, intensity and duration—in recognition of the orderly way in which the brain grows.

And how does the brain grow?

> Brain growth is dynamic—it can be stopped or slowed, but most significantly it can be *speeded.*

The brain grows by use.

There are very few sentences composed of only five words that contain more power to change the world than this one:

The brain grows by use.

Just like the biceps, the brain grows by use.

Those who use their biceps very little have small, undeveloped, weak biceps. Those who use their biceps an average amount have average biceps. Those who use their biceps an extraordinary amount have extraordinary biceps.

There is no other possibility.

The same is true of the brain, because the brain grows by use.

It was our hurt children who proved this to us.

When we began to treat our brain-injured children successfully, they began to develop normal function. Children who had been unable to move began to move. Children who could not walk began to walk. Children who had poor understanding began to understand the world around them.

A characteristic of brain-injured children is that they are physically small. They have very poor physical structures compared to their healthy peers. The majority of the children that we see are below the tenth percentile in their physical measurements. They have very small chests. They often have small heads, and their overall stature is much less than their healthy brothers and sisters.

They are not small because they have inferior genes; they are small because their brain injury has prevented them from having normal function. That lack of function is responsible for their poor structure.

There is an old law of nature that says that *function determines structure.*

The brain-injured child demonstrates that the opposite is also true. *A lack of function creates a lack of structure.*

We believed that if we could successfully treat the brain, the child would begin to increase his function, and that as this happened his structure would begin to change.

This is exactly and precisely what happened.

As children began to see for the first time and understand for the first time and move for the first time and walk for the first time, their structures started to change.

They began to grow like weeds.

Children whose height had been ten centimeters below their well

All we do to speed development is to provide visual, auditory, and tactile stimulation with increased frequency, intensity, and duration.

peers began to grow at twice the rate at which a well child of the same age was growing. Children who had tiny chests and had suffered from chronic upper respiratory problems experienced chest growth that in some cases was three to five times faster than their well peers, and they stopped having upper respiratory infections.

We were delighted but not surprised. This physical growth and development made total sense.

The ability of Mother Nature to make up for lost time has a name—it is called the "Catch-up Phenomenon."

What did surprise us, however, was a physical change that we were not expecting. Many of the brain-injured children we were treating were older than six years of age. In fact, some were not children at all, but adults. Although we did meticulous head measurements on all of the brain-injured children and adults who came to us, we really did not expect to see much growth in the circumference of the heads of children who were over six years of age.

After all, we knew, as everyone knows, that brain growth is essentially over at six, and so the size of the head changes very little after this point.

Babies raised in an environment rich in stimulation develop better brains.

We were wrong.

When we started to look at the changes in head growth of our brain-injured children who were well over six years of age, we were astounded by what we found. Although the head growth of their well peers was very slight, our brain-injured children's heads were growing two, or three, or sometimes even four times faster than their well peers.

There was clear physical evidence that the brain grows by use.

We have been watching this phenomenon for fifty years.

The physical structures of brain-injured children who are not getting effective neurological treatment become worse with each passing day.

But brain-injured children who are given the correct stimulation and the opportunity to function develop bigger and better chests, arms, legs, and brains.

Likewise, *well* babies who are raised in an environment that is rich in stimulation, and where they have increased opportunity to function, also develop bigger and better chests, arms, legs, and—most important of all—brains.

5

The Newborn Baby

We adults have always assumed that being a newborn baby is a rather happy, halcyon state. A baby's primary jobs seem to be eating and sleeping, and since we do not regard either as very difficult, we regard the newborn as enjoying a kind of baby honeymoon in which he has all the time in the world to get settled and comfortable in his new home.

In fact, the newborn baby lives in no such world.

He arrives having just completed what is arguably the most dangerous journey he will ever make. Even if he has had an easy delivery, he has still had a lot of work to do.

We make much of the labor of mother in delivering a baby, as well we should, since it is physically hard work. But delivery is a partnership and the younger member of the team works as hard as the older member, if not harder, to get himself delivered.

Once he has arrived he must adjust with amazing rapidity to the fact that he is no longer in an aqueous environment. He must not only learn to move his arms and legs without the support of this aqueous environment, but he must also quickly master the rudiments of breathing if he is to survive.

It is astonishing that he does both of these things within seconds of being delivered.

Once things have settled down and he has been given the once over by doctors, nurses, mother, and father, he must get down to the formidable task of figuring out what's what.

At birth he cannot see. He is functionally blind. However, since he is exposed to light for the first time at birth he will immediately begin to try to use his vision. He will respond to light even though at first he can do so only briefly. His attempts to see will be short-lived. He will quickly grow tired and fall asleep after making an effort to see.

He also cannot hear very much. It has been demonstrated that babies in utero respond to certain sounds and voices if they are loud enough. However, at birth the baby is, in a functional sense, deaf. He can hear some loud sounds but most sounds he cannot hear at all. Often the baby is born into an environment full of loud sounds. This creates auditory chaos for the baby. This blurred sound will be hard for him to hear.

The baby has tactile sensation, of course, but it is a very crude sensation. He can use his sense of smell to locate mother, and if he is in good shape neurologically he will be able to suck and swallow shortly after birth.

Newborn babies are struggling to overcome blindness, deafness, and immobility.

He can move his arms and legs freely but forward motion is difficult at best, especially since he is usually bundled up like a mummy and placed on his back in the nursery.

He can cry, but his respiration is not yet good enough for him to be able to differentiate the sound that he makes. So he has one cry that he will have to use to communicate everything.

He can grasp a finger placed into his hand at birth. Parents are often impressed with the strength of their newborn baby's grasp. However, while he can grasp very well and appears to be quite strong, he doesn't have the ability to let go even if he wants to do so.

Overall the newborn baby exists in a blind, deaf, relatively insensate world in which he cannot move or use his hands, and has difficultly making sounds.

This is not a happy state in which to be.

Newborn babies are not the happy little bundles that we like to imagine they are. Instead they are very intent human beings struggling against very difficult circumstances to overcome blindness, deafness, and immobility.

They are deadly serious and they should be.

It is not easy or safe to be a newborn baby.

The baby thinks it is his job to learn to see, hear, feel, and move at the earliest possible moment. He will use every waking moment to do this. The only real question is whether we will help him to get his job done or get in his way.

No sane parent ever set out to get in the way of her newborn baby, but unwittingly we do it all the time.

Some of our modern methods of delivery and early child care have developed with little rhyme or reason as to what we do or why we do it. When there is a reason for what we do, it is often simply our own convenience. Tragically, what may appear to be convenient or efficient in the adult world is often very bad for the tiny baby.

Let's take a look at the typical environment of the newborn baby and ask this question: Is it set up for his benefit or ours?

After being delivered he is usually taken away from his mother, wrapped up, and put on his back, and often placed, if mother permits, in a nursery with many other babies.

Is this good for him or is it simply more convenient for the hospital staff to keep an eye on him?

Nature has arranged a one mother/one baby ratio so that the newborn baby has mother watching and observing him at all times. We frustrate nature's design and take baby away so that he is one of a litter of babies that are watched over, not by their own mothers, but by a few conscientious nurses.

To help the nurses keep an eye on so many babies at once, they are placed on their backs so that the nurses can be sure that they are breathing.

The babies are covered in blankets because the nursery is not warm enough for them to be naked. If we made the nursery warm enough for the babies to be naked, then it would be too hot for the nurses.

Although the babies cannot see or hear their mothers very well at birth, they can smell their mothers. When they arrive at the nursery they cannot smell mother any more. This is very upsetting for the baby.

His survival imperative tells him, "Keep mother by your side at all times!" Therefore he will cry to call mother to his side. Since mother is a hundred yards away down the hall, she cannot hear his call and does not respond to it. Thus the baby knows his mother is not there and his attempts to call her go unanswered.

This is not a comforting condition for the newborn.

This frightening situation is compounded by the fact that he can hear the loud and repeated cries from the other babies in the nursery who are also trying to call their mothers.

And we call this a "nursery"?

Our intentions may be good but we have set up the environment to suit adult convenience. This environment could hardly be worse

> Is the typical environment of the newborn set up for his benefit or our own convenience?

for the baby if we had set out intentionally to confuse, frighten, and frustrate him.

When the baby arrives home he will continue to be bundled up no matter what time of year it is. We cool or heat our homes based on what is comfortable for us. But the baby needs a warmer environment than suits us, so he must be bundled up in the first few months of life.

Wrapped up in blankets and dressed in clothing that fits like a snowsuit, he has a hard time moving at all. He already has a very chubby body that is hard enough to move, but dressed in thick diaper, a long-sleeved and long-legged baby suit, and then wrapped up in blankets, he would have to be a sumo wrestler to escape from the padding that envelops him.

And he is desperate to move.

He will move his arms and legs frantically at those rare times when he is freed from the confinement of his clothes and blankets. This is why diapering can be such a trial. It is usually the only time in the day when, for a fleeting instant, he is free. He struggles like mad, which usually drives us crazy since we are trying to put a diaper on him.

How much time is the baby free to move unencumbered on his belly? Almost zero time.

It is not just the clothing and the blankets that frustrate his attempts to move. He is almost invariably placed on his back right from birth. In this position he is like a turtle turned upside down. All of the wonderful propulsive movements of his arms and legs are useless in this position. They produce no forward motion for him.

However, when he is placed right-side up on his belly on a smooth, warm surface, all those seemingly random motions of his arms and legs become productive motions that produce forward movement. Whenever he is placed on his belly he will begin to make the thousand and one experiments that he must make to discover how to use his arms and legs to crawl. Nature has provided him with a rage to move his body, and he needs all the time he can get in order to do so.

If you calculate how much time the modern baby is free to move unencumbered on his belly on a smooth, warm surface, you find it is almost zero.

Even when we give him some opportunity to move, we restrict his playing field severely by placing him in a crib, playpen, swing, stroller, or "walker." Each of these devices was invented to act as a kind of remote babysitter. They are designed to restrict the baby so that we can go about our affairs without having to watch the baby so closely. This may seem like a necessary convenience or even a safeguard for the baby, but, in fact, it is neither convenient in the long run nor safe in the short run.

There is nothing convenient about arranging the environment so that the baby cannot, try as he may, develop the vital abilities to crawl and creep freely.

We know now that these are not just incidental stages in his development; crawling and creeping are critical to all aspects of neurological development. What may seem convenient today will turn out very inconvenient if his lack of creeping and crawling as a baby leads to difficulties later in life.

As for safety, with a tiny baby there is no substitute for real vigilance. Every device that allows us to put distance between ourselves and the baby is a device that lulls us into a false sense of security.

We have a clinic full of brain-injured children who *were* well children who climbed out of their cribs and fell on their heads or climbed out of their playpen and fell into the swimming pool.

The lesson is simple—the closer the baby is to mother *and* the floor, the safer he will be in both the short run *and* the long run.

As parents and as a society, we need to take a careful look at what our priorities are when we decide to bring a baby into this world.

When we take a closer look, we may see that we have been selfish, insensitive, and extremely short-sighted to design the baby's environment almost totally for our comfort and convenience, thus denying the baby his birthright to move and explore and develop his abilities to their fullest.

The baby's environment should be designed to ensure his safety and long-term growth and development.

Although we have not meant to do so, we have gotten in the way of our babies' development.

The needs of the newborn are much more important than our own temporary convenience. The environment should be designed to ensure his safety and long-term growth and development.

The family and society as a whole stand to benefit hugely from the increased ability and happiness of babies who are raised in a way that meets their neurological needs.

6

Making the Alarm Clock Go Off

We have said much about what we should not do but we have only hinted at what we *should* do to create a better environment for our babies.

Now let's take a closer look.

It has long been believed that the key milestones in a child's development are achieved automatically, purely as a result of the child's growing older over time.

This theory dictates that the child walks at age one due to some kind of built-in mechanism—rather like an alarm clock set to ring at twelve months that triggers the ability to walk.

Simultaneously the alarm clock for talking rings, and he begins to say words. The same theory postulates a preset alarm clock for each and every significant stage of development. This theory suggests that the mere passage of time leads to the development of human ability and that the acquisition of ability is as inevitable as the sunrise and the sunset.

The concept of "readiness" is nonsense.

This is called "readiness." For example, the alarm clock rings at six years of age and the child supposedly has "reading readiness."

The concept of "readiness" and the whole alarm clock theory are patent nonsense.

If reading readiness takes place at six years of age as the conventional thinking says it does, then how can we explain that thirty percent of the children in our school system will fail to learn to read properly by the age of eighteen? Why did their alarm clocks fail to ring at age six or seven? Why has it still not gone off by the time they are eighteen?

It is even harder to explain the thousands of brain-injured children who have learned to read splendidly by the age of three. They were more than ready. They think reading is the greatest invention since mothers.

Why did their reading "alarm clocks" ring early?

It is true that at twelve months of age the average child will walk. But is this a cause-and-effect relationship? Is it the passage of time that has brought about this new ability?

Obviously not.

Why do children who are raised in a superb environment walk, talk, and use their hands earlier than their peers?

After living night and day with well children who were given a superb environment in which to develop from birth, we had to ask ourselves, "Why do they walk and talk and use their hands earlier than their peers?"

Why do their alarm clocks go off *before* they are supposed to do so? Why are they learning earlier?

One of the most exciting discoveries we were to make was that the process of growth and development is a product of the amount of stimulation in the child's environment. It is not determined by a preset alarm clock.

We therefore began to look for every way we could to "set off the alarm clocks" for our brain-injured children, and we have found hundreds.

We discarded the model of the preset alarm clock. What we had discovered was a simple and elegant truth:

The brain grows by use, not a preset alarm clock.

Brain growth can be speeded by increased stimulation at any point in life, but most especially at those times when it is growing fastest: in the first six years of life.

The first six years of life are precious because during this time the brain grows at a tremendous rate. Brain growth is most dramatic in the first year.

The development of the newborn's visual pathway offers clear proof of the dramatic growth of the brain in the first year of life.

As we have pointed out, a well newborn is, like other little creatures, functionally blind in a practical sense. He can see only light and dark. He has a "light reflex." This means that if we shine a light into his eyes, the pupil will constrict to prevent too much light from entering the visual pathway. If we turn off the light, the pupil will again dilate to allow an acceptable amount of light to enter his visual pathway.

Now consider three children:

1. A baby born two months premature in Chicago, who is now exactly two months old.

2. A healthy, full-term newborn conceived on the same day as the premature baby, also born in Chicago.

3. A healthy, three-month-old baby of a Xingu tribe in Brazil's Mato Grosso.

If the alarm clock theory were true, the healthy three-month-old Xingu baby should see the most, the full-term Chicago baby should see less, and the premature baby conceived the same day should see the least.

In fact, the exact reverse is the case.

How is this possible?

Let's begin with our disadvantaged two-month-old baby who was born premature, ejected too soon from the friendly environment of his mother's uterus.

We examine him at birth and find that in his case the prematurity has not affected his vision. He has a normal light reflex and sees light and dark.

Our full-term Chicago baby, conceived on the same day, was born exactly two months later than our disadvantaged premature baby. We examine him and find that he too has normal vision. He has a light reflex and therefore sees light and dark.

Both of these babies have the same "alarm clock" age. Based on the instant of conception, they are exactly the same age.

At birth the full-term baby sees only light and dark while the disadvantaged premature baby (now two months old) already sees outlines and silhouettes, which is normal for a healthy two-month-old baby.

We have seen this over and over. What does it mean?

Why does the disadvantaged premature baby now see outlines while the full-term baby, the exact same age from conception, only sees light and dark?

It is obvious, isn't it?

The disadvantaged child has had a world to see for two whole months, while the advantaged child has not.

Nobody ever read a book who didn't have a book to read.

Nobody ever played a violin who didn't have a violin to play.

Nobody ever swam who didn't have water in which to swim.

Nobody ever saw a world who didn't have a world to see. It takes a month or two of seeing to grow the visual pathway of the brain to the stage at which it can begin to sort out what it sees.

What about our three-month-old Xingu baby in the great savannahs of Brazil? These people were still so isolated 40 years ago that the legendary Villas-Boas brothers were the only outsiders who had ever seen them. So when The Institutes team arrived in 1966, we were the third, fourth, fifth, and sixth people outside of their own culture who had ever met and lived with them.

Our Xingu baby is something in excess of three months old. He was raised with his Xingu tribe in the Mato Grosso of Brazil Centrale.

If the model of the preset alarm clock were true, then surely our three-month-old Xingu baby would be able to see better than the disadvantaged premature baby or the full-term newborn.

The reality is just the opposite.

The disadvantaged, two-month premature baby will see the most. The advantaged newborn will, within a few days, see less. Our Xingu baby will see nothing at all.

How can this be so?

In the absence of appropriate opportunity in which to see, the passage of time is not an advantage. It is, in fact, a disadvantage.

What happened to our little Xingu baby?

He was a very beautiful baby, as are all Xingu babies. His people live in very large grass huts that have no windows and only one very small opening. These small openings serve to protect those who live within. It is impossible to enter a Xingu home without bending and bowing one's head. Intruders are easily dealt with by a blow to the head. The result is that Xingu huts are very, very dark. Indeed, there is almost no light at all inside the hut.

When a Xinguano baby is born, for reasons known only to the Xinguanos, the baby is kept inside the hut for approximately the first year of life.

When our team visited these beautiful people of the Mato Grosso, it was one of the few times in our lives that ignorance stood us in good stead.

Being unaware of this custom, we asked a family with a baby, who was at least three months of age, if we could see him and photograph him. So mother and father brought baby out into the sunlight so we could get better photos of the baby.

We examined his stage of development in terms of sight, hearing, and touch.

He had a light reflex, but saw only light and dark. At three months of age he demonstrated no ability to see outline or detail.

How could it have been otherwise?

During this year the babies are not brought outside into the light at all. As a result of this custom, the babies cannot see when they are finally brought out of the huts. They have a light reflex, which is to say their pupils constrict in the presence of light as do a newborn baby's pupils, but beyond this they cannot see.

So our three-month-old Xinguano baby was the oldest of the three chronologically, but in the sense of his visual development he was at the stage of a newborn.

The premature disadvantaged baby has had two whole months in which to see before he was even scheduled to be born. He is chronologically the youngest from conception but he has had two months more stimulation than the well newborn. He is visually a full five months ahead of the Xinguano baby. He has the visual age of a two-month-old.

This is because there is no preset alarm clock. *The brain grows by use,* not by a preordained timetable.

Consider three families living side-by-side in suburbia. In one lives the Green family, in the next the Brown family, and in the last the White family.

On the exact same day, each mother gives birth to a baby.

Five weeks later, Mr. Green comes home and Mrs. Green says, "Guess what? The baby followed me with his eyes this morning. He was lying on his belly in bed and when I walked in between him and the window and it was very clear that he could see me even though I was across the room."

And Dad says, "Is that all?" Mother says, "Wait a minute. He's five weeks old and our pediatrician says babies don't follow visually until they are ten weeks old. We have a very bright baby."

Ten weeks after the babies are born, Mr. Brown comes home and Mrs. Brown says, "Hey, guess what? The baby followed me with his eyes today." And Dad says, "Is that all?" Mother says, "He is ten weeks old today and that's exactly when a baby is supposed to be able to follow with his eyes. We have a nice healthy baby."

Fifteen weeks after the babies are born, Mr. White comes home and Mrs. White says, "Honey, we have to have a talk tonight." Since

> The brain grows by *use,* not by a preordained timetable.

her tone is decidedly serious Dad says, "It's about money; let's talk now." Mother says, "No, it's not about money; it's much more important than that. It's about the baby. You know our baby is fifteen weeks old today and he still does not follow me with his eyes. And Dad says, "Is that all?" Mom says, "Wait a minute; he should have started to do that five weeks ago. Our baby's got a problem."

Each of these mothers has come to a conclusion. Mrs. Green concludes that she has a very, very bright baby. Mrs. Brown concludes that she has a nice normal, healthy baby. And Mrs. White concludes that her baby has a problem.

And they are right, all three of them.

But to what do they attribute it?

Mrs. Green says to herself "I'm bright, my husband is bright, so we have a nice bright baby."

Mrs. Brown says to herself, "I'm normal, my husband is normal, we both come from very normal families, so we have a nice normal baby."

Mrs. White says to herself, "I'm absolutely normal and so is my husband, but I am not so sure about my husband's family. He had an Aunt Mabel who. . ."

Basically, all three mothers assume that their babies are the way that they are for predetermined genetic reasons.

But their three very different babies are not a product of genetic differences.

Each of them is a product of their environment.

The Green baby is a product of an enriched environment (even though in the Green family this happens to have been a happy accident).

The Brown baby is a product of a visually average environment, and this too is an accident.

The White baby is a product of an environment very low in visual stimulation. Unhappily, this too is an accident.

How very sad that we raise our children by accident.

We feed their stomachs with the best food we can buy.

We feed their brains by accident.

We should above all other things give our babies the most important of all rights, the right to achieve their full human potential. And that, after all, is why you are reading this book. This book will show you how to grow your precious baby's brain, rather than waiting for the non-existent preset alarm clock to ring.

Each baby is a product of his environment.

Remember: *The brain grows by use.*

In the case of the Green, Brown, and White families, the difference was in the stimulation of the visual pathways of the brain, which combined with the other pathways, actually comprise the brain.

Each of the three babies is a product of how many times mother or father turned the light on and off. The sun comes up and the sun goes down. That's two stimuli for the baby. Beyond that, what's critical is how many times the "accident" of the light reflex occurs.

When we turn the lights on in a dark room this stimulates the light reflex. The pupil will reflexively constrict in the presence of light and will dilate in the darkness. In most households this happens several times a day by accident.

What father in history ever came home and said to his wife, "How many times did you turn the light on and off for the baby today?"

But in the households of our families at The Institutes for The Achievement of Human Potential, that is exactly what happens. Fathers and mothers of blind, brain-injured children arrange for this "accident" to happen hundreds of times a day so that their blind children can develop, improve, or strengthen their light reflex, which is the first all-important step to being able to see.

Fathers and mothers of well newborn babies arrange for this "accident" to happen dozens of times a day so that their well babies can improve and strengthen their light reflex and thereby gain the ability to see more rapidly.

The importance of the well baby gaining the ability to see more rapidly is not simply so we can say, "How nice. He is growing faster than other babies his age." What good is that to the baby?

The significance of gaining the ability to see earlier is far greater. The average baby is trapped in a visually ordinary room at the very moment when his brain is growing at its fastest rate. He is capable of taking in a tremendous amount of information but his visual pathway is not sufficiently developed to do so.

The newborn who is stimulated, and thereby gains the ability to see weeks or even months earlier, has the wonderful opportunity to see everything that is around him during the period when his brain is growing so very rapidly.

This visual ability then leads to the maturation of other pathways. Once he can see, he begins to understand more easily what we

> The newborn who is stimulated has the opportunity to see during the period when his brain is growing very rapidly.

are saying to him. When he can see, his need to move is hugely increased. As a result, he tries harder to move and moves more. This movement both stimulates his sense of touch and helps to further develop his vision. His increased movement helps his chest to grow and as a result his respiration improves. This better respiration allows him to make sounds more easily so he can communicate his needs better.

Thus begins a happy cycle of events, each one touching off yet another spark, each spark igniting yet another new ability.

The more the brain is used the more it grows, and the more capable the baby becomes. This is the very definition of using the brain.

This stimulation should be done on purpose, not by accident.

The brain-injured child cannot afford to be stimulated by accident and, in truth, neither should the well newborn baby.

The ability of the child is a product of stimulation and opportunity, not of a preset alarm clock or a predetermined genetic design.

The *reality* of how the brain really develops turns out to be much better than the old *idea* of how the brain develops. The truth turns out to be much better than the fiction.

Here we have seen how the *visual* pathway begins to grow by use. The brain is composed of *six* pathways that *all* grow by use. It's time to have a look at what those six pathways are.

Stimulation should be done on purpose, not by accident. The more the brain is used the more it grows, and the more capable the baby becomes.

7

The Institutes Developmental Profile

The Institutes Developmental Profile is a delineation of the significant stages of development that normal children pass through as they progress from birth to six years of age. It reflects progressive brain development. The Profile was developed after years of research and study of how children develop.

We found that there are six abilities that characterize human beings and make them different from every other creature.

These six functions are unique to human beings and all of them are functions of our unique cerebral cortex.

Three of these functions are motor in nature, and they are entirely dependent upon the other three, which are sensory in nature.

The three unique motor functions of all human beings are:

1. To walk and run in an upright position and in a true cross pattern (with opposite limbs moving together).

2. To speak in a complex symbolic vocal language invented and maintained by agreement and convention, such as English, Chinese, Spanish, Japanese, Italian, etc.

3. To write that invented, symbolic language by opposing thumb to forefinger.

These three motor functions are absolutely unique to human beings and each is a function of the unique human cortex.

These three motor skills are based on three unique sensory skills:

1. To see in such a way as to read the invented, symbolic language.

2. To hear in such a way as to understand that invented, symbolic language.

3. To feel in such a way as to be able to identify an object by touch alone and without confirming what it is by seeing, hearing, smelling, or tasting it.

Each of these three sensory functions is unique to human beings and each is a function of our unique human cortex.

After studying the early development of both brain-injured and well children, we found that each of these six functions developed through seven stages, beginning at birth and ending at six years of age.

The seven stages of function correspond to seven stages of development of the brain. This occurs as different parts of the brain, which all exist at birth, develop and become functional.

Stage I   Early Brain Stem and Cord

Stage II   Brain Stem and Early Subcortical Areas

Stage III   Midbrain and Subcortical Areas

Stage IV   Initial Cortex

Stage V   Early Cortex

Stage VI   Primitive Cortex

Stage VII   Sophisticated Cortex

We found that in average children these stages become functional at approximately the same time on the road to reaching each of the six functions. These seven critical periods, though highly variable, are, roughly:

Birth

2.5 months

7 months

12 months

18 months

36 months

72 months

With these pieces of the puzzle in place, it was possible to create a chart that shows the six vital and unique human functions and the seven stages at which they occur in a well child (see Figure 7.1 on page 42).

Once we had determined the significant stages that a baby must go through in order to complete his development, we needed to determine which functions are critical to human growth and development.

This involved careful observation of hundreds of well babies at all stages of development. This study has spanned the last fifty years and continues to the present day.

If The Institutes are remembered a hundred years hence it will more than likely be because of The Institutes Developmental Profile, which is the fruit of much of our labor.

This Profile is a description of the growth and development of the human brain from birth to the point of maturation of the brain at six years of age.

It is a no-nonsense document that is designed to be clear and straightforward so that any parent can study it and, what is much more important, use it easily.

The challenge of creating the Developmental Profile was to decide not what to *include* but rather what to *exclude.* There are literally thousands of events that take place during the first six years of development. Gesell and his staff spent years cataloging those events. It was a monumental task.

Essentially they had documented everything that a child did in those all important years between birth and five years of age.

But we wanted to know a much more important thing: Of all the thousands of things a well child does in the process of growing up from birth to six, which things matter?

In short, of the multitude of things that a baby does, which things are causes and which things simply results?

Which would prevent him from developing normally if they were removed from his life?

Each of these seven stages of development are the responsibility of a different stage of the brain. While all these stages of the brain *exist* in the newborn at birth, they *become functional* in successive order, from the lowest stage at birth to the highest stage of development at six years of age in the average child.

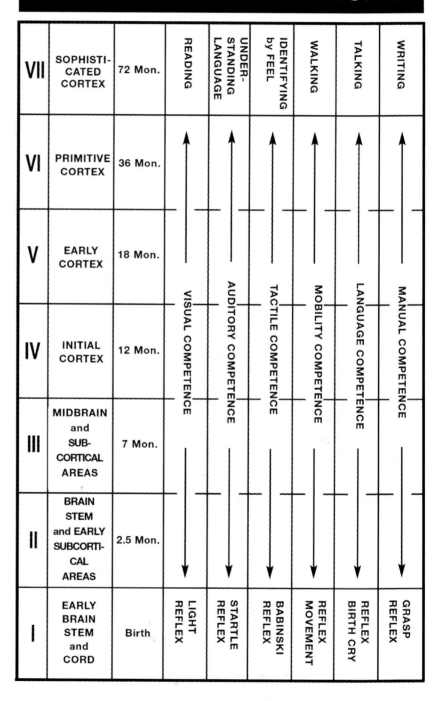

THE DEVELOPMENTAL PROFILE

			READING	UNDERSTANDING LANGUAGE	IDENTIFYING by FEEL	WALKING	TALKING	WRITING
VII	SOPHISTICATED CORTEX	72 Mon.						
VI	PRIMITIVE CORTEX	36 Mon.						
V	EARLY CORTEX	18 Mon.	VISUAL COMPETENCE	AUDITORY COMPETENCE	TACTILE COMPETENCE	MOBILITY COMPETENCE	LANGUAGE COMPETENCE	MANUAL COMPETENCE
IV	INITIAL CORTEX	12 Mon.						
III	MIDBRAIN and SUB-CORTICAL AREAS	7 Mon.						
II	BRAIN STEM and EARLY SUBCORTICAL AREAS	2.5 Mon.						
I	EARLY BRAIN STEM and CORD	Birth	LIGHT REFLEX	STARTLE REFLEX	BABINSKI REFLEX	REFLEX MOVEMENT	REFLEX BIRTH CRY	GRASP REFLEX

Then we needed to add:

1. A diagram of the human brain with its successive stages of development.

2. The specific brain function itself in each of the forty-two blocks.

3. A color code to distinguish each of the brain stages.

Thus a child's progress can be plotted, stage by stage and column by column on the Profile.

This enables parents to ascertain their child's correct overall neurological age and handle any weak points that are found.

Actually the Profile gives us six neurological ages: a visual age, an auditory age, a tactile age, a mobility age, a language age, and a manual age.

Mother evaluates her baby in each of the six columns to find out which abilities in each area her baby has and which abilities he does not have. A line is then drawn across the top of the highest stage that the baby has achieved in each of the six columns. Parents sometimes expect that the highest stage will be the same in all six columns but this is seldom the case.

The sensory side of the Profile is, by necessity, higher than the motor side. The child must gain a good bit of sensory input before that input will become motor output. In short, the information must go into the brain before we can expect it to come out. For this reason the motor side of the Profile will often be somewhat behind the sensory side.

It is possible that a lower area in some of the columns is not perfect. It is possible to achieve a higher stage before all lower stages are perfect. However, the child will not achieve perfection at the top of the Profile (Stage VII) until he has perfected all lower stages.

Finally, we had what has become known as The Institutes Developmental Profile (see Figure 7.2).

As we have said, in the past it was theorized that this progression was a predestined and unalterable fact that resulted from predetermined genetic inheritance superimposed upon a rigid schedule of time and sequence.

We have shown this to be untrue.

The order in which the significant stages of development take place (visual, auditory, and tactile on the sensory side of the Profile, and mobility, language, and manual development on the motor side) is a function of the brain's development as successively higher stages are brought into play.

The timetable is highly variable and depends upon two things:

1. The frequency, intensity, and duration of the stimuli provided to the brain by the child's environment.

2. The neurological condition of the child.

Figure 7.2.
The Institutes
Developmental Profile

	PREDOMINANT BRAIN STAGE	TIME FRAME		VISUAL COMPETENCE	AUDITORY COMPETENCE	TACTILE COMPETENCE
VII	SOPHISTICATED CORTEX	Superior	36 Mon.	Reading with total understanding	Understanding of complete vocabulary and proper sentences	Tactile identification of objects
		Average	72 Mon.			
		Slow	144 Mon.	*Sophisticated human understanding*	*Sophisticated human understanding*	*Sophisticated human understanding*
VI	PRIMITIVE CORTEX	Superior	18 Mon.	Identification of visual symbols and letters within experience	Understanding of 2000 words and simple sentences	Ability to determine characteristics of objects by tactile means
		Average	36 Mon.			
		Slow	72 Mon.	*Primitive human understanding*	*Primitive human understanding*	*Primitive human understanding*
V	EARLY CORTEX	Superior	9 Mon.	Differentiation of similar but unlike simple visual symbols	Understanding of 10 to 25 words and two couplets	Tactile differentiation of similar but unlike objects
		Average	18 Mon.			
		Slow	36 Mon.	*Early human understanding*	*Early human understanding*	*Early human understanding*
IV	INITIAL CORTEX	Superior	6 Mon.	Convergence of vision resulting in simple depth perception	Understanding of two words of speech	Tactile understanding of the third dimension in objects which appear to be flat
		Average	12 Mon.			
		Slow	24 Mon.	*Initial human understanding*	*Initial human understanding*	*Initial human understanding*
III	MIDBRAIN and SUBCORTICAL AREAS	Superior	3.5 Mon.	Appreciation of detail within a configuration	Appreciation of meaningful sounds	Appreciation of gnostic sensation
		Average	7 Mon.			
		Slow	14 Mon.	*Meaningful appreciation*	*Meaningful appreciation*	*Meaningful appreciation*
II	BRAIN STEM and EARLY SUBCORTICAL AREAS	Superior	1 Mon.	Outline perception	Vital response to threatening sounds	Perception of vital sensation
		Average	2.5 Mon.			
		Slow	5 Mon.	*Vital perception*	*Vital perception*	*Vital perception*
I	EARLY BRAIN STEM and CORD	Superior	Birth to .5	Light reflex	Startle reflex	Babinski reflex
		Average	Birth to 1.0			
		Slow	Birth to 2.0	*Reflex reception*	*Reflex reception*	*Reflex reception*

The Developmental Profile details the development of every child from birth to six years of age, when neurological development is effectively complete.

In creating this Profile we have not used the conventional psychological, developmental, or medical terms. These terms often represent an observable chronology that accompanies a child's development, and while these events may be true, they are none-

THE INSTITUTES DEVELOPMENTAL PROFILE BY GLENN J. DOMAN	MOBILITY	LANGUAGE	MANUAL COMPETENCE
	Using a leg in a skilled role which is consistent with the dominant hemisphere *Sophisticated human expression*	Complete vocabulary and proper sentence structure *Sophisticated human expression*	Using a hand to write which is consistent with the dominant hemisphere *Sophisticated human expression*
	Walking and running in complete cross pattern *Primitive human expression*	2000 words of language and short sentences *Primitive human expression*	Bimanual function with one hand in a skilled role *Primitive human expression*
	Walking with arms freed from the primary balance role *Early human expression*	10 to 25 words of language and two couplets *Early human expression*	Cortical opposition bilaterally and simultaneously *Early human expression*
	Walking with arms used in a primary balance role most frequently at or above shoulder height *Initial human expression*	Two words of speech used spontaneously and meaningfully *Initial human expression*	Cortical opposition in either hand *Initial human expression*
	Creeping on hands and knees, culminating in cross-pattern creeping *Meaningful response*	Creation of meaningful sounds *Meaningful response*	Prehensile grasp *Meaningful response*
	Crawling in the prone position culminating in cross-pattern crawling *Vital response*	Vital crying in response to threats to life *Vital response*	Vital release *Vital response*
THE INSTITUTES FOR THE ACHIEVEMENT OF HUMAN POTENTIAL® 8801 STENTON AVENUE WYNDMOOR, PENNSYLVANIA 19038	Movement of arms and legs without bodily movement *Reflex response*	Birth cry and crying *Reflex response*	Grasp reflex *Reflex response*

theless not significant to his development.

In addition, many of these terms mean different things to different people. That diminishes their usefulness as reliable tools, and it accounts for widely differing reports by various observers as to when specific abilities occur in the average child.

The Profile was devised because of the need for a precise standard of comparison as we dealt with children who ranged from brain-injured to superior. While the children varied from developmental norms, they had to be measured against those norms and averages.

Our goal with each child is to help him go through these stages of healthy development in their proper order, and to do it with the greatest possible speed while achieving excellent function.

We use The Institutes Developmental Profile as a standard of normal progression. We measure each child's progress against it, and then we design an appropriate home program to speed that progress.

The forty-two functions in the Profile are the key factors in a child's life from birth to six. How quickly and how well he achieves them will strongly influence his intellectual, physical, and social function for the rest of his life.

The accomplishment of each of these forty-two vital functions is an unadulterated product of the number of times a child has the opportunity to perform each of the functions.

8

Evaluating Your Newborn Baby

I t is very important to evaluate the basic functions of a newborn baby, and it is not difficult to do so.

This first evaluation should take place as soon after birth as possible. Ideally, it should be within the first twenty-four hours of birth, and if not then, as soon as mother can manage.

If you find that any of your baby's functions or responses are less than perfect, it is not a signal for panic or fear, but for thoughtful and appropriate action. The whole point of doing this evaluation is, in fact, to help design an effective neurological program for your baby, whatever the outcome of this initial evaluation may be.

With a newborn, mother and father need only evaluate Stage I of the Developmental Profile. These are all the functions at the bottom of the Profile, in red. This is the reflex stage of development. All of these functions should be present at birth in the well newborn baby.

At birth the baby has reflexes. These can be elicited and observed immediately after delivery. He arrives with all levels of the brain present and ready to be used, but it is the medulla and early subcortical areas that are functioning at birth.

VISUAL COMPETENCE: STAGE I

The Light Reflex

At this stage mother simply needs to evaluate her baby's *light reflex*. The light reflex is the response of the pupil to light. In the absence of light the pupil dilates to allow more light to enter. In the presence of light the pupil constricts. This constriction of the pupil is called the light reflex.

Materials Needed:

• household flashlight

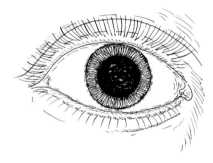

Figure 8.1. Pupil dilates in dark

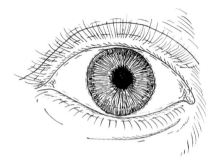

Figure 8.2. Pupil constricts in light

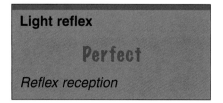

Light reflex

Perfect

Reflex reception

Figure 8.3. Perfect light reflex

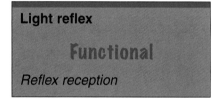

Light reflex

Functional

Reflex reception

Figure 8.4. Functional light reflex

This is a very important reflex that is in use throughout life. The state of this reflex provides us with a small but important window through which we can see, to some degree, whether the brain is functioning normally or not.

In order to evaluate the light reflex in a newborn baby, it is important to know, as a standard for comparison, what a normal reflex looks like. Since it is generally easier to see the reflex in an adult, mother should gain experience by observing father's light reflex, and father should practice checking mother's light reflex.

You will need a regular household flashlight and a dark room, as dark as possible. Wait a minute or so for the eyes to adjust to the dark. The pupils will expand to maximum dilation (see Figure 8.1). Then gently cover the left eye and, holding the flashlight six to eight inches from the right eye, turn it on and shine it briefly into the eye. You will see the pupil constrict instantly when you flood the eye with light (see Figure 8.2). That constriction should be immediate and the pupil should constrict to a pinpoint. This is a normal response.

Now wait ten seconds. Gently cover the right eye and repeat the process with the left eye. You should see the same response.

If the response of the left eye seems to be less than the right eye it may be because you have not waited long enough between stimulating the right eye and the left eye. Even though you have covered the left eye while you stimulate the right eye it will still have a sympathetic response. This is why you need to wait between stimulations.

Now you have evoked and observed a normal light reflex. To increase your confidence, do it again several times, and try it on others to be sure you know what you are looking for. If it seems pretty easy, you are on the right track. It *is* easy.

Now you are ready to evaluate this important reflex when your baby is born.

You may find that evaluating a newborn baby is somewhat more difficult than evaluating an adult. Remember, you are looking for an immediate and complete constriction of the pupil in both eyes. If you find it, then write "Perfect" on the light reflex box of the Profile and draw a blue line across the top edge of this box (see Figure 8.3).

A less-than-perfect response would be a reflex that is slow in either eye or in both eyes, or incomplete in one or in both eyes. An incomplete response would be one in which the pupil did not constrict fully. If either eye is slow or incomplete, write "Functional" in blue in the light reflex box of the Profile and draw a blue line across the top edge of this box (see Figure 8.4).

A blind child sometimes has no light reflex whatsoever in either eye. When this is the case, we draw the blue line at the bottom edge of this box (see Figure 8.5).

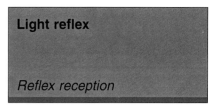

Figure 8.5. Zero light reflex

AUDITORY COMPETENCE: STAGE I

The Startle Reflex

The next reflex to evaluate in your newborn is the *startle reflex*. The startle reflex occurs in the presence of a sudden, sharp, loud noise. When such a sound occurs unexpectedly, we will jump or startle. We have all experienced this reaction.

In the newborn this reaction appears to be the result of conscious fear, since the newborn's body stiffens so suddenly. However, a true startle reflex is in no way a conscious act since it is, as the name states, a reflex and is therefore at a much lower stage.

The startle reflex is not only normal but desirable in the newborn and in all human beings.

The startle reflex will occur in the presence of a sharp, loud sound. The sharpness of the sound is more important than the loudness, although both are factors.

The startle reflex is therefore much more likely to be seen when a door is slammed, a plate dropped, or, when a person clears his throat suddenly than when a sound gradually becomes louder, such as a fire siren.

The purpose of the startle reflex is to place us instantly on the alert in the presence of a sudden, loud sound that by its very nature might be threatening to us.

Again, mother may wish to elicit a startle reflex first on father. For simplicity's sake we use two thick blocks of wood. Two pieces of 2" x 4" lumber, 6 to 8 inches long, will do nicely. When banged

Materials Needed:

• 2 blocks of wood
(L 6"/ W 4"/ D 2")

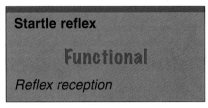

Figure 8.6. Perfect startle reflex

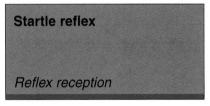

Figure 8.7. Functional startle reflex

Startle reflex

Reflex reception

Figure 8.8. Zero startle reflex

together the blocks will create a sound that is sufficiently loud to elicit a startle reflex.

In order to do this with an adult you must do it unexpectedly. This will not make you popular, but you will get to see a nice healthy startle reflex. Father can be encouraged to retaliate at an equally unexpected moment and then mother will have the opportunity not only to evaluate the startle reflex but to experience it.

You will then be ready to evaluate baby's startle reflex. Take the blocks of wood and hold them *at least two feet away* from the baby and clap them together. You should see the baby instantly startle, usually by a stiffening of his entire body.

If you see an immediate and complete response, write "Perfect" on the startle reflex box of the Profile and draw a blue line across the top edge of the box (see Figure 8.6).

If there is a delayed response rather than an immediate one, mark "Functional" on the startle reflex box and draw a blue line across the top edge of the box (see Figure 8.7).

A child with an auditory problem will show some indication that he heard the sound but will not startle. A deaf child will not hear the sound at all and will not startle. In the case of both of these children, we draw the blue line at the bottom edge of the startle reflex box (see Figure 8.8).

TACTILE COMPETENCE: STAGE I

The Babinski Reflex

Now we need to evaluate the *Babinski reflex*, which is seen in the feet. It is present in the healthy child from birth until approximately twelve months of age. At that time it is replaced by the plantar reflex, which we retain for the rest of our lives.

The Babinski reflex can be elicited by running the flat part of the thumbnail along the outside edge of the sole of the baby's foot from the heel to the toes. When this is done the baby's big toe will go up and the remaining toes will fan outward (see Figure 8.9).

The plantar reflex can be seen in adults. If mother scratches the sole of father's foot from heel to toe, his toes will bend down instead

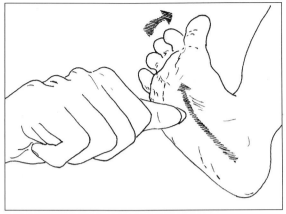

Figure 8.9. Babinski reflex

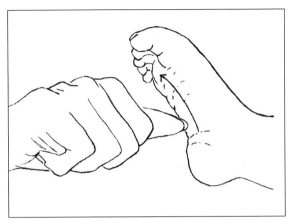

Figure 8.10. Plantar reflex

of extending upward. He will, in effect, be withdrawing the sole of the foot from the stimulus (see Figure 8.10).

Since this is the case, parents will not be able to use each other to see a Babinski reflex. Instead, mother should evaluate this response on a number of well babies from birth to twelve months.

The purpose of the Babinski reflex is to help the newborn baby to gain traction with his feet in order to crawl. When the big toe goes up and the little toes fan outward, this helps him to dig in and makes it easier for him to move forward. Once he can crawl and creep he no longer needs this reflex. In fact, it would not be helpful in the process of walking. When he begins to walk he will lose this reflex and acquire the plantar reflex.

If you see the correct response in both feet when you evaluate the Babinski reflex in your newborn, write "Perfect" in the Babinski reflex box on the Profile and draw a blue line across the top edge of this box (see Figure 8.11).

If there is the correct response in one foot but not the other, write "Functional" in the Babinski reflex box and draw the blue line across the top edge of the box (see Figure 8.12).

An insensate child sometimes has no Babinski reflex. When we evaluate such a child, we draw the blue line across the bottom edge of this box (see Figure 8.13).

Figure 8.11. Perfect Babinski reflex

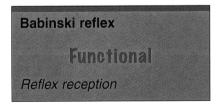

Figure 8.12. Functional Babinski reflex

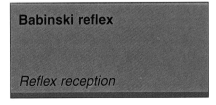

Figure 8.13. Zero Babinski reflex

MOBILITY COMPETENCE: STAGE I

Freedom of Movement

Movement of arms and legs without bodily movement
Perfect
Reflex response

Figure 8.14. Perfect movement

At birth babies can move all four limbs freely. This should be very easy to observe. Again it may be helpful for mother to observe other babies who are only a few days or a few weeks of age, before her baby is born.

It is easy to observe the free motion of all four limbs when the baby is on his back. This is the position in which motion and function at Stage I should be evaluated.

If your newborn baby can move all four limbs freely, write "Perfect" on the movement of arms and legs box of the Developmental Profile and draw a blue line across the top edge of this box (see Figure 8.14).

Movement of arms and legs without bodily movement
Functional
Reflex response

Figure 8.15. Functional movement

If your baby does not move one or more of his limbs or the movement is restricted in comparison to the other limbs, write "Functional" on the movement of arms and legs box of the Profile (see Figure 8.15).

A paralyzed child will sometimes have no movement whatsoever in one or more limbs. In this case, we draw the blue line at the bottom edge of this box on the Profile (see Figure 8.16).

Movement of arms and legs without bodily movement
Reflex response

Figure 8.16. Zero movement

Also, at the earliest possible moment after birth, put your baby *on his belly, naked,* and observe his movement. A healthy baby who has had an easy delivery will actually be able to move forward somewhat, even within a few moments of birth.

It is a tradition in some cultures that immediately following birth the baby is placed on his mother's body, at the hip, and given the opportunity to crawl from her hip up her body to find the breast in order to nurse. This is a very sane custom. It demonstrates that the newborn can, in fact, crawl a bit if he is given immediate opportunity to do so.

LANGUAGE COMPETENCE: STAGE I

The Birth Cry

The *birth cry* of the newborn baby is surely the most ancient of all evaluations as to the well-being of the new baby. Once the baby has arrived, he should have a good, loud, lusty cry.

If your baby has a good, loud cry at birth, or shortly thereafter, write "Perfect" on the birth cry box of the Profile and draw a blue line across the top edge of this box (see Figure 8.17).

If your baby has a weak or very soft cry, write "Functional" on the birth cry box and draw a blue line across the top edge of this box (see Figure 8.18).

Some hurt children have no cry whatsoever at birth or shortly thereafter. In this case we draw the blue line at the bottom edge of the birth cry box (see Figure 8.19).

MANUAL COMPETENCE: STAGE I

The Grasp Reflex

The *grasp reflex* is very apparent in the healthy baby at birth.

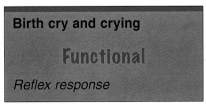

Figure 8.17. Perfect birth cry

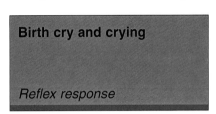

Figure 8.18. Functional birth cry

Birth cry and crying

Reflex response

Figure 8.19. Zero birth cry

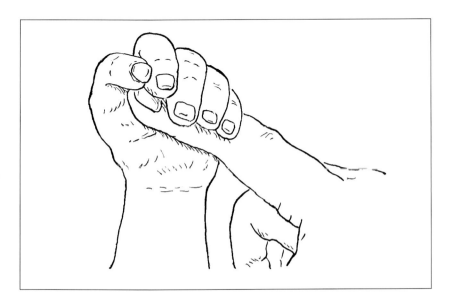

Figure 8.20.
Grasp reflex

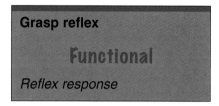

Figure 8.21. Perfect grasp reflex

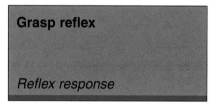

Figure 8.22. Functional grasp reflex

Grasp reflex

Reflex response

Figure 8.23. Zero grasp reflex

When something is put into the hand of the baby, he will reflexively grasp whatever has been placed there. This is called the grasp reflex. This reflex allows the baby to hang onto something, if need be, immediately after birth.

The easiest way to evaluate this reflex in your newborn baby is to put your baby on his belly, then place your right index finger into his fisted left hand as you place your left index finger into his fisted right hand. Then gently pull the baby toward you with your index fingers. As the baby feels the pressure of your index fingers you will feel his grasp tighten significantly. This is the grasp reflex (see Figure 8.20).

If your baby has the correct reflex in both hands, write "Perfect" on the grasp reflex box of the Developmental Profile and draw a blue line at the top edge of the box (see Figure 8.21).

If one hand is clearly not as good as the other or if either hand does not have a grasp reflex, write "Functional" on the grasp reflex box and draw a blue line at the top edge of the box (see Figure 8.22).

Some hurt children have no grasp reflex at birth. In this case we draw a blue line at the bottom edge of the grasp reflex box (see Figure 8.23).

SUMMARY

You have now completed the first evaluation of your baby. You have drawn a blue line across each of the six columns of the Developmental Profile and you have marked each of the six boxes at the reflexive level as they pertain to your newborn baby.

This first evaluation gives you *a neurological baseline* for your baby. Mark this very first Profile in blue. Blue always denotes the first evaluation.

The completely well baby will have a blue line at the top edge of each of the six red boxes on the Profile and will be marked "Perfect" in each of these boxes.

If there is any area marked "Functional," you immediately know which sensory area needs increased levels of stimulation or which motor area needs more opportunity in order to develop completely. It is as simple as that.

When there is any area where the blue line is drawn across the bottom of a red box on the Profile, we know that the baby has a significant problem.

The sooner you know this the sooner you can take action to design an effective neurological program. This will insure that the baby will be able to gain the functions that he lacks and move up the Profile at the earliest possible moment.

Now you have taken the first important step by learning how to use The Institutes Developmental Profile to evaluate your newborn.

We are now ready to learn how to use the Profile to design an effective program to stimulate brain growth and development in your newborn baby.

9

The Sensory Program for Your Newborn

We are now ready to design a specific program to grow your baby's brain—not by accident but on purpose. We will tailor that program to fit your baby's neurological condition, but first you must understand a bit more about the structure of the brain.

The brain is divided physically into two major sections, the back and the front. The back half of the brain and the spinal cord is devoted to incoming pathways. These incoming pathways are one-way roads into the brain. They are our five senses: seeing, hearing, feeling, tasting, and smelling.

All that Leonardo, Shakespeare, Beethoven, and Thomas Jefferson knew about the world they learned through these five pathways. Of these five, seeing, hearing, and feeling are the pathways vital to human beings. These pathways will become, by six years of age, reading, understanding, and sophisticated tactile perception. Since these are entirely one-way paths into the brain, we must feed them by means of stimulation.

The front half of the brain and the spinal cord is comprised of the motor pathways. Their purpose is to act upon the information that the brain has received through the sensory pathways. These motor pathways are mobility, language, and manual competence. They are also vital to the child because they will later become walking, talking, and writing.

Since the motor pathways are one-way roads leading *out* of the brain, it is impossible to grow them by stimulation as we do with the sensory pathways, which are incoming. To grow the outgoing pathways, we must give babies the maximum opportunity to move, make sounds, and use their hands.

There is, of course, a connection in the brain between the incoming and the outgoing pathways. Engineers call it a "cybernetic loop." It enables us to be affected by our environment and to act on the environment in response.

The following diagram depicts this connection, or "cybernetic loop" (see Figure 9.1).

Obviously we cannot design a good program to help the new baby develop his potential without knowing exactly where he is on the Developmental Profile. That is why we began with a careful evaluation. Even if you are using this book to help a child who is not a newborn, a careful evaluation, using the Developmental Profile, is the first step.

After completing the evaluation it is very important to have the correct tools to design a sensory program, the purpose of which is to enhance the growth and development of the baby. For the well baby this means giving him a true head start. For a baby who is behind in any area, this means helping him to close the gap.

The Developmental Profile is not only very easy to use to evaluate the baby but also to create the best sensory program for the baby.

The sensory side of the Profile is composed of three of the five pathways that lead into the brain. It does not deal with taste and

Figure 9.1.
Cybernetic loop

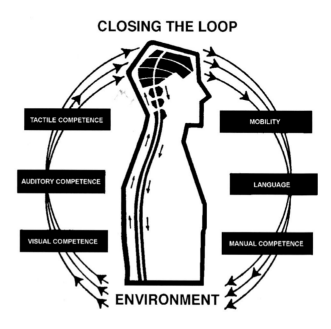

smell, as they are far less important to neurological development than the other three sensory pathways.

In order to develop these sensory pathways, the baby needs visual, auditory, and tactile stimulation. The sum total of this stimulation will come from mother, father, and the environment they create for the baby.

If there is any area on the sensory side of the Developmental Profile where your child is not as high as he should be for his age, that area becomes the top priority when creating your sensory program. However, the sensory program must also be designed to *reinforce* those abilities that your child already has.

It is a common mistake to believe that once a child has achieved a stage of development he no longer needs stimulation at that stage. Actually, achieving the new stage is just the beginning. The baby needs tremendous reinforcement at each stage in order to reach the next stage, which will occur much sooner than if left to accident.

The sensory stimulation program is a natural and happy process that helps the baby begin to see, hear, and feel for the first time. This is of enormous benefit to the tiny baby. Afterall, it is not easy to be functionally blind, deaf, and insensate. There are those who argue that the baby must wait for seeing, hearing, and feeling to develop by accident because this is more "natural." But there is nothing natural or worthwhile about being functionally blind and deaf and insensate for weeks or even months longer than is necessary. The truth is that the every child has a natural and insatiable hunger to experience and to know about the world around him. Seeing, hearing, and feeling *are* the basis for this exploration.

SUMMARY

1. Parents provide sensory stimulation in the form of visual, auditory, and tactile stimulation.

2. Any area that is below age level on the Profile is addressed first in the program.

3. The primary focus of the program is to reinforce the stage that baby has achieved.

4. The program should also provide sensory stimulation for the stage just above the level of baby's present function.

THE SENSORY STIMULATION PROGRAM

We know that the newborn baby is essentially living in a blind, deaf, and relatively insensate world, so our job is extremely clear. We must provide the baby with as much stimulation as we can so that the baby can graduate as quickly as possible from the confusing and difficult world into which he was born.

In the sensory world of the newborn, seeing, hearing, and feeling are actually hard work. It is an effort for the baby to use his vision, his hearing, and his tactile sense.

We adults see, hear, and feel so effortlessly that it is hard to imagine the eager and earnest effort that the newborn makes in order to see, hear, and feel.

We must make an environment in which it is easy to see, easy to hear, and easy to feel. This will encourage the baby to turn on his vision, hearing, and feeling more often.

We are not forcing him to do these things. We are simply stimulating these pathways and giving him the opportunity to respond.

We must never forget the basic fact: *The brain grows by use.*

The visual, auditory, and tactile pathways are part of the brain.

The child's visual pathway from the eyes to the brain grows by use.

The child's auditory pathway from the ears to the brain grows by use.

The child's tactile pathway from the skin to the brain grows by use.

This means that every time he sees, his visual pathway actually grows. This makes seeing easier and better. This cycle of improvement proceeds until his visual pathway is totally, completely, and fully mature.

A program of sensory stimulation will help to determine whether this visual maturation happens by the age of three, which is splendid, or by the age of six, which is average, or by the age of nine, which is a serious problem, or never, which is tragic and is called blindness. The different results depend on how soon, how often, and how thoroughly the child has the opportunity to develop that visual pathway and, of course, the neurological well-being of the child.

The same principles apply to the auditory and tactile pathways as well as the olfactory and gustatory pathways. However, taste and smell are far less important to survival and healthy neurological development in human beings than they are in animals.

VISUAL COMPETENCE: STAGE I

The Visual Program

Your baby's first visual stimulation program will consist of *stimulating the light reflex*. This will make the light reflex faster and stronger, and help him to achieve the next visual stage more quickly.

Materials Needed:
• household flashlight

Objective: To establish, improve, or reinforce the light reflex

Purpose: Stimulation of the light reflex

Frequency: 10 times daily

Intensity: Regular household flashlight

Duration: About a minute

Content: 5 stimulations for each eye

Environment: A completely dark room

Technique: Cradle the baby in your arms or place the baby on his back in a comfortable position. Give him a kiss and a hug then gently cover the left eye with your hand. Hold the flashlight six to eight inches from your baby and shine the light into the right eye. Observe the constriction of the pupil. This usually takes about one second or so. Turn the light off and wait five seconds in the dark. Now gently cover the right eye with your hand and shine the light in the left eye. Observe the constriction of the pupil. Wait five seconds in the dark and repeat the above process. Alternate between the two eyes. You should be able to provide five stimulations for each eye in one minute.

Please Note: You may find that sometimes your baby's light reflex is much better than at other times. This may be disconcerting, especially if it was perfect the very first time you evaluated it. Do not be alarmed. The newborn baby will be inconsistent. When he is well-rested you will see a response that is clearly better than when he is sleepy or a bit under the weather. As you continue to stimulate this reflex and the auditory and tactile reflexes, you will see that each of them becomes more and more consistent. As you shine the light each time, say to your baby in a loud, clear, voice "light." This provides your baby with auditory stimulation and teaches him the word "light." When you have finished, cuddle him again and tell him how much you love him.

AUDITORY COMPETENCE: STAGE I

The Auditory Program

Materials Needed:

• 2 blocks of wood
(L 6"/ W 4"/ D 2")

Your baby's first auditory program will consist of *stimulating the startle reflex*. This will make his startle reflex more consistent if it is somewhat inconsistent, and it will mature his response so that it becomes less of a full body startle and more like the milder adult startle.

This process of reinforcing and stimulating the startle reflex will help your baby to achieve the next auditory stage more quickly and easily.

Objective:　To establish, improve, or reinforce the startle reflex

Purpose:　Stimulation of the startle reflex

Frequency:　10 times daily

Intensity:　Banging two blocks together

Duration:　10 seconds

Content:　3 stimulations

Environment:　A quiet room

Technique:　Place the baby on his back in a comfortable position where you can observe his face easily and he can see yours. Smile at him and tell him, "Now you are going to hear blocks!" Hold the blocks two feet away from him and bang them together loudly once. Observe your baby's response. Wait three seconds and bang them together again. Observe your baby's response. Again wait three seconds and bang the blocks for the final time. Each time you bang the blocks together say in a loud, clear voice "blocks." When you finish ask him, "Did you like the blocks?" or "Is Mommy banging those blocks again?" Make every moment with your baby light-hearted and fun.

Please Note: You may find that at first your baby has a bigger response after the second or third stimulation. This is typical of the immaturity of the newborn. He needs the cumulative effect of one or two stimulations in order for the message to arrive in the brain. As you continue to stimulate the baby he will begin to respond consistently the very first time. A consistent response is the hallmark of a more mature sensory pathway. When you see that consistent response you know that the pathway is growing because you provided an opportunity for the baby to *use* it.

TACTILE COMPETENCE: STAGE I

The Tactile Program

Your baby's first tactile program will consist of *stimulating the Babinski reflex*. This will make his Babinski reflex faster and stronger, and will help him to achieve the next tactile stage *and* the next mobility stage more easily.

Objective: To establish, improve, or reinforce the Babinski reflex

Purpose: Stimulating the Babinski reflex

Frequency: 10 times daily

Intensity: The thumbnail pressed against the sole of the foot

Duration: 30 seconds

Content: 3 stimulations for each foot

Environment: Normal environment

Technique: Place the baby on his back in a comfortable position. The baby should have bare feet. Gently take the baby's left leg and hold it with your right hand. Using your left hand, press the flat part of your thumbnail along the outer sole of your baby's foot, starting from the heel and going toward the toes. Observe the baby's response. Then gently take the baby's right leg with your right hand and repeat this procedure. If you are left-handed you may find that you are more comfortable holding the baby's leg with your left hand and stimulating his foot with your right hand.

Each time you touch the baby to elicit the Babinski reflex, say in a loud, clear voice "touch."

Saying "light," "blocks," and "touch" stimulates the auditory pathway, but more than that it is part of the natural exchange between mother and baby. Mothers know intuitively that it is important to tell the baby what is going on. It is very important to establish this line of communication from mother to baby right from birth.

THE SENSORY PROGRAM FOR PROFILE STAGE I

Daily Checklist

Visual Competence:

Stimulating the light reflex: 10x daily for approx. 60 seconds

☐ ☐ ☐ ☐ ☐
☐ ☐ ☐ ☐ ☐

Total time: 10 minutes

Auditory Competence:

Stimulating the startle reflex: 10x daily for 10 seconds

☐ ☐ ☐ ☐ ☐
☐ ☐ ☐ ☐ ☐

Total time: 1 minute 40 seconds

Tactile Competence:

Stimulating the Babinski reflex: 10x daily for 30 seconds

☐ ☐ ☐ ☐ ☐
☐ ☐ ☐ ☐ ☐

Total time: 5 minutes

Changes Noted Today: _____

_____

Date: _____

10

The Motor Opportunity Program for Your Newborn

The motor side of The Institutes Developmental Profile represents all the pathways coming out of the brain.

In order to grow these three critical outgoing pathways, the baby needs opportunity to move, make sounds, and use his hands. Mother and father need to create an environment that gives their baby maximum opportunity to do this.

Please do not be discouraged if there is an area on the Developmental Profile where your baby is below where he should be for his age. The very purpose of the Profile is to show us which areas need attention. We know to make these lower areas a priority when creating a good program.

Just as with the sensory program, the motor program should reinforce the abilities that your baby already has. This will allow him to achieve the next stage much sooner than he would have otherwise.

SUMMARY

1. Parents provide motor opportunity in the form of mobility opportunity, language opportunity, and manual competence opportunity.

2. Any motor area that is below age level on the Profile is addressed first in the program.

3. The primary focus is on reinforcing the motor stage that the baby has already achieved.

4. The program should provide opportunity for the motor stage *above* where the baby is currently.

THE MOTOR OPPORTUNITY PROGRAM

We move, make sounds, and use our hands so effortlessly that it is hard for us to imagine the tremendous effort that the newborn makes in order to do these things. Our job is very clear—to provide ample motor opportunity for the baby so that he can do these things *without effort* and graduate from this vulnerable state as quickly as possible.

The more he uses his abilities the easier it will be to move, to make sounds, and to use his hands. As it becomes easier, he will be more willing to use these abilities. In this way, he becomes more able every minute.

Figure 10.1.
Beatriz gives her newborn, Maria, an opportunity to crawl in her track.

THE MOBILITY PROGRAM

Since it is almost impossible for your baby to move while he is on his back, like an overturned turtle, the first and best thing you can do for him is to create a safe floor environment where he can spend as much time as possible on his belly. This will give him the maximum opportunity to use his arms and legs to learn how to move forward. This will help him to achieve the all-important stage of crawling.

This program will be divided in two parts: specific short sessions in which we encourage the baby to move, and large amounts of opportunity in which the baby is completely free to move in an environment carefully set up for this purpose.

Figure 10.2.
Maria uses the side of
the track to push off.

The Infant Crawling Track

We have developed the infant crawling track as the ideal environment for the newborn baby to move his arms and legs in order to learn to move forward. The infant track is safe, clean, warm, smooth, and cushioned. These are the important elements that together create an excellent mobility environment for the baby.

The track is wide enough to enable the newborn to move his arms and legs easily, yet narrow enough to enable him to push off the sides with his feet. This makes movement much easier.

Materials Needed:

• infant crawling track

Because the track is straight, it keeps the baby moving in a straight line. This is helpful to the newborn who otherwise tends to move backwards or pivot in circles when he first begins to move. This is frustrating for him since he clearly is trying to go forward (see Figure 10.3).

The track is made of plywood or hardwood, with one inch of foam rubber padding covering the floor and sides of the track. Leatherette is secured on top of the foam padding. The result is a well-insulated and cushioned surface that gives the correct amount of friction, spring, and comfort for the newborn baby to move.

The protective sides form a barrier against drafts and protect the newborn from falling out of the track. The surface is easy to keep clean. Use mild soap and water, and rubbing alcohol to keep it disinfected. Allow time to dry.

It is important that the infant crawling track be made *before* your baby is born. Detailed instructions for constructing it are included in the Appendix of this book.

How quickly a newborn learns to use his arms and legs to move forward is a function of how easy or difficult it is for him to move in the first few days or weeks of life. Make sure he has an excellent environment, set up for his needs, then give him as much time as possible to *use* that environment.

Figure 10.3.
Isolda crawls in the flat track with her mother's encouragement.

Part I—The Inclined Infant Crawling Track

Objective: To establish, improve, or reinforce the ability to move arms and legs

Purpose: Create opportunity to move arms and legs in the prone position

Frequency: 10 times daily

Intensity: Gentle incline from 6" to 24"

Duration: 10 to 30 seconds

Content: 1 trip down the inclined crawling track

Environment: A well-lighted room with an infant crawling track (made according to instructions in the Appendix of this book). The room must be warm enough so that the baby is comfortable in very little clothing.

Technique: Dress your baby so that his arms and legs are bare, such as in a diaper and a T-shirt or little baby bodysuit commonly called a "onesie." Place your baby on his belly at *the top end* of his crawling track. Then go to the bottom of the track and get down on the floor so that your baby can see, hear, and even feel that you are

Figure 10.4.
Isolda crawls in the inclined track as her mother cheers her on. Isolda began to crawl at birth.

at the end of the track. Your baby's objective will be to get to you. Each day he will be able to see, hear, and feel you better than he could the day before.

The track should be inclined by raising it at the top end. It should be raised anywhere from 6 to 24 inches, depending on what height is best for your baby. You determine this height by seeing how steep the incline must be in order for your baby to move down the track in less than 60 seconds (see Figure 10.4).

Please Note: Your baby may need to cry in order to move his arms and legs with enough force to come down the inclined track. This is all right. Most newborns need to cry a little in order to increase the rate and depth of their breathing so that they can move. This is rather like a weightlifter who grunts with the effort of lifting a heavy weight, or a tennis player shouting as she hits the ball. As all mothers know, there is a difference between crying and screaming. If your baby is screaming, end the session on the track immediately and find out why he is screaming.

Most of the time the baby will struggle to move his arms and legs in order to come down the inclined track. Cheer him on so that he comes to know that you love to see him move and you appreciate the effort he makes to move. This is an important athletic feat, and no small achievement for the baby.

Part II—The Flat Infant Crawling Track

Objective:	To grow the mobility pathway by establishing, improving, or reinforcing the ability to move arms and legs
Purpose:	Providing maximum opportunity to move arms and legs in the prone position
Frequency:	Done as a way of life
Intensity:	Flat infant crawling track
Duration:	3 to 4 hours daily
Content:	Unlimited opportunity to move in the inclined crawling track
Environment:	A well-lighted room with an infant crawling track. The room must be warm enough so that the baby is comfortable in very little clothing.

Technique: Now that you have created the ideal environment, you only need to add your own enthusiasm and company to complete the equation. Place the baby and his crawling track in whatever room you are working, not only to watch over and protect the baby but to talk to him and encourage him to move down the track and explore his world. At this stage your family should live on the floor with the baby as much as possible. He should not feel abandoned when he is on the floor. Even though he may not be able to see, hear, and feel very well at this point, he does have the ability to sense your presence or absence.

> Newborns move more while they sleep than during the day.

Please Note: The newborn baby will move a great deal in his sleep. In fact, in the first few weeks of life many babies will move more during their sleep than during their waking hours. This means that the floor environment is very important during a baby's sleeping time. This precious time will be wasted if we create an environment in which the baby cannot move.

The infant crawling track can be placed right alongside your bed so that he can sleep safely by your side and have an excellent mobility environment in which to move at night (see Figure 10.5). See the Appendix for more information on the topic of baby's sleeping position.

> A track that wraps around the bed allows the baby to crawl throughout the night.

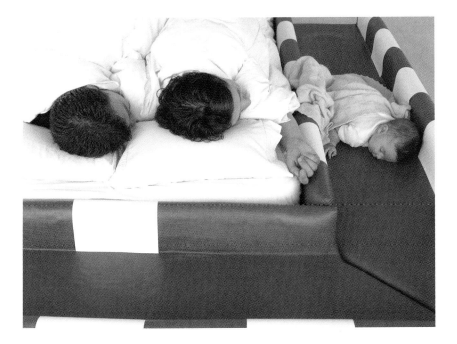

Figure 10.5.
Isolda is close to Mom and Dad but has the maximum freedom to move safely as she sleeps.

There is the added benefit that when the baby awakens to be fed, mother can simply roll over, nurse the baby, put him back in his track, and go right back to sleep. Many mothers have discovered that this is very helpful not only to the baby but to their sleep and well-being.

Part III—Balance Activities

Objective: To grow the balance areas of the brain by establishing, improving, and reinforcing the ability to move through space

Purpose: To provide the maximum opportunity to move through space in a variety of ways

Frequency: 15 times daily

Intensity: Slow and careful movement

Duration: 15 seconds, working up to 45 seconds

Content: 1 balance activity per session

Environment: An open space that is free from obstructions so that you are not in danger of bumping into anything as you do these activities with your baby. The baby should be dressed comfortably and in a way that you can easily maintain a good grasp on his arms, legs, torso, hands, and feet.

Technique: Each of the following activities should be introduced very gradually. Begin with only a few seconds of each activity and by evolution increase the length of each session up to 45 seconds. You should always tell the baby what you are doing before and while you are doing it.

Always stop each activity *before* the baby wants to stop so that he will look forward to his next opportunity.

CAUTION—
Always support the baby's head and neck when you move him.

1. Carry your baby around in this way: hold your hands palm up; with one hand support the back of his head; with the other hand hold his bottom. Now simply carry him around, moving him gently through the air and up and down. Move him up and down, back and forth, and from side to side. Take him around the house, talking to him and telling him where he is and the names of things. Also, let him look out the window and talk about what is outside (see Figure 10.6).

2. Lie on your back and hold the baby under his arms and around his torso. Then raise the baby up so that you are eye-to-eye with him. Gently move him to the right and to the left, then up and down (see Figure 10.7).

3. Sit in a rocking chair with the baby sitting on your lap and rock back and forth with the baby.

4. Place the baby on his belly on a pillow or small mat. You may do this on the floor or on the bed. Gently pick up one side of the pillow and rock the baby to the right, then pick up the other side of the pillow and rock him to the left (see Figure 10.8).

5. Move the baby and the pillow so that baby's head is toward your one hand and baby's feet are toward your other hand. Use a gentle pitching motion to rock him forward and backward (see Figure 10.9).

Figure 10.6. Isolda enjoys moving in all directions with her father's help.

Figure 10.7. Mother moves Isolda side to side in the air.

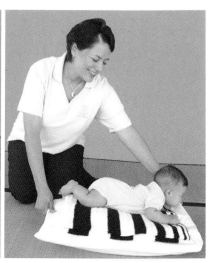

Figure 10.8. Mother rocks Isolda side to side on a pillow.

Figure 10.9. Mother pitches Isolda head to toe on a pillow.

Figure 10.10. Mother accelerates Isolda backward and forward on a pillow.

Figure 10.11. Father slides Isolda to the left and to the right.

6. Place the pillow on the floor, and put the baby on the pillow on his belly. The baby's head should be at your one hand and his feet at your other hand. Pull the pillow to move the baby forward. Then do the opposite so that the baby moves backward (see Figure 10.10).

7. Using the same pillow or mat, rotate the baby so that he is facing you. Slide the mat to the right and then to the left so that the baby experiences side-to-side movement (see Figure 10.11).

8. Keeping the baby on his belly on the pillow or mat, place him so that his head is close to the edge. Take the edge of the mat where his feet are and gently rotate the baby clockwise (see Figure 10.12).

9. Repeat as above, but rotate the baby counterclockwise.

10. While you are standing, place the baby belly-down over your shoulder and gently spin in one direction, then gently in the opposite direction. Be careful not to get dizzy and lose your balance (see Figure 10.13).

11. Repeat as above, but place the baby on his left side on your right shoulder. Spin gently in both directions.

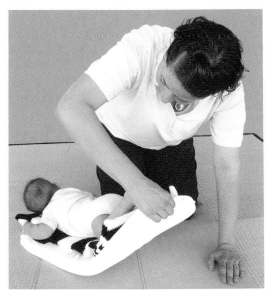

Figure 10.12. Mother rotates Isolda clockwise
and counterclockwise as she lies on a pillow.

Figure 10.13. Isolda enjoys a gentle spin
on her father's shoulder.

12. Repeat as above but place the baby on his right side on your left shoulder. Spin gently in both directions.

13. Kneel down and place the baby on his back on the mat, with his feet towards you. Place your hands under the baby's arms and around his body while supporting his neck. Gently lift him up to eye level and then gently back down again (see Figure 10.14).

14. Put the baby on his back on the floor. Kneel at the baby's feet so that they touch your knees. Place your left thumb in the baby's right hand. The baby will grasp your thumb automatically. Then say "Pull" to the baby and gently pull your left hand so that the baby rolls over onto his left side and then onto his belly.

    Do the same thing with your right thumb in the baby's left hand, so that he rolls to his right side and then onto his belly.

Figure 10.14. Father lifts Isolda up and down.

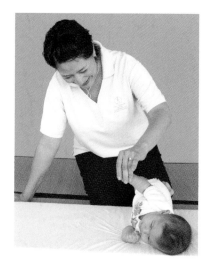

Figure 10.15. Isolda holds her mother's thumb independently, as mother rolls her from her back onto her tummy.

Figure 10.16. Mother clasps Isolda close to her body as she trots around the house.

Alternate back and forth between left and right. Be careful not to put the baby's arm in an uncomfortable position when turning him onto his side (see Figure 10.15).

15. Hold your newborn close to your body so that he is very secure and his head is stabilized. Gently trot through the house. The baby will feel the up and down motion of your body. As his vision improves, he will also begin to see the moving world around him (see Figure 10.16).

You now have fifteen different activities that teach the baby how it feels to move through space. Each activity gives him the opportunity to feel motion and gravity in a different orientation.

It is helpful to name each activity for the baby as you do them. Just as you say "light," "blocks," or "touch," say "up," "down," "spin," "rock," "roll," etc., so that your baby begins to understand what is about to happen and what it is called.

Alternate between these 15 activities throughout the day. As your baby matures, these activities will become among his favorite moments of the day.

Please Note: Remember to begin slowly and gradually increase the duration of each activity. Hold the baby carefully at all times. Be sensitive to your baby. Watch and observe him. If he appears upset or startled, slow down or stop what you are doing. Find out what has upset or startled him.

THE LANGUAGE PROGRAM

Clearly every mother and father gives their newborn the opportunity to cry and make sounds.

What can parents do to enhance their baby's ability to make sounds?

The best way to increase language development is through improving the immature respiration of the newborn.

When the baby is born he must immediately adapt to an entirely new environment. He has enjoyed nine months in an aqueous world where his oxygen supply was guaranteed by his mother's ability to breath. At birth he must take over this process and miraculously he does. However, his breathing at birth is barely adequate for his survival. He does not go from no ability to breathe to a perfect ability to breathe in the few minutes after delivery. Instead he goes from no ability to breathe to just about being able to breathe, if all other systems are functioning perfectly.

Mothers of newborns are instinctively concerned about the breathing of their babies. They check their babies' breathing many times during the day. At night, it is commonplace for the mother of a newborn to creep into the baby's room many times to check his breathing. Often mother will even touch the sleeping baby to awaken him. When the baby awakens and cries mother is happy, and she returns to tell father that the baby is fine. Father often wonders why did she wake up the baby? Mother woke up her sleeping baby for a very, very good reason: she couldn't see him breathing.

Mothers of tiny babies are obsessed about being able to *see* their babies breathe. They think that tiny babies do not breathe very well, and once again, mothers are absolutely correct.

Tiny babies do not breathe very well.

Mother's natural concern about respiration is justified. Newborn babies have very immature breathing, that is to say that they breathe shallowly and irregularly. Sometimes they stop breathing briefly and then start again. Sometimes they stop breathing and mother just happens to be right there to say "Wake up and breathe." And so, the baby awakens, takes a breath, and breathes again.

Mothers are right to be concerned. This is the most vulnerable area of function for the newborn. Every effort should be made to help the baby develop deeper and more regular breathing at the earliest possible moment.

A baby's language development is very dependent on the development of his respiration. It is a simple fact of life that in order to make sounds the baby has to be able to inhale and exhale. Furthermore, he needs to be in control of the process of *when* he will inhale and exhale.

If his respiration is immature, he cannot pull in enough air to make a very loud or sustained sound. This means that his ability to make sounds will be hampered and require more effort. As a result, he will not be able to communicate with mother and father as well or as often as he should.

If his respiration is developed so that he can breathe more regularly and more deeply, it will be easier for him to make sounds. This means that each day he will be able to communicate with mother and father more readily and more often, since it will take less and less effort to do so.

A baby who can breathe deeply and regularly is a safer baby than one who cannot.

A baby who can make sounds easily is a safer baby than one who cannot.

What is the best way to promote the maturation of the newborn baby's respiratory system?

Mobility.

There is no better program for getting deep, regular breathing than movement of the arms and legs, and crawling. In fact, when the baby wants to make sounds we can watch him pump himself up by moving his arms and legs more rapidly. He is then able to fill his lungs with air, which allows him to achieve a good loud cry.

Movement is critical to the development of better respiration. The more time a baby has to be on the floor to move, and the more opportunity he has to move down his inclined infant crawling track, the faster his respiration develops. It is as simple as that.

It is wise for parents to be vigilant about their baby's breathing in the first few weeks of life. It is very important to place a high priority on giving the baby opportunity to be on his belly. This will bring about the maturation of his respiratory system as quickly as possible.

This is the very best language development program for the newborn.

THE MANUAL COMPETENCE PROGRAM

Your baby's first manual program will consist of stimulating the grasp reflex.

This will make his grasp reflex faster and stronger than it is presently. This process of reinforcing and strengthening his grasp reflex will help him to achieve the next manual stage more easily.

Objective:	To grow the manual competence areas of the brain by establishing, improving, or reinforcing the grasp reflex
Purpose:	To evoke the grasp reflex
Frequency:	10 times daily
Intensity:	Gentle pressure

Duration: 10 seconds increasing to 60 seconds

Content: One opportunity to grasp mother's index fingers, increasing to 6 opportunities

Environment: The floor or a bed, with the baby in the prone position

Technique: Place the baby on his back in a comfortable position facing you. Gently place your right index finger or thumb in the fist of your baby's left hand and your left index finger or thumb in the fist of your baby's right hand. Now gently and slowly begin to pull the baby toward you. As the baby feels the pressure of your fingers, you will feel his grasp tighten. Again, this is the grasp reflex, which is what you want to elicit. As he grasps your finger, say in a loud, clear voice "grasp." This will help him begin to understand the word and the action. Have the baby maintain this grasp for a few seconds before lowering him gently onto his back. Tell the baby what a good job that he has done and then gently remove your fingers.

Please Note: At first these sessions should be only a few seconds in duration, but you will quickly notice that your baby's grasp reflex is becoming stronger. As this happens, make each opportunity a little bit longer than the one before. Also, after a brief pause, give the baby a second opportunity and then a third until by evolution you are up to a one-minute session. In this way you will promote your baby's neurological development, as you build up his strength (see Figure 10.17).

Figure 10.17. Caleb grasps his mother's fingers before she slowly lifts him.

THE MOTOR PROGRAM FOR PROFILE STAGE I

Daily Checklist

Mobility Opportunity

Opportunity to move arms and legs in the prone position:
Inclined track: 10x daily for 10 to 30 seconds

☐ ☐ ☐ ☐ ☐ ☐ ☐ ☐ ☐ ☐

Total time: 1 minute 40 seconds to 5 minutes

Flat track: 3 to 4 hours daily

Total time today: _____

Opportunity to move through space in a variety of ways:
(15 different activities, 1 activity per session)
15 sessions daily, each 15 seconds increasing to 45 seconds

☐ ☐ ☐ ☐ ☐ ☐ ☐ ☐ ☐ ☐

Total time: 3 minutes 45 seconds to 7 minutes 30 seconds

Language Opportunity

Maximum opportunity to move in the prone position to improve respiration,
which makes it easier to make sounds.

See Mobility Opportunity above.

Manual Opportunity

Opportunity to use the grasp reflex:
10x daily for 10 seconds, working up to 60 seconds

☐ ☐ ☐ ☐ ☐ ☐ ☐ ☐ ☐ ☐

Total time: 1 minute 40 seconds to 10 minutes

Changes Noted Today: _____

_____

_____

Date: _____

THE MOTOR PROGRAM FOR PROFILE STAGE I

Daily Checklist

Balance Activities

Opportunity to move through space in a variety of ways.

Note: 1 activity done per session

15 different sessions daily, working up to 45 seconds each

Total time: Up to 11 minutes 15 seconds

1.   Carrying baby around ☐ ☐

2.   Moving side to side ☐ ☐

3.   Rocking with baby in lap ☐ ☐

4.   Rocking side to side ☐ ☐

5.   Rocking front to back ☐ ☐

6.   Accelerate front to back ☐ ☐

7.   Accelerate side to side ☐ ☐

8.   Rotation prone, clockwise ☐ ☐

9.   Rotation prone, counterclockwise ☐ ☐

10.   Horizontal rotation, prone ☐ ☐

11.   Horizontal rotation, on left side ☐ ☐

12.   Horizontal rotation, on right side ☐ ☐

13.   Lift baby up and down ☐ ☐

14.   Roll baby back to belly, both directions ☐ ☐

15.   Trot around house with baby ☐ ☐

Duration of each activity: _____

Changes Noted Today: _____

_____

_____

Date: _____

11

Your Baby's Second Evaluation

After one month of giving your baby a consistent program of sensory stimulation and motor opportunity, it is wise to evaluate your baby again. Since you have already done this once, it will be easier this time. Before getting started you will need to understand Stage II on the Profile, and how to evaluate the six functions at this stage.

The first part of this second evaluation, however, is to repeat the Stage I evaluation to check the progress your baby has made in the few weeks since you did it. In fact, you should always begin any new evaluation by repeating your evaluation of the lower stages. This will let you see what functions have become stronger, quicker, or more consistent. You may be surprised at how much the quality of your baby's responses have improved, even in those areas that you previously marked "Perfect."

As we move to higher stages of the Profile, it becomes increasingly important to choose the best time of day for the baby in order to get an accurate evaluation. Avoid those times when he is cranky, hungry, or tired. We want to be able to evaluate him at his best, so choose those times when he is well-rested, happy, and generally in good form.

At this evaluation we will look at Stage II, shown in orange on the Profile, which covers all the *vital responses* that are part of a tiny baby's development.

VISUAL COMPETENCE: STAGE II

Outline Perception

At this stage the parent needs to evaluate baby's ability to perceive

Materials Needed:

• penlight

outline. This is the ability to locate or follow a dark object against a light or bright background.

For example, when mother walks in front of a window where sunlight is flooding into the room, the stage is set for the baby to locate or follow mother as she moves in front of the window.

Since this opportunity does not often present itself, we will have to simulate it. To do this, you will need a penlight rather than a large household flashlight. Again, it is important to place yourself and the baby in a totally dark room so that you can create a complete contrast between darkness and light. This will help the baby to see the light.

Place the baby on the floor on his belly or comfortably in father's lap. Turn off all the lights. Once you are in darkness, hold the penlight two or three feet away from the baby and turn it on. Hold the light still and give the baby an opportunity to locate the light. It may take several seconds for him to do so. Do not talk or make sounds. If you do so he may turn toward the sound of your voice and only appear to locate the light. In order to get an accurate evaluation it is important to introduce only one element of sensory stimulation at a time.

When he successfully locates the light tell him what a good boy he is and give him a few moments to look at it. Then turn off the light for several seconds, change your location quietly, and turn the light on again. Once more give him several seconds to locate the light, making sure you are not giving him auditory clues as to your whereabouts.

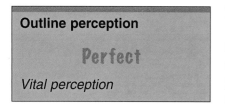

Figure 11.1. Perfect outline perception

When he locates the light again, hug him and give him a kiss so he knows you know he spotted the light. Give him a chance to look at it, and turn it off again. Repeat the process. Locating the light is enough. Three opportunities to do this is plenty. If you do more than this at one session, baby may well become tired and simply turn off his vision.

If he can locate the light consistently, wait a few hours and evaluate him again. This time, however, instead of holding the light still, move it slowly, and see if he can follow it. This is more difficult, so you should not start moving the light until you are sure he can locate it consistently when it is stationary.

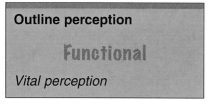

Figure 11.2. Functional outline perception

When the baby can consistently follow a moving person or can consistently follow a moving light in the darkness, without any other clues, write "Perfect" in red on the outline perception box of the Profile and draw a red line across the top edge of this box (see Figure 11.1).

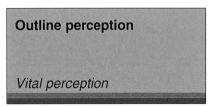

If a baby can follow a moving person or a moving light in the darkness without any other clues, but only *inconsistently,* write "Functional" in red on the outline perception box of the Profile and draw a red line across the top edge of this box (see Figure 11.2).

Figure 11.3. Zero outline perception

If a baby cannot locate, or follow, a person or a light in a dark room, draw a red line on top of the blue line from the previous evaluation to show that he is still at the same stage in his vision (see Figure 11.3).

AUDITORY COMPETENCE: STAGE II

Vital Response

The next step is to evaluate your baby's vital response to threatening sounds. This response is built upon the startle reflex but adds the next stage of sophistication. The startle reflex occurs in the presence of any sudden sharp sound. However, not all sudden sharp sounds are life-threatening. The purpose of this next stage is for the baby to be able to distinguish a merely unexpected sharp sound from a threatening sound.

Materials Needed:

• air horn

This ability is clearly a life-saving mechanism. It allows the baby when he hears such a sound to let out an appropriately frightened cry that will bring mother or father to his side instantly and will, in some cases, literally save his life.

This vital response to threatening sounds is present in all human beings at all stages of life.

Brain-injured children who do not have this vital response sometimes suffer additional serious injury because they do not respond appropriately to a threatening sound.

Again, it is always best for mother and father to evaluate any new function on each other before evaluating the baby. In order to evaluate the vital response you need a sound that will be perceived as life-threatening. An air horn, of the sort used to start boat races and generally found in a sporting goods store, is easy to use and very portable. You could also use the car horn if the person you are evaluating is close enough to the car to get the full brunt of the horn.

Children at play like to elicit a vital response by sneaking up on each other and saying "Boo" in a loud and frightening voice. This is very effective on unsuspecting adults as well. However, it does not have great enough intensity to be effective with the tiny baby.

Using any of the above methods, elicit a vital response from your spouse at a moment when he or she does not expect it, and encourage him or her to return the favor at another time for you.

When you are ready to evaluate your baby, *make certain that the baby is at least ten feet or more away from the car horn or the air horn.*

If you are using the air horn, put the baby in a safe and comfortable position on his belly on the floor. Position him so that you can see his face easily. Now sound the air horn for a second or so. Turn off the air horn and wait several seconds. Now sound the horn again. You may find that the very first time you evaluate this stage it takes two or three one-second soundings of the horn punctuated by a few seconds of silence before your baby responds.

Often at the first sounding he will look very attentive, at the second his face will begin to look concerned, and at the third he will burst out crying.

This is a fascinating and completely normal series of responses.

It is fascinating because the evaluation *itself* will have brought about the *creation* of the vital response.

On the first sounding he does not respond vitally, yet he clearly hears the sound. On the second sounding he is concerned and suspicious, but again he does not have a vital response. On the third sounding the intensity of the full blast arrives and he perceives that the sound is indeed threatening, and now he has a truly vital response.

In this brief evaluation we have the opportunity to see the actual growth of the auditory pathway. At the start of the evaluation there was not a vital response. Three stimulations later the vital response is born. Although for a while, this response may be somewhat inconsistent, the baby now has a vital response for the first time.

When your baby does experience a vital response, pick him up and comfort him so that he knows that he is safe and that the threat has been handled. Tell him it was a loud sound that he heard and that he is safe.

It may also happen that your baby develops a vital response to a threatening sound very quickly and that he cries loudly at the very first sound of the air horn. In this case, you need only do one stimulation, not three.

When your baby responds immediately, the very first time you blast the air horn, he has a perfect vital response. Write "Perfect" " in red on the vital response box of the Profile and draw a red line across the top edge of this box (see Figure 11.4).

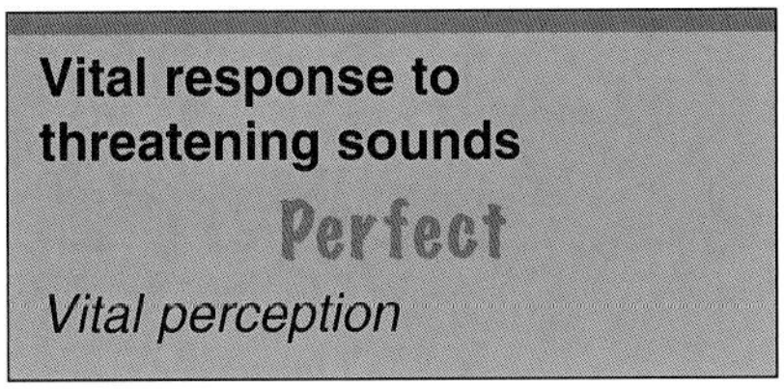

If your baby has a vital response to threatening sounds most of the time but not all of the time, write "Functional" in red on this box and draw a red line across the top of this box (see Figure 11.5).

If your baby does not have a vital response to threatening sounds, draw a red line on top of the blue line from the previous evaluation to show that he is still at that stage of development (see Figure 11.6).

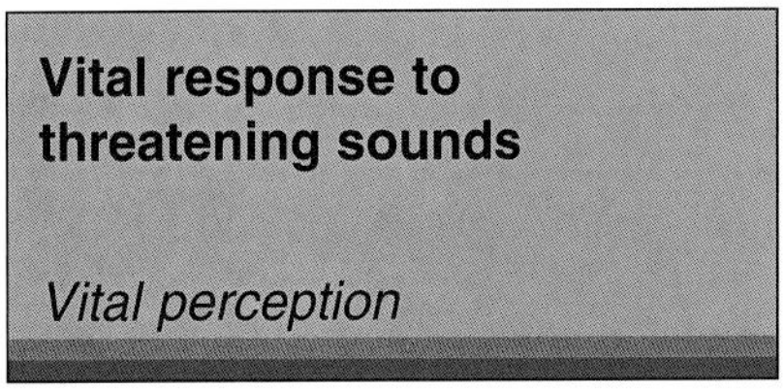

Please Note: Air horns are generally used as starters' signals for field and track events or boat races. A well-equipped sporting goods store usually has them or can order them.

These horns make a very loud, penetrating sound that is excellent for this purpose. However, they should be kept out of the reach of your other children since they would give older children quite a scare if set off inadvertently.

Remember: Always stand at least ten feet away from your baby when using the air horn.

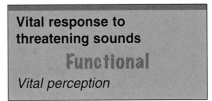

Figure 11.4. Perfect vital response

Figure 11.5. Functional vital response

Figure 11.6. Zero vital response

TACTILE COMPETENCE: STAGE II

Perception of Vital Sensation

Now we are ready to evaluate the baby's ability to perceive vital sensation. This is the baby's ability to feel strong tactile sensation such as sharp pain or extremes of hot and cold. In brief, these include those tactile sensations that would be life-threatening to the baby if they were permitted to persist. This ability is very basic to all creatures and is, of course, highly developed in human beings.

A true vital response is a good loud, lusty, angry cry. However, since we ourselves have never been very good at pinching babies, or sticking pins in them hard enough to make them cry, we can hardly recommend this to other mothers and fathers.

Therefore we recommend just enough pressure, or hot or cold, to bring about withdrawal, but not enough to make the baby cry.

Materials Needed:

• ice

• warm towel

This is surely the least popular part of any sensory evaluation since it involves painful stimulation. Happily we often find it is not necessary to evaluate this very important function since babies are frequently subjected to some degree of pain accidentally, or because of inoculations that they receive in the first few weeks of life.

No one wants to subject a baby to pain, even briefly. Fortunately mothers are very good about remembering how the baby responded when he received an injection, or was accidentally stuck with a diaper pin.

Although we all know what it feels like to be pricked with a pin or pinched or the sensation of hot and cold, it is still best for mother and father to evaluate these things on each other. This will give mother a sense of how much intensity is needed to produce a vital sensation. It is actually a good bit less than one might imagine. It will also help to allay our fears about hurting the baby since when this is done properly the slight pain is momentary.

One simple way to evaluate this stage is to lightly pinch the baby. If you have long nails, cut them, so that you can gently grasp a little bit of baby fat rather than having your nails scratch the baby's skin. When the baby feels the pinch he should withdraw as we would do.

It is important to evaluate the baby's torso and each of his arms and legs. Some areas may be more sensitive than others. Sometimes one side of the body reacts more quickly and consistently than the other side. It is good to have this information. Mother may also observe that when she pinches an area once there is no response but after the second or third pinch the baby does respond.

This is the same phenomenon that we discussed in the evaluation of the auditory pathway. Three stimulations may be required by an immature pathway in order for the message "pinch" to arrive.

After a program of stimulation the tactile pathway grows and matures, and then it requires only one pinch for the message to arrive. Again, if this is the case in the beginning, mother should note it and look for it to improve in the future.

Another way to elicit a vital response is to use hot or cold sensation. This can be done by taking a small piece of ice and touching the baby at different points all over his body. In order to use hot stimulation take a wash cloth and soak it in hot water. Then wring it out and wait until it cools from very hot to a hot which is uncomfortable but not in any way harmful. Touch the baby with the towel at various points all over his body and observe his response.

Please remember that we recommend enough pressure, or hot, or cold, to bring about withdrawal, but not enough to make the baby cry.

When you are evaluating a desperately brain-injured and possibly insensate child, the need for such a careful and detailed evaluation is critical to the ultimate well-being of the child. In such cases we do need to understand precisely what, if anything, will bring about a vital response. But with the essentially well baby there is no need for this.

When your baby has a consistent and immediate response to vital sensation all over his body, write "Perfect" on the vital sensation box of the Profile and draw a red line across the top edge of the box (see Figure 11.7).

If one area of your child's body, or several areas, respond inconsistently or have a delayed response, or require several stimulations to get a response, or have no response, write "Functional" in red on the vital sensation box on the Profile and draw a red line across the top edge of this box (see Figure 11.8).

When a child has no response whatsoever anywhere on his body to vital sensation, draw a red line on top of the blue line of the previous evaluation to show that he has not yet achieved this stage of development (see Figure 11.9).

Perception of vital sensation
Perfect
Vital perception

Figure 11.7. Perfect vital sensation

Perception of vital sensation
Functional
Vital perception

Figure 11.8. Functional vital sensation

Perception of vital sensation
Vital perception

Figure 11.9. Zero vital sensation

MOBILITY COMPETENCE: STAGE II

Crawling

At this stage of development parents need to observe their baby's ability to crawl. Since mother and father have already devoted a good bit of time and energy to providing a good floor environment so that their baby has the opportunity to crawl, evaluating the baby's ability to do so is quite easy.

Crawling is the ability to move forward on the abdomen using the arms and legs.

At first the baby will crawl using whatever method he can. His movements will appear random, with no pattern. However, as he becomes more experienced he will begin to coordinate his arms and legs so that he develops a cross-pattern form to his crawling. This cross-pattern crawling is a product of turning his head to the right and flexing his right arm while extending his right leg, and extending his left arm while flexing his left leg. Thus the right arm and left leg are flexed at the same time and then, as he moves forward, the left arm and right leg are flexed simultaneously (see Figure 11.10).

Figure 11.10. Isolda crawls in a cross pattern.

This represents the most efficient and advanced means of crawling.

It is important to choose a good time to evaluate your baby's ability to move. Put him in his infant crawling track or on a floor surface that is smooth, warm, and clean. Make sure that he is wearing as little clothing as possible so that he can get maximum traction with his arms and legs on the smooth surface.

Now lie down on the floor about six feet away and call him to come to you. From your previous time on the floor together he should have a pretty good notion of what you would like him to do. Give him two or three

Crawling in the prone position culminating in cross-pattern crawling
Perfect
Vital response

Figure 11.11. Perfect crawling

minutes to crawl towards you. Encourage him and applaud whatever effort he makes to do so.

When he can crawl a distance of six feet in less than three minutes, using a cross-pattern movement, mark "Perfect" in red on the crawling box of the Profile and draw a red line across the top edge of this box (see Figure 11.11).

When he can crawl six feet in less than three minutes using random movements, or some other pattern, write "Functional" on the crawling box of the Profile and draw a red line across the top edge of this box (see Figure 11.12).

If the baby is not able to move six feet in less than three minutes, draw the red line on top of the previous blue line to show that he has not yet reached this stage of mobility (see Figure 11.13).

> **Crawling in the prone position culminating in cross-pattern crawling**
>
> **Functional**
>
> *Vital response*

Figure 11.12. Functional crawling

> **Crawling in the prone position culminating in cross-pattern crawling**
>
> *Vital response*

Figure 11.13. Zero crawling

LANGUAGE COMPETENCE: STAGE II

Vital Crying

By the time mother and father are ready to evaluate a baby's ability to have a vital cry, life has frequently intervened and provided more than ample opportunity for the baby to demonstrate this ability.

When a baby perceives a life-threatening situation he should have the ability to cry in a way that is quite different from his normal cry.

By the time a baby is a few weeks old, mother and father have become quite familiar with the baby's normal method of calling them. This cry is not an alarming cry at all. It is rather a signal that the baby is alive and well and would like to announce this fact. It is a comforting sound to mother and father because it indicates to them that the baby *is* alive and well.

The vital cry is different—it means "something is wrong, help me immediately." The first time mother hears this cry she comes running. There is no mistaking it.

Anything that the baby perceives as a threat will bring about this cry. Two forms of sensory input that we have already mentioned—the threatening sound and the threatening sensation—are common reasons for a baby to use a vital cry.

In the event that you have not yet heard your baby respond to a life-threatening situation using a vital cry, it is necessary to evaluate this ability.

One method is to use the air horn that we discussed earlier in the auditory section of this chapter. If the baby responded consistently to that evaluation with a vital cry, mark "Perfect" in red on the vital cry box of the Profile, and draw a red line across the top edge of this box (see Figure 11.14).

Vital crying in response to threats to life

Perfect

Vital response

Figure 11.14. Perfect vital cry

If your baby responds inconsistently to life-threatening situations with a vital cry, then you must make a decision. Is his *perception* of the threatening situation inconsistent or his *response*?

In the majority of babies it will be the *sensory* pathway that is still immature. The problem will seldom be in the motor pathway response. It is important to make this differentiation, otherwise you may find yourself marking your baby "functional" *twice* when, in fact, his vital cry may be perfect but his perception of vital sounds is still inconsistent. In other words the baby is not hearing consistently yet, but at those times when he does hear he has a good and appropriate vital cry.

Vital crying in response to threats to life

Functional

Vital response

Figure 11.15. Functional vital cry

This phenomenon is easy to demonstrate in the baby who has a consistent vital cry whenever he is in pain but is inconsistent when a vital sound is made. In such cases, it is clearly the auditory pathway that is immature.

If you find that your baby has a weak or inconsistent vital cry, and you are confident that it is the cry that is the problem rather than the perception of the threat, write "Functional" in red on the vital cry box of the Profile and draw a red line across the top edge of this box (see Figure 11.15).

Vital crying in response to threats to life

Vital response

Figure 11.16. Zero vital cry

When a baby has no vital cry, even though it is clear that he can hear and feel and perceive a threat to his life, draw a red line on top of the blue line of the previous evaluation to show that he has not yet achieved this stage (see Figure 11.16).

MANUAL COMPETENCE: STAGE II

Vital Release

Now you are ready to evaluate your baby's vital release. As we have said, a newborn has a strong grasp but no ability to let go. The second stage of his manual development will be to gain the ability to release an object in his hands when there is a life-threatening reason to do so. Again, this is vital to the safety of the baby.

A baby often picks up something dangerous that may be life-threatening. He not only must perceive the danger but have the motor ability to respond appropriately by releasing the object instantly. In a modern household the most common such threat would be a hot iron, or pot, or a wire of some kind.

Mother Nature takes few chances. This ability to release the object will develop in the baby before he has the ability to reach out and pick something up.

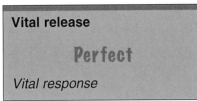

Figure 11.17. Perfect vital release

This vital response can be evaluated very easily by placing an object in your baby's fist so that he gets a good grasp on it and then giving the palm of the hand with the object a firm pinch. This pinch should be strong enough that the baby opens his hand and lets go of the object. This is a vital release. This ability should be evaluated in both hands. Mother may find that one hand is better than the other. Again, this should be noted.

When your baby consistently has an instant vital release in both hands, write "Perfect" in red on the vital release box of the Profile and draw a red line across the top edge of this box (see Figure 11.17).

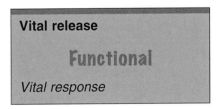

Figure 11.18. Functional vital release

If your child has a slow or inconsistent response in one or both hands, write "Functional" on the vital release box of the Profile and draw a red line across the top edge of this box (see Figure 11.18).

When a child does not have a vital release in either hand, draw the red line on top of the blue line of the previous evaluation to show that he has not yet achieved this stage (see Figure 11.19).

Figure 11.19. Zero vital release

12

Expanding Your Sensory Program

Now that you have completed your second evaluation you have a very clear idea of those areas in which your baby has matured and progressed. You should also have a clear picture of those areas in which the baby may need more stimulation and opportunity.

Before expanding your newborn program, you will want to strengthen the program you already have by increasing the frequency of stimulation in the areas at Stage I that are still inconsistent, or less than perfect. Also, based on your second evaluation, you can decrease the frequency in those areas that are now perfect.

Time is the most precious of all commodities in the life of a tiny baby and his mother. Therefore, mother should be certain that each element of her program is tailored to the precise neurological needs of her baby. The Institutes Developmental Profile provides you with the information that you need to make the correct choices about what frequency, intensity, and duration is needed for each part of your sensory program.

For example, after your second evaluation you may find that your baby now has a perfect startle reflex. It is now very consistent whereas at his first evaluation it was inconsistent. You can now decrease his startle reflex stimulation from 10 times a day to 5 times a day. However, this stimulation should be continued in order to help stimulate Stage II.

After the second evaluation you may find that his light reflex is improved but it is still not perfect in both eyes. You would be wise to increase from 10 light reflex sessions daily to 15 sessions daily so that your child can develop a perfect light reflex more quickly.

After reviewing Stage I in each column of the Developmental

Profile in this manner, you will have reshaped your program to reflect the new abilities of your baby. Now you are ready to expand your program to include stimulation for Stage II on the Developmental Profile.

THE SENSORY STIMULATION PROGRAM

Our job now is to make it easy for baby to see, hear, and feel at Stage II, just as we did at Stage I. Contrast continues to be of the greatest importance. The baby's world should be, in a sense, black and white, not just in terms of what he sees but also in what he hears and touches. It will be easier for baby to see, hear, and feel when there is a good deal of contrast in his environment (see Figure 12.1).

When the baby is in a gray or pastel world he goes back to being blind, deaf, and to some degree insensate. It is our job to create an environment that says to the baby, "Wake up! Open your eyes! There are things to see, things to hear, and things to feel!"

It is true that very young babies need a lot of sleep, but it is also true that bored babies who lack adequate stimulation sleep a good deal more than stimulated and interested babies do.

Remember: Babies are intensely curious, but very helpless. They need us. If there is not much to see, hear, or feel, the intelligent baby simply tunes out and falls asleep. If we create an environment in which it takes less effort to see, to hear, and to feel, the baby will add his own natural curiosity and energy to turning on his vision, hearing, and tactility.

We provide baby with the help he needs by using contrasting stimulation with the appropriate frequency, intensity, and duration.

When mother and baby are both moving toward the same goal, baby develops more rapidly.

Figure 12.1. Maria takes a good look at the checkerboard floor that her parents created to provide excellent visual contrast.

VISUAL STIMULATION

At Stage II a parent needs to stimulate outline perception in addition to reinforcing the light reflex. This is the stage where the baby begins to see a dark object against a light background.

At this stage contrast continues to be vital to the baby. He needs ample opportunity to see a dark object, or form, on a light or white background. This may occur once a day by accident, but we want to give the baby many such opportunities a day on purpose so that his visual pathway matures and he begins to see at the earliest possible moment.

Objective: To stimulate, establish, improve or reinforce the ability to see outline

Purpose: To stimulate outline perception

Part I—Contrasting Environment

Frequency: Every waking moment

Intensity: 10" by 10" black and white checkerboard squares

Duration: Every waking moment

Environment: A very well-lighted room or corner of a room. Take two large pieces of foam core board, approximately 30" by 40", and make a checkerboard on them. Use black construction paper or black poster board in 10" by 10" squares. The core board is already white so you do not need to make white squares to get the checkerboard affect that you want. The lighting on the checkerboarded area should be twice the normal ambient light. It should never be in the baby's eyes, but directed toward the checkerboarded area. Incandescent light is preferred (see Figure 12.2).

Technique: The two 30" by 40" pieces of foam core checkerboard should travel around the baby's environment wherever he goes, and so they must be light and easy to transport. If he is on the floor in the living room, they should be placed near to him at right angles, creating a kind of corner. The checkerboard will provide the baby

Materials Needed:

- 2 large pieces of white foam core board (30" x 40")

- 12 squares of black poster board (10" x 10" each)

Figure 12.2. A large checkerboard provides a visually contrasting environment.

Figure 12.3. Two large checkerboards placed at a right angle provide greater visual stimulation.

with a contrast of black and white that he can actually begin to see. A white wall, or a wall of some pastel color, does not provide any contrast, and so it is hard for the baby to see (see Figure 12.3).

If he is going to take a nap in his room, the checkerboards should go with him so that he can look at them as he goes to sleep and again when he awakens.

If he goes to grandmother's house, grab one of the boards and take it with you. This will help him to enjoy this outing even more. Once he arrives at grandmother's (or any new environment), he finds that everything is different and hard to see. Often he cries or goes to sleep, but his checkerboard will provide him with something he *can* see. This stimulation and familiar environment make the visit a lot happier for him.

The lighting of the checkerboard is very important. The greater the ambient light, the easier it will be for the baby to see the black and white squares. The dimmer the lighting, the harder it will be for the baby to notice the contrast in his environment. Track lighting is particularly good for this purpose since you can direct the light on to the checkerboard and make it more visible.

Please Note: It is also very helpful to the baby to place 10-inch-wide vertical black and white stripes down the sides of the infant crawling track (see Figure 12.4). This gives the baby more opportunity to use his vision. As he moves down the track he is aware of his forward motion because of the visual feedback of the alternating black and white stripes. This quite literally helps him to make one of the most important discoveries he will ever make—that he is moving!

In an environment where there is no contrast, and where there is only the usual lighting, the baby would see almost nothing. He would not be visually aware that he is moving down the track.

The relationship between mobility and vision is critical at all stages of development but nowhere is it more critical than at this moment in the baby's life.

Figure 12.4. Isolda appreciates the visual contrast of the light and dark stripes on her infant crawling track.

Part II—Spotting a Light

Materials Needed:
• penlight

Frequency: 10 times daily

Intensity: Penlight or a small, intense lamp

Duration: 1 minute

Content: 6 to 10 stimulations

Environment: A completely dark room

Technique: If mother and father are doing this together, it is best for one parent to cradle the baby in his or her arms while the other uses the light. If only one parent is doing this, it is best to lay the baby on his back on the floor in a comfortable position.

Turn off the lights so that the room is totally dark. Then turn on the penlight and shine it on your open hand or some other relatively reflective surface, not further than 18 inches from the baby's face (see Figure 12.5). *Do not shine the penlight in the baby's eye.* This light is more intense than the flashlight used in the initial sensory program. Hold the light and your hand still and wait for the baby to find the light. This may take some time, so be patient.

You may want to encourage him by saying, "Find the light."

When he turns toward the light say, "Good boy, you found the light!"

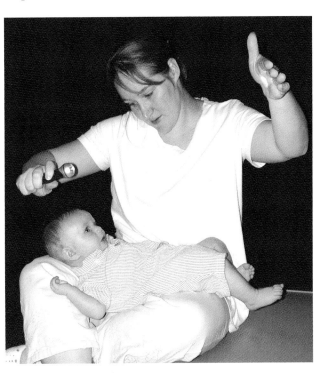

Let him look at it for a few seconds then turn it off. Wait in the dark for two or three seconds before moving the light to a different location. Once again turn on the light, holding it within 18 inches of his face, and say, "Find the light."

Figure 12.5. Caleb spots the light shining on his mother's hand in a dark room.

Each time he succeeds, be sure to tell him that he did so with a warm and enthusiastic voice. Provide as many stimulations as you can in the one-minute session and then stop.

Please note: At first the baby may not be able to see the lighted hand at all, but persist. We want to give the baby this ability. Do not

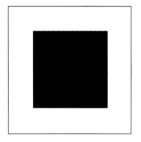
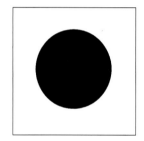

do this when the baby is hungry or tired. Choose the best times in the day to do this.

Sometimes you may find the baby is very good at spotting the lighted object and at other times he does it poorly. This is typical of a baby who is just beginning to see outline. It will improve daily if you keep at it. Sometimes there is a tendency to want to sweep the lighted object across the baby's field of vision to attract his attention. *Do not do this.* A moving target is a lot more difficult to spot than a stationary one.

Once baby can consistently spot the lighted object, you may move it slowly and let him follow it with his eyes.

Part III—Outline Bit of Intelligence Cards

Thinking and reasoning cannot operate without data or without the sensory pathways to take in that data. Here we introduce the use of special cards, identified by the trademark Bit of Intelligence® cards ("Bit" cards). These "Bit" cards are data. We are able to enhance and grow the baby's visual and auditory pathways and offer him useful and interesting information at the same time.

We begin with simple "Bit" cards, and as the sensory pathways grow the "Bit" cards become more sophisticated visually and intellectually.

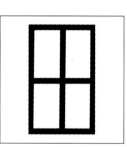

 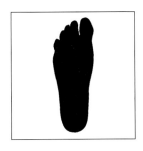  

Frequency: 10 daily

Intensity: Black images on white 11" by 11" posterboard

Duration: 5 to 10 seconds

Content: 1 to 3 Bit of Intelligence cards

Environment: A well-lighted room with extra light shining on the Bit of Intelligence cards as they are shown.

Technique: Each of these Bit of Intelligence cards is a simple, large, black image mounted on a white posterboard card. We commonly use a square, circle, triangle, star, banana, foot, hand, cup, spoon, fish, cat, tree, elephant, window, eye, mouth, butterfly, bird, flower, scissors, and spider. (see Figure 12.6).

Week #1 to Week #3

Start with the "square" because it is one of the simplest images. Use this same card for the entire day. Cradle your baby gently in your arms or place him in a comfortable position on his back on a bed or on the floor. Hold the card 12" to 18" from his face and say, "square."

Now wait and give him time to find the card. This may take several seconds. When he finds the card repeat in a loud, clear voice, "square."

Figure 12.6.
Basic outline "Bit" cards enhance and grow the baby's visual pathway.

Now give him a hug and a kiss and tell him what a good fellow he is. At first do only one card per session. Any more than this will tire him out. You always want him to end a session feeling that it is easy to see, not with any sense of fatigue. If for any reason you feel that you have chosen a bad moment to show the card, put it away immediately and come back at a better time. He has to be in very good form to be able to do this, especially at first. It is important to be sensitive to your baby's condition.

Repeat this same basic session ten times, each time waiting for him to locate the Bit of Intelligence card and then repeating the name of the card. Those hugs and kisses at the end of each session are important too, so don't neglect them.

At the end of the first day, retire the "square" card temporarily and choose another simple image, the "circle," for the following day. *Show a new card every day for one week.* At the end of the week go back to the "square" card and cycle through these same seven Bit of Intelligence cards again, one each day.

Do this for three weeks. This means that the baby will have seen the "square" card on three different days, ten times each day, or thirty times in all. Now you are ready to move on and start adding new outline cards.

Week #1 to #3

- square
- circle
- triangle
- star
- banana
- foot
- hand

Week #4

Choose one old card from the week before (#1–7) and one new card (#8–14). Now show both of these cards at each session for one day. Repeat this process each day, showing a different old (#1–7) card and a different new card (#8–14) every day for one week.

Week #4

- cup
- spoon
- fish
- cat
- tree
- elephant
- window

Week #5

Retire cards #1–7 used in the first four weeks. Replace the retired cards with seven more new cards (#15–21). Now each session has two cards, one from Week #4 (#8–14) and the other brand new (#15–21). Each evening choose two different cards for the following day.

At the end of the fifth week you will have cycled through all 21 basic outline cards needed at this stage.

The purpose of this careful progression is to provide adequate frequency for the baby to recognize the old outline "Bit" cards and to

Week #5

- eye
- mouth
- butterfly
- bird
- flower
- scissors
- spider

introduce new outline "Bit" cards only in combination with "Bit" cards he already knows.

Please Note: In the beginning make certain that there is extra ambient light aimed at the cards as you present them to the baby. However, once you get started and are feeling more confident of what you are doing, you can sometimes do a session in a darkened room where the light shines only on the "Bit" card. This can help your baby locate the Bit of Intelligence card you are showing.

A variation of this is to turn the light on and off while showing a "Bit" card, so that you create a blinking effect. This further draws the baby's attention and interest to the card.

You must be careful to time the on and off cycles. If the light goes on and off too quickly, the baby cannot find the card before the light goes out. This will frustrate and annoy him. Begin by leaving the light on for at least two seconds and turning it off for one second. Through trial and error you will find the timing and the rhythm that is best for your baby.

AUDITORY PROGRAM

Now you are ready to provide the opportunity for your baby to develop a vital response to threatening sounds. The development of Stage II abilities gives the baby a consistent vital response. By definition these responses help him to save his own life should he need to do so.

After your second evaluation you may have been surprised to learn that he had no such auditory response or that his response was inconsistent. Now we can provide the stimulation he needs to develop that consistent and life-saving response.

Objective:	To stimulate, establish, improve, or reinforce the vital reflex
Purpose:	To stimulate a vital response by using threatening sounds
Frequency:	5 times daily
Intensity:	The sound of an air horn at least ten feet away from the baby
Duration:	3 to 10 seconds
Content:	1 to 3 stimulations

Environment: A quiet room

Materials Needed:

• air horn

Technique: Place the baby on his back in a comfortable position where you can observe his face easily and he can see your face. Now move at least ten feet away from the baby and push down the lever of the air horn for one second. Observe your baby's response. Wait two or three seconds and again sound the air horn for one second. Observe your baby's response again. Again wait two or three seconds and then sound the air horn for one second.

Please note: As mentioned in the last chapter, you may find that your baby's response to the air horn builds after each stimulation. At first the baby may not have any response until the final stimulation. Again, persist. This response is created by increased opportunity to hear a threatening sound.

When your baby does have a vital response, which is the goal of this part of his sensory stimulation program, pick him up so that he knows that he is safe and that the threat has been handled. As you did when you were evaluating this stage, tell him that he heard a loud sound and that now he is safe.

It may also happen that your baby develops a vital response to a threatening sound very quickly. If he cries loudly at the very first sound of the air horn, you can stop after the first stimulation. Continue to give one stimulation five times a day for three days so that you can be sure that he has a consistent response. Then you no longer need to do this. He has the response and is ready for the next stage of stimulation.

TACTILE PROGRAM

Now you are ready to design a tactile program that will help your baby to greatly improve his vital sensation.

The sooner the baby has a consistent vital response to threatening tactile stimulation, the safer he will be.

Objective: To stimulate, establish, improve, or reinforce vital tactile sensation

Purpose: To provide threatening tactile stimuli

Frequency: 12 times total daily
(4 times cold)
(4 times hot)
(4 times pressure)

Intensity:	1. Cold
	2. Hot
	3. Pressure

Duration: 30 seconds

Content: Ice pack, warm towel, and moderate pressure pinch on the arms, legs, hands, feet, and torso of the baby

Environment: An environment warm enough for a naked baby

Technique: Place the baby on his back in a comfortable position on the bed or the changing table. The baby should be naked so that you can go over his entire body.

Materials Needed:
- ice
- warm towel

As mentioned in the previous chapter about tactile evaluation we recommend using just enough pressure, or hot or cold, to bring about withdrawal, but not enough to make the baby cry.

You will gain a sense of how much intensity is needed to produce a vital sensation of cold, hot, or a moderate pressure pinch when you are doing the tactile evaluation.

Begin with cold stimulation. As you did in your evaluation, take a small piece of ice and touch the baby at different points all over his body. In order to use hot stimulation, take a wash cloth and soak it in hot water. Then wring it out and wait until it cools from very hot to a temperature that is uncomfortable but not harmful. Touch the baby with the towel at various points all over his body and observe his response. To stimulate with pressure, use a moderate pinch as you did in your evaluation.

When you begin it is helpful to establish a set pattern, a routine for covering all parts of his body and the sequence in which you do them. Talk to the baby as you go. Say, "Can you feel the ice on your hand?" If he does not withdraw his hand, persist a little bit. He may need the cumulative affect of several seconds of stimulation in order for the message "cold" to arrive. When he withdraws his hand a little, stop and say, "Good boy, you felt the ice, didn't you?" Now proceed to his other hand and do the same thing. Then go to his feet, arms, legs, abdomen, back, and neck, always telling your baby what part of his body you are stimulating. Continue this for thirty seconds. At the next session use heat stimulation, and at the following session use pressure. Alternate between cold, hot, and pressure throughout the day.

You will quickly be able to observe varying degrees of response as you move from one area of the baby's body to another. These responses will tell you which areas are sensitive to vital touch and which are still dull. Emphasize the dull or inconsistent areas and skip the areas where there is a consistent immediate response.

When all areas respond consistently, your baby has a perfect response to vital sensation. You may stop this part of your program and start preparing to work on Stage III.

Please remember that we recommend enough cold, hot, or pressure to bring about withdrawal, but not enough to make the baby cry.

SOME PRACTICAL HINTS

Diaper Bag Contents:
- flashlight
- penlight
- blocks
- air horn
- outline "Bit" cards
- towel

An easy way to organize your baby's program is to get a second diaper bag to carry your sensory stimulation program materials. Since the baby is diapered over and over again throughout the day, it is easy to do two or three parts of your sensory stimulation program at every diaper change. This has worked very well for many mothers. It also makes a diaper change a lot more interesting for both of you!

Another aid in organizing your program is to make a daily checklist that includes each element in your program. Sensory stimulation programs are, by nature, high-frequency/low-duration programs. The number of individual items may seem large, but when you look at how briefly each item is done it is actually quite easy.

Check off a box each time a session is done. At the end of each day, take a minute to write down your observations. Keep the checklists in a notebook, and as baby matures change the checklist to reflect the changes in the program.

You will quickly become quite good at doing these programs, and can begin to teach father how to do them as well. This helps father to become an important part of his baby's development. When father takes over the program for mother, he simply follows the checklist. In some families it is father who spends the majority of time with the baby; in this case it is father who teaches mother.

You will learn very quickly how to complete the checklist and do everything else that needs to be done in a day.

THE SENSORY PROGRAM FOR PROFILE STAGE II

Daily Checklist

Visual Competence

Stimulating the light reflex:
10x daily for approx. 60 seconds

☐ ☐ ☐ ☐ ☐ ☐ ☐ ☐ ☐ ☐

Total time: 10 minutes

Stimulating outline perception:
Checkerboard environment—During waking hours   ☐

Spotting a light
10x daily for 60 seconds

☐ ☐ ☐ ☐ ☐ ☐ ☐ ☐ ☐ ☐

Total time: 10 minutes

Seeing outline Bit of Intelligence cards:
10x daily for 5 to 10 seconds

☐ ☐ ☐ ☐ ☐ ☐ ☐ ☐ ☐ ☐

Total time: 50 seconds to 1 minute 40 seconds

Auditory Competence

Stimulating a vital response:
5x daily for 3 to 10 seconds (1 to 3 stimulations)

☐ ☐ ☐ ☐ ☐

Total time: 15 seconds to 50 seconds

Tactile Competence

Stimulating a vital response:
12x daily for 30 seconds

☐ ☐ ☐ ☐ ☐ ☐ ☐ ☐ ☐ ☐ ☐ ☐

Total time: 6 minutes

Changes Noted Today: _____

_____

_____

Date: _____

SUMMARY

You now have a clear program that will provide your baby with the stimulation he needs to develop mature and consistent vital responses in visual, auditory, and tactile areas.

These are life-protecting responses that will serve him throughout his entire life. Each of these responses gives him a clear and effective means of communicating with you when he is in danger or when he thinks he is in danger. Your prompt response to his call lets him know that you are there when he needs you. This is a very important lesson for him to learn. It means that he is a much safer baby and a much more secure and happy baby. And when the baby is secure and happy, so are his parents.

13

Expanding Your Motor Opportunity Program

Information must go in before it can be expected to come out again.

The level of the outgoing motor responses of the tiny baby are totally dependent on the level of maturity of the incoming sensory pathways. This is why it is so important to provide an environment that is rich in sensory stimulation for the baby if you want him to develop good motor responses.

This may appear to be obvious, but it is astonishing how often the baby is expected to give a motor response when he has never received adequate sensory stimulation that would permit him to develop such a motor response.

Therefore the first and most important element in your motor program is an excellent sensory program. This must be done consistently so that the baby develops the sensory pathways that will tell him when he is threatened. He is not going to be inspired to crawl away from a threat if he cannot see, hear, or feel a threat—this is a certainty.

The second step in expanding your motor opportunity program is to review each of the reflexive functions at Stage I on the Profile. Again, any area that is not yet consistent should be given extra opportunity in order to make it perfect as soon as possible.

At this stage of development you are not going to decrease or eliminate any of the basic motor opportunities that you began when your baby was a newborn. He still needs to reinforce and improve those reflexive motor responses. However, we can now add new opportunities that will further help him to achieve Stage II on the Developmental Profile.

THE MOBILITY PROGRAM

It is still of the greatest importance that your baby spends the maximum time possible on the floor. In fact, during the first year of his life this is vital.

Continue to divide his floor time between short sessions in which you encourage him to move and large blocks of time in which he can experiment in an environment designed to make it easy for him to move.

Each day the tiny baby grows heavier and heavier. He needs to be that much stronger and fitter to be able to pull that added weight along. In this respect, time is not his friend. He is working against the clock to gain the ability to crawl—and crawl well—before his body becomes so heavy that forward movement is almost impossible.

At this stage of development, there is a striking difference between the floor baby and the baby who has been bundled up and not permitted to explore and develop his mobility.

The floor baby is a little dynamo who is exploring the world. Each day he becomes more and more capable and confident. He eats well and he sleeps well. He is a very happy little fellow.

Materials Needed:

• infant crawling track

The other baby is more likely to be fat and sluggish. He cannot get to the things that he wants because he is all bundled up or penned up in one device or another. When he discovers this, he often gives up before he has even tried. As he gains weight he finds it even more difficult to move. He sleeps a lot because he is often bored. He is a lot less happy because he cannot do much, see much, or achieve what he wants to achieve. His natural right to explore and develop has been frustrated.

Part I—Opportunity in the Track

Objective:	To establish, improve, or reinforce the ability to crawl
Purpose:	To provide maximum opportunity to crawl
Frequency:	Every waking moment possible
Intensity:	Flat infant crawling track
Duration:	Minimum 4 hours daily Maximum 18 hours daily

Content: Opportunity to crawl in his track and in any other area that meets his requirements. Each day the baby should increase his total crawling distance by approximately one foot.

Environment: The floor area must be safe, clean, warm, smooth, cushioned, and flat. The baby should wear a T-shirt and a diaper so that he has bare elbows, knees, and feet.

Technique: Place the baby on his belly in his track, which is placed near household activity. Mother, father, and brothers and sisters are working and playing nearby, occasionally coming over to encourage him and cheer him on in his efforts. They give him many hugs and kisses whenever he crawls off his track (see Figure 13.1).

   Please Note: As his vision improves, he will begin to be attracted by large objects that have a good visible outline and are well-lighted. At this point, placing blinking or twinkling lights in his floor environment is a very good idea.

   However, be careful not to create such a stimulating and amusing environment for the baby while he is in his track that he has no need to move out of it.

   Position objects in his floor environment so that they create a need for him to move. Place them so that he can find the light, or touch the big red ball, or get to older brother only by moving, not by staying still and remaining passive. This creates a need for the baby to explore, and that exploration causes him to develop (see Figure 13.2).

Figure 13.1.
Maria comes down her track like a champ and has a conversation with her grandmother.

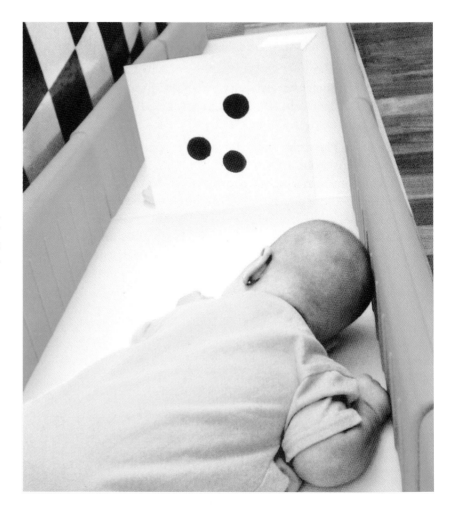

Figure 13.2.
Maria heads down her
crawling track to get a
closer look at three dots.

All too often the modern baby is placed in an environment in which he has no need to do anything but sit and do nothing. This is great training for a couch potato, but not much fun for the baby who is naturally curious and wants to move and learn more about his environment.

Part II—Opportunity on the Floor

Frequency: 15 times daily

Intensity: Flat Infant Crawling Track, evolving to a smooth floor surface

Duration: 1 minute

Content: Opportunity to crawl in his track and in any other area that promotes mobility

Environment: The floor area must be safe, clean, warm, smooth, cushioned, and flat. The baby should wear a T-shirt and a diaper so that he has bare elbows, knees, and feet.

Technique: Place the baby on his belly in his track or on a clean, smooth, warm floor.

Please note: At this point the long-range objective is for the baby to crawl 150 feet in a day. It is important to keep track of the number of times he moves down his track each day or the distance he travels when he is on the floor during the day. Keep a simple, but accurate, record sheet of the distance the baby crawls each day.

LANGUAGE COMPETENCE PROGRAM

The Language Competence Program for Stages I–IV is outlined in Chapter 14. Please refer to this chapter for the language program.

MANUAL COMPETENCE PROGRAM

By now you have given your baby many opportunities to use his grasp reflex. This will have helped the baby to develop his next manual milestone—the ability to let go of an object, which is called vital release.

Materials Needed:
• small objects

At this point the baby may be dropping objects that have been placed in his hands, but usually he does this after holding the object for a long time. In this case he does not really let go of the object but instead drops it because the grasp reflex has gone into fatigue. This is not a vital release. The development of the vital release is important. It is a life-saving ability since it allows the baby to let go of something that may be dangerous or life-threatening. If he picked up something very hot or something very sharp, he needs to have the tactile understanding of the vital sensation *and* the manual ability to let go instantly.

Part I—The Vital Release

Objective: To establish, improve, or reinforce the vital release

Purpose: To provide the maximum opportunity to grasp an object and evoke a vital release

Frequency:	10 times daily
Intensity:	Gentle pressure, then a brief sharp pinch
Duration:	6 seconds
Content:	2 opportunities to grasp and release an object (one for each hand)
Environment:	This should be done in a position that is comfortable for you and the baby.

Technique: Place in the baby's hand an object that he can grasp easily. When you see that he has a firm grasp, say, "Now let go" and gently pinch the palm of his hand holding the object. At first the baby may feel the pinch but actually tighten his grasp. This is a baby who is developing a good vital sensation but does not yet have a vital release. Persist with the technique. The more you give him this opportunity, the faster he will develop a good, consistent vital release.

After doing this once with one hand, switch to the other hand and repeat the process. Whenever the baby releases the object immediately or shortly after the pinch, tell the baby, "Good boy, you let go!"

When the baby is able to release the object instantly and consistently, stop this part of the manual program. The baby now has this ability.

Please Note: You will discover the proper intensity for the pinch during your evaluation of this stage. As always, the point is not to upset the baby but rather to give him the opportunity to develop a life-saving ability.

Part II—Strengthening the Grasp Reflex

Materials Needed:

• ¼" wooden dowel (L 24")

Now the baby is ready to strengthen his manual ability to grasp, and the process by which he does that will increase his chest growth and development. Chest growth has two great advantages for the baby: improved respiration and creating a bigger reservoir for oxygen. Better respiration will be very important for the baby's language development. Since oxygen is the primary nourishment for the brain, improved oxygenation will enhance all functions.

Frequency:	15 times daily
Intensity:	Gradually building up to the pressure created by the weight of the baby

Duration: 2 to 30 seconds

Content: An opportunity to grasp mother's fingers or a dowel

Environment: Done on the floor or a bed, with the baby on his back

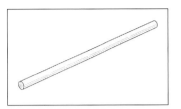

Figure 13.3. Give your baby the opportunity to hang from a ¼" dowel at this stage.

Technique: Have the baby grasp your thumbs or index fingers as in the first manual program that was designed to create a strong grasp reflex. When he has a good grasp, raise your hands until the baby is in a sitting position, and then continue to lift him until he is in a standing position. If you feel his grip loosen, gently lower him back onto the bed. Have the rest of your fingers ready to grab him in case he loses his grip entirely.

Once you have the baby in the standing position, you will feel him take some of his weight on his feet. Now you can actually lift him off the bed. He will then, even if only for a moment, take his entire weight (see Figure 13.4).

Before he tires, lower him gently onto the bed. You will find that he can hold a little bit longer each time.

When you feel confident about his ability to hold on for ten or fifteen seconds, begin to use a one-quarter-inch wooden dowel. Use the exact same procedure whether you are using your fingers or the dowel. Continue to use your fingers in half of his daily sessions. If you find he does better with your fingers, use fingers only for this technique.

Please note: These sessions are very short to begin with, but as the baby's ability becomes better the sessions become a little longer. Stop before your baby wants to stop so that he always enjoys doing this with you. Tell him what a wonderful baby he is. This is a great achievement. (If you have any doubts, try hanging from a bar yourself—your respect for your baby will multiply.)

Figure 13.4. Maria enjoys using her grasp reflex to hang independently from her mother's thumbs.

THE MOTOR PROGRAM FOR PROFILE STAGE II

Daily Checklist

Mobility Opportunity

Maximum opportunity to crawl:

Flat crawling track—Every waking moment possible (4 to 18 hours)

☐ ☐ ☐ ☐ ☐ ☐ ☐ ☐ ☐ ☐
☐ ☐ ☐ ☐ ☐ ☐ ☐ ☐ ☐ ☐

Each box = 1 hour

Flat crawling track and/or smooth floor

15x daily for 60 seconds

☐ ☐ ☐ ☐ ☐ ☐ ☐ ☐ ☐ ☐
☐ ☐ ☐ ☐ ☐

Total time: 15 minutes

Manual Competence

Opportunity to use a vital release:

10x daily for 6 seconds

☐ ☐ ☐ ☐ ☐ ☐ ☐ ☐ ☐ ☐

Total time: 1 minute

Opportunity to strengthen the grasp reflex:

15x daily for 2 to 30 seconds

☐ ☐ ☐ ☐ ☐ ☐ ☐ ☐ ☐ ☐
☐ ☐ ☐ ☐ ☐

Total time: 30 seconds to 7 minutes 30 seconds

Changes Noted Today: _____

_____

_____

Date: _____

14

The Language Development Program from Birth to 12 Months

The baby goes through very distinct stages in his mobility and manual development. These stages are very easy to discern, and each demands a new set of programs and techniques. We will work our way up The Institutes Developmental Profile one stage at a time so that as the baby enters a new stage of development mother has the new program information she needs.

This approach applies less precisely in the area of language. This critical ability does not demand a series of changing programs and techniques so much as a good understanding of how language actually develops. For this reason it is best to discuss language development between birth and 12 months of age as a whole. We will want to create the very best environment for the baby's language to grow and develop right from birth.

The first priority is to develop good, regular, mature breathing. The initial newborn program covers this in some detail. This means that crawling is essential for the baby's language development at Stage I. That program will have a profound effect on the baby's ability to make sounds, and to use those sounds to communicate with mother.

The second part of developing the baby's language ability is the Sensory Stimulation Program. This program provides the baby with the stimulation and opportunity to develop and use a vital cry to call out to his mother and protect himself. This is a very important part of the Language Program at Stage II.

While these are fundamental, there is more that mother can do to enhance the language environment for the baby.

The purpose of this chapter is to show parents how they can cre-

Language development is dependent upon good, regular, and mature breathing.

ate the ideal language environment for their baby from his first days after birth until he has reached Stage IV and is beginning to talk.

THE LANGUAGE DEVELOPMENT PROGRAM

Objective: For the baby to use two or more words of speech spontaneously and meaningfully

Purpose: Providing abundant opportunity for the baby to talk with mother and be understood

Part I—Listening

While some adults talk to a very young baby, very few adults ever *listen* to a tiny baby. There is a general assumption that babies do not have anything to say, and that it will be months, if not years, before they do have anything to say.

This is simply not true.

Luckily mothers do talk to their babies and babies do their very best to talk back.

From the moment a baby is born, his greatest single need is to communicate. This is part of being human.

Baby first needs to communicate that he is alive. Very shortly after that he needs to communicate that he is hungry. As his awareness grows, which it does very rapidly, he may need to communicate that he is alarmed, happy, annoyed, uncomfortable, contented, or tired.

One of baby's most critical needs, which he will often want to communicate, is to be in close contact with mother or father and to be reassured that they are there when he needs them.

The baby is, after all, trapped in a chubby little body that does not allow him to satisfy his own needs. He must communicate those needs or go without. As every mother knows, babies are not famous for contentedly going without. They want what they want when they want it.

The idea that the tiny baby has nothing to say is absurd. He is desperate to talk to mother and he will use every means available to do so from the moment he is born until the day that both mother and father understand his every desire perfectly.

The single most important thing that mother should know about her baby's language is this:

> The baby is desperate to talk to mother and he will use every means available to do so.

All sounds are language.

Every sound that a baby makes is language. The sounds a baby makes are not merely *like* language, they *are* language. These sounds are not *like* English, they *are* English. They are just very poor quality English (or Spanish or Japanese or whatever language is spoken in your household) but they *are* that language.

From the baby's point of view, his first problem is basic: Is anybody out there listening to me?

The baby sends out messages to find out the answer to his question, "Is anybody home?"

If, as is often the case, adults are *not* listening (because we have been raised to believe that babies don't have anything to say), we do not get the message. Baby is left unanswered. Since he is very determined, he discards those actions that do not work and keeps looking for ways to communicate. If he can only get our attention, he will ultimately succeed.

When this happens mother will be shocked. No one has prepared her for the fact that her two-month-old baby is trying to talk to her.

In her excitement and enthusiasm she will go to her pediatrician, or to the next-door neighbor, and announce proudly, "My one-month-old baby is trying to talk!"

She will then be told in a matter-of-fact, even patronizing tone that the sounds her baby is making are a result of gas.

Gas?

This is when the conspiracy of silence is born. Mother learns not to mention that her very young baby is trying to talk because people simply think that she is crazy. And so this invaluable piece of developmental knowledge becomes a hidden artifact that each new mother must discover and unearth like a jewel buried in a box. Mother then learns to hide the jewel again exactly where she found it.

Sadly, some mothers never do find this jewel and their little babies spend the first 12 months of life trying, in vain, to talk to them. These babies are doomed to being talked at with no chance to express themselves until they can make those sounds that we adults recognize as "words."

It is a long wait.

All sounds are language.

When mother knows and understands this fact she has the first and

> The sounds a baby makes are not *like* language, they *are* language.

best piece of information she needs. She then will begin to listen to her baby and learn what he has to say.

Very young babies are geniuses at cause and effect. They are constantly pushing the edges to see what works and what does not work. There is no area where this is done with more precision and determination than in the creation of language.

Consider little Derek. When Derek was five weeks old his mother would ask him, "Derek are you hungry?" After a brief pause, he would stick out his tongue and make small but audible gasping sounds. He looked and sounded exactly like a man dying of thirst on a desert.

One wonders how could a five-week-old know that this is the classical representation of a man dying of thirst?

The answer is, of course, that he does not know. But he is hungry, and since he has a very immature respiratory system he cannot make a specific sound to show us what he needs and wants. So he does the next best thing—he pantomimes.

His response is entirely consistent. If you watch mother nurse Derek and then ask, "Derek, are you hungry?" he will look contented and happy.

This drives us crazy. Adults always want an answer. But babies are very pragmatic. When they are in need they will answer by making a sound or sign. If their needs have been met, however, they simply communicate this by looking content.

This clear look of contentment is an answer. It is a "No, thank you. I am fine at the moment."

Adults often want a clear "yes" response *and* a clear "no" response. The look of contentment, which *is* the "no" response, is not strong enough for us. Sometimes when adults do not understand this they are apt to believe that the clear "yes" response they got was not real but imagined, and they pay less attention to what the baby is trying to communicate.

By the time Derek was nine months old he would indicate that he needed to nurse by saying, "Chi-chis, chi-chis," and mother would, of course, nurse him. He could now make a specific sound because his respiration had matured. However, the message was identical to the one he had been sending since he was five weeks old.

As it happens, Derek was a young man who was fond of nursing, and so one day when he was three years old he came into the

Babies are geniuses at cause and effect.

kitchen where mother was preparing dinner and started to chant, "I want to nurse, I want to nurse!"

Mother pointed out that everyone was hungry and that after dinner was prepared and eaten if he wanted to nurse she would nurse him but until then he would have to wait. He then started chanting, "Chi-chis, chi-chis."

Mother proved deaf to the request. His eight-year-old sister tugged on mother's arm and pointed at little Derek who was sitting in the middle of the kitchen floor with his mouth open, his tongue hanging out, making little gasping sounds. His sister reminded mother that he had not done that since he was an infant. Mother laughed and said, "Yes. He is going back to what *always* worked."

This is precisely right—he was going back to what always worked.

If mother is listening to and watching her baby, she gets the message and responds in some way. The baby is thrilled. It worked. He thinks: "There is intelligent life on earth after all." He will then use this same method of communicating again because it worked.

So the first key ingredient in the program to help baby communicate is that *you must be listening.* Be on the alert to hear what the baby is trying to say. Begin this process *at birth.* Each day the sounds he makes will change. When the baby knows that you are listening, he will do his very best to communicate as often as possible. The more he does, the more skillful he becomes. The more his respiration improves through crawling and building a bigger chest, the easier it is for him to make sounds.

> When the baby knows you are listening, he will communicate as often as possible.

Part II—Having a Conversation

Frequency: 10 times daily

Intensity: Loud, clear voice

Duration: Approximately 60 seconds

Content: 1 question and time for the baby's answer

Environment: Quiet, free from distractions

Technique: Once mother understands that all sounds are language, there are many ways she can help her baby use his sounds to communicate. There are certain things she asks the baby over and over throughout the day: "How are you?" / "Are you hungry?" / "Are you sleepy?" / "Are you wet?"

There are other things she tells the baby over and over again: "I love you," "These are your toes," "This is your nose."

There are simple instructions that she gives the baby: "Open your mouth," "Look at Daddy," "Push with your feet."

There are certain greetings that the baby hears over and over again: "Good morning," "Hi," "Bye-bye."

Since these are the things that the baby hears frequently, they are the first things that he begins to decode and understand. But even before he fully understands these messages he tries to respond.

Several years ago a mother called us and before we could inquire as to who she was and what she wanted she clicked on a cassette recorder. A very tiny baby's voice could be heard, first some sounds and then, "Hi," "How are you?" and "I love you."

The tape recorder clicked off and mother was back on the line. Well, she asked, "Did you hear it?"

We told her the three things we had heard. She let out a huge sigh of relief and said, "That is my baby and he is 11 weeks old!" And having said so she hung up.

Another victim of the conspiracy of silence, no doubt.

Now what was that all about?

How many times do you suppose that a tiny baby hears, "Hi," "How are you?" and "I love you" in the first few weeks of life? Probably a thousand times.

Be consistent about the way you talk to your baby.

Is it really surprising that he wants to try to send the message back? We do not need to debate whether he understands the full meaning of the word "love." It is not the point. He hears language and he wishes to use the language that he hears.

It may be the music of the language that interests him at first, but he will very quickly learn that the words and the music together exercise a powerful effect on mother and father.

At this early stage you need to be consistent about the way you talk to your baby. When baby hears these often repeated greetings, questions, statements, and simple instructions in the same way each time, he can recognize them. It helps him to learn the rules of conversation, the first of which is to listen to what the other fellow is saying. Eliminate the noise and chaos in the household. Turn off the radio, the CD, and the television so the baby can hear you. Speak in a loud, clear voice, and make certain that you are nose-to-nose with the baby so he can listen with rapt attention.

Now add a second magic ingredient. When you finish asking,

"How are you?" stop, look enthusiastically at the baby, and wait. Wait 10 seconds, 20 seconds, 30 seconds, maybe longer. The younger the baby, the more patient you must be.

At first, you may not get an answer, but as the baby realizes that this is not a one-sided conversation but rather a *real* conversation—and that he has the opportunity to participate—he *will.*

For example, say to the baby, "How are you?" then smile and wait and the baby will begin to move his arms. This is to pump-up his respiration so that he can make a sound. Then his body may wiggle a bit and he may say "Ah" or whatever sound comes out.

He has little control over the actual sound. He is simply trying to get a hold of one good exhalation and add some sound to it.

When he makes this sound, whatever it may be, add another piece of magic. Say, "Really? I am glad to hear that!" In other words, respond to what he has just said.

One may ask whether this is an appropriate response since you do not know what "Ah" means.

At first we do not know exactly what the baby means. Just as he is listening to our meaningful sound to hear if we are happy or sad, we must listen to his meaningful sound. You will become very good at knowing whether it was a happy "Ah" or an irritated "Ah" and will respond appropriately. Even if you get it wrong, you are right in the baby's eyes because *you are listening and responding, and that is what he wants.*

Now for the first time he can have a real conversation. You say something and he listens attentively. Then you are quiet and listen attentively and he says something. Then you respond and the conversation is over.

This is a real conversation.

The baby is not yet two months old and he is perhaps ten months from saying the first sound that the world at large considers to be a "word."

What a relief not to have to wait that long to have a conversation with mother when you are as smart and as eager as this little fellow!

Now you will arrange to have many little conversations throughout the day. Make a little ritual of each of them. Hold him in the same way, sit in the same comfortable chair, and even prepare him each time by saying, "Do you want to talk to Mommy now?"

As he comes to understand that this is the cue to begin these much-loved talks, he will wiggle and kick and show how happy he is.

Listen to your baby and answer him. This is what he wants.

Objective:	Opportunity for the baby to have a conversation with mother
Frequency:	At least 10 times daily
Intensity:	A loud, clear voice
Duration:	1 to 2 minutes
Content:	1 question that requires only a 1-word answer
Environment:	A quiet room with minimal distractions of any kind. Sit with the baby on your lap, facing you.

Technique: Ask, for example "Are you hungry?" Watch your baby carefully and listen intently. Wait for your baby to respond. Be patient—it may take 30 to 60 seconds for your baby to answer you. Be silent once you have asked the question. Do not keep repeating the question. This will make it harder for your baby to respond. When the baby responds with a sound, answer him.

Part III—Creating Specific Sounds

Materials Needed:

• simple rhyme

Once mother has begun these little conversations throughout the day she can add a second step. Now she creates a simple little rhyme for her baby. She chooses a good time and with great enthusiasm she recites the little poem to him. As before, he is sitting in her lap facing her.

Little Marlowe's first rhyme was:

When I come home
I say, "Hi."
When I go out
I say, "Bye."

This was a very clever poem for his mother to write, as we shall see. His mother repeats this rhyme throughout the day. After several days she begins to give the baby a part in the poem, but she does so in a very predictable way. She recites the poem in the same way, but when she reaches the last word of the last line she stops. She does not say "Bye." This is going to be the baby's word, and he will have the choice to say it or not.

She waits and looks at him enthusiastically, as she does during their conversations. Since he has heard the poem many times he knows there is the sound "Bye" at the end and that it is missing. He wants to fill it in for mother. He starts moving his arms, he wriggles his body. He pumps up his breathing, and after 30 seconds or so of this he says, "Ah."

Mother is thrilled.

Baby is thrilled.

Baby knows that the sound "Ah" stands for "Bye." (He just can't say "Bye" yet.)

Mother knows that the sound that baby just said stands for "Bye."

But what is much more important—the baby knows that mother knows that "Ah" stands for "Bye."

And thus together mother and baby have broken the code.

The baby knows that mother knows that he is trying to talk but that it doesn't always come out the way he wants it to come out.

This is a very, very important moment for mother and baby.

Many mothers say that these stolen moments—when they leave the noise and the chaos and chores of everyday life and sit down with their babies to recite their poems together—are the most wonderful moments they ever share with their tiny babies.

These sessions do for language development what nursing does for nutrition.

When the baby can fill in the last word of the poem with any sound whatsoever, mother continues to give him more opportunity to participate.

Now she recites the poem but when she gets to the last word of the second line she stops. Now she waits for him to make a sound for the word "Hi." At first he may not, but as she repeats this opportunity he realizes that he has yet another word for himself. Once again he makes a sound—perhaps the same "Ah" or perhaps something completely different.

Mother continues to recite the same poem. Each day she notices that the sounds the baby is making are changing. Now once in a while she hears what sounds like "Hi" for "Hi." Now the baby is beginning to make specific sounds.

Yuuki's mother chose:

> Hey diddle diddle,
> The cat and the fiddle,
> The cow jumped over the moon,
> The little dog laughed to see such sport
> And the dish ran away with the spoon.

It is vital for your baby to know that *you* know that he is *talking.*

By the time little Yuuki was six weeks old mother would say:

> "Hey diddle diddle
> The cat and the _____"

After a five-second pause Yuuki would softly say "iddle." mother would continue:

> "The cow jumped over the _____"

And Yuuki would say "Aah."
Mother would finish:

> "The little dog laughed to see such sport,
> And the dish ran away with the _____"

And Yuuki would conclude with "oon."

He could make two specific sounds before he was two months of age. This is a wonderful accomplishment for such a tiny baby. But what was more wonderful was the joy that mother and Yuuki experienced every time they said their poem together.

By the time young Zachary was seven weeks old he could fill in the last word of each line of:

> The owl and the pussy <u>cat</u>
> Went to <u>sea</u>
> In a beautiful pea green <u>boat</u>,
> They took some <u>honey</u>
> And plenty of <u>money</u>
> Wrapped up in a five-pound <u>note.</u>

When the baby does his poem with you, he experiences the satisfaction of actively participating, not merely listening.

The sounds were crude but each one was clearly a *specific sound* meant to be the word in question.

Again, no one is proposing that these babies have the foggiest notion what "a five-pound note" is, but neither did you or I when we first heard this poem as a child. It did not prevent us from enjoying it again and again. Each time we understood it a little bit better than the time before. The baby experiences the same basic pleasure, and—what is more—the intense satisfaction of being able to *participate* in the recitation.

Mothers and babies create a language together that they will use until the baby can make much more specific sounds that we adults think of as words.

Here is the simple program that you can follow:

Goal:	For the baby to fill in several words of a short poem with any sound consistently
Frequency:	5 times daily
Intensity:	Loud, clear voice
Duration:	1 to 2 minutes
Content:	1 recitation of a very short poem
Environment:	A quiet room with minimal distractions of any kind. Sit with the baby on your lap, facing you.

Materials Needed:

• short poem
• audio recorder

Technique: In the beginning it is best to create a simple poem just for your baby. In this way you can choose words that are familiar to the baby, such as the names of family members. You should choose easy, one-syllable words like "Hi" and "Bye" for ending lines. It is also good for the little poem to have some end lines that rhyme.

Memorize the poem and begin to recite it to your baby. Do this only at the very best times in the day, when the baby is well-fed and rested and when you are full of energy and enthusiasm. Recite the poem with great excitement and meaningful sound in your voice. Do this five times daily for five days. On the sixth day you are ready to let the baby have a part in the poem. Recite it in the same way, but stop when you reach the last word of the last line. Do not say the last word. Instead, look at the baby intently and wait.

From this recitation onward this last word of the last line will be the baby's word, to say or not to say as he chooses. Never say this word in the poem again as this would break the contract you are making with the baby. Once a word is dropped, it belongs to the baby.

Now it is very important at this moment for you to wait because it might take the baby 30 seconds to be able to respond. You will gradually learn how long your baby needs to make a sound.

When the baby is able to make a sound, you are naturally thrilled. Hug and kiss him so he knows that you got the message. If the baby makes no sound after a minute, say, "Did you like your poem?" Wait to see if he wishes to respond to this question, and then you are finished.

When the baby can consistently make any sound whatsoever for the final word of the poem, then and only then should you begin to drop the last word of another line. If the baby is still only five or six weeks old, these two words will be enough. You will see how hard he works to pump up his respiration as soon as he knows that you are about to recite his poem.

As you see that the poem is getting easier for him, you can move on to a new poem. Once he really starts to crawl for transportation his respiration will improve in leaps and bounds. This will give him a much better ability to communicate.

Now he will almost start to interrupt you as you are reciting the poem. He wants more words than you are giving him. At this point, follow the same sequence given but now drop three or four words in the new poems. In the example below the numbers indicate the sequence in which the words are dropped:

Once the baby is crawling for transportation, his respiration will improve dramatically.

> Twinkle, twinkle, little <u>star</u> (2)
> How I wonder what you <u>are</u> (3)
> Up above the world so <u>high</u> (4)
> Like a diamond in the <u>sky</u> (1)

When the baby can easily do this, continue to drop words:

> Twinkle, <u>twinkle</u> (5) little <u>star</u> (2)
> How I <u>wonder</u> (6) what you <u>are</u> (3)
> Up above the <u>world</u> (7) so <u>high</u> (4)
> Like a <u>diamond</u> (8) in the <u>sky</u> (1)

When you reach this stage, try to give the baby the most interesting words in the body of the line. If the word has two or three syllables you may help by taking one syllable for example you may say, "Like a dia____ in the ____."

This allows the baby to increase his participation but not be stopped by the long words that come up.

Any sound that the baby makes is fine. Remember that you are not expecting words here. You are giving the baby the opportunity to use his sounds and to make them more specific when he is able to do so.

In this way you and your baby build up a repertoire of poems. Occasionally return to an old poem and do it again with the baby. You will find that the baby uses more specific sounds than he did before.

Please note: It is very wise to record some of the sessions. When you play these recordings back you can turn up the volume and actually hear the baby better than you did originally. You will not only hear things that you did not hear at all the first time, but you

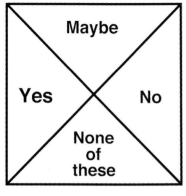

Figure 14.1.
A beginning choice board

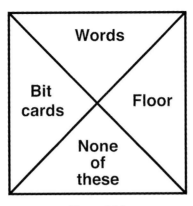

Figure 14.2.
"What's next?" choice board

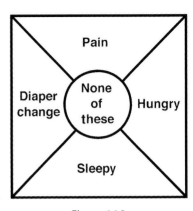

Figure 14.3.
Daily life choice board

will notice that some of the sounds are specific sounds. The baby's voice tends to be soft and difficult to hear, so these tapes can be invaluable. They will also become one of the most precious mementos of your baby's early childhood.

Part IV—Using a Choice Board

We live in unusual times. One part of society still thinks that babies understand very little while another part of society has discovered that very little babies can learn sign language. It is true that babies can learn sign language, and this gives them yet another option for communication. If you know sign language you should go ahead and teach your baby—he will learn quickly. If you have a member of your family who is deaf, it will be a great advantage for your baby to be able to communicate with that family member easily. However, if you do not know sign language or do not have someone in your household who is deaf, we propose that you use the precious time you have with your baby to teach him how to use a simple choice board instead of sign language. This will quickly give your baby another way of communicating and will bring you and your baby closer together. The choice board will begin as a very simple "yes" and "no," but as you and your baby gain experience and confidence, you can make the choices more specific and more sophisticated.

You will increase communication by providing your baby with a simple choice board.

Goal: To discover what your baby needs and wants

Purpose: Opportunity for the baby to communicate using a simple choice board.

Frequency: At least 10 times daily

Intensity: A loud, clear voice

Duration: A few seconds to 30 seconds, or as long as it may take for your baby to make a choice.

Materials Needed:

- choice boards
  (11" x 11")

Content: Ask your child a question and hold his hand or arm lightly. Using your baby's hand, point to the choices "yes" and "no" as you say those words. Then gently pull the baby's hand back and relax your arm so that the baby can point to his answer. Your baby will strongly or lightly push towards the answer he wants.

If you cannot feel his push to "yes" or "no," you should bring his arm back again to the resting position and begin the process again-starting from your question, then pointing to each answer, and then giving him an opportunity to choose. You may need to repeat this several times initially. He needs to get the idea of what you want. Never, never, never guide his hand to an answer. The answer comes from him or it does not. It is as simple as that.

Try not to miss any sign of response your baby may give. Be patient with yourself. This process involves sensitivity and skill. You may be uncertain of yourself at the start. Everyone is. But if you believe in your baby's ability, he will respond. Sometimes you will make mistakes. If you sense you have made a mistake or you are simply unsure, ask another question to confirm that the first answer was the one your baby wanted.

Say, "I am getting 'yes'. Is that your answer?" Babies are wonderful. They don't expect us to be perfect, they just expect us to *try,* and when we do they are remarkably patient and forgiving.

When you are comfortable doing "yes" and "no" questions, you may gradually add other choices, such as "I don't know" and "none of these answers." It is possible that baby may not answer because he does not *have* an answer to the question, or the answer he wants is not one of the choices available to him.

Ask *real* questions. This not a game-it is a chance for real communication. It is also not a test to see what the baby knows or does not know. Ask questions that will *matter* to your baby.

As you begin to consistently feel your baby's hand push toward the answer, you may add more choices to the board.

Have fun. Your baby's little choice board will prove to be an invaluable tool for you to get to know him better.

Part V—Assigning Meaning to a Specific Sound

Now consider the first word of a baby born in the United States. It is almost certain to be "Mama." As it happens this is a very easy specific sound to make. When a little American baby says "Mama" for the first time mother comes rushing over to him and smothers him with kisses, "Yes, I am Mama!" she tells the baby. Every time the baby repeats the sound "Mama" the same thing happens. That night she proudly tells father, "The baby called me *Mama* today!"

The truth is when the baby first says *Mama* we do not have the ghost of an idea what the baby means. He may mean "mother," he may mean "blanket," or he may mean "food."

Who knows?

Let's assume this particular baby meant "blanket" but every time he says *Mama* he gets mother, not the blanket. At some point he says to himself, "Well, I am not getting my blanket with this but since I always seem to get mother I guess I'll use this sound when I want mother and find some other way to say *blanket.*

If we ask a French mother, "What is the first word a baby says in France?" She will say, "Why, *Mama,* of course!"

And when we ask "But what does it mean?" she will say, "It means me! It means mother."

Again we have no idea what the little French baby means when he first says "Mama" but our French mother also assumes he is talking about her and the baby quickly learns the effect that "Mama" has upon his mother.

If we go to Japan (feeling very confident now) we say to a Japanese mother, "Is *Mama* the first word that Japanese babies say?"

When she confirms that it is, we say, "And it means mother?"

She will stop us in our tracks and say, "No, *Mama* means food."

Now can we propose that when a Japanese baby says "Mama" for the first time we don't have a ghost of an idea what he means. He may mean "mother," he may mean "blanket," or he may mean "food." But every time the Japanese baby repeats the sound "Mama" he either gets a bottle to drink from or a breast to nurse from or a spoon full of food. He learns very quickly not to say "Mama" unless he is hungry.

The truth is that when the baby first says "Mama," we have no idea what the baby means.

In assuming that her baby wants food, the Japanese mother shows that she is a bit less egocentric than the rest of us. She is also probably closer to the truth.

Thus the word "Mama" is created by mother and baby. But let us not be fooled as to who is teaching whom. It is the baby who is the teacher in this case and the mother who is the student.

The baby is looking at what works with mother and what does not work. When he sees that she responds consistently, he will repeat the successful action. When the sound he makes does not produce a result, he abandons it.

If he makes sounds and no one listens to him or responds to him, he will stop making sounds or will make them infrequently.

SUMMARY

The newborn baby will begin the process of trying to communicate with mother and father at birth. He will show tremendous determination in doing so. Listening is the key. In this chapter we have looked at five effective ways that we can help the baby. These things can and should be done concurrently—one part of the language development program does not replace another. There are very simple and very basic rules that parents can follow to help their baby in his struggle to communicate.

First, remember: **All sounds are language.**

Following these simple guidelines will help to create a wonderful, safe, and sane environment for the baby in which he can quickly learn how to use his sounds to communicate with mother and father. These guidelines should also be used to create a standard for everyone in the household to follow. Make sure that brothers, sisters, and grandparents understand the baby's right to be heard and respected.

When a baby can communicate with mother and father, and he knows that they want to talk to him, then he can use all of his energy and creativity in a positive and happy way. He will not spend his time frustrated and annoyed because no one pays attention to him or because he cannot get what he wants.

Such frustration and annoyance makes for an unhappy, grumpy baby, who may conclude that we adults are not very smart after all.

That would be a great shame, because we adults have a great deal to teach the tiny baby. The foundation for all our teaching is the

When it comes to language, it is the baby who is the teacher and his mother who is the student.

establishment of respectful communication between the baby and mother and father.

This communication should not wait until the child is four or five years of age. It should start at the earliest possible moment. When it does, the love and respect between mother and father and the baby will blossom.

Respectful and effective communication between the baby and his family is essential.

| THE RULES OF THE LANGUAGE DEVELOPMENT PROGRAM ||
DO	DON'T
1. Always listen to the baby.	1. Don't use "baby talk" with the baby.
2. Look as if you are listening.	2. Don't ignore the baby.
3. Be willing to wait for a response.	3. Don't ask a question and leave no time for him to answer.
4. Accept the fact that the baby decides whether to respond or not; it is his choice.	4. Don't neglect to answer him.
5. Respond to what he says.	5. Don't imitate or make fun of the sounds he makes.
6. Welcome enthusiastically every effort the baby makes to talk.	6. Don't correct his pronunciation.
7. Assign meanings to the specific sounds that baby says repeatedly.	7. Don't try to force him to answer or respond.
8. Use real words when talking to the baby.	

THE LANGUAGE PROGRAM FOR PROFILE STAGES I TO IV

Daily Checklist

PART I

Opportunity to talk and be listened to by parents:

Mother or Father listening to all sounds baby makes—Every waking moment　☐

PART II

Opportunity to have a conversation:

10x daily (minimum) for 60 seconds

☐　☐　☐　☐　☐　☐　☐　☐　☐　☐

Total time: 10 minutes

PART III

Creating specific sounds in a poem:

5x daily for 1 to 2 minutes

☐　☐　☐　☐　☐

Total time: 5 to 10 minutes

PART IV

Using a choice board:

Number of times board was used today: _____

Interesting answers today: _____

_____

PART V

Assigning a meaning to a specific sound:

New specific sounds today: _____

_____

Changes Noted Today: _____

_____

_____

Date: _____

15

The Third Evaluation: Meaningful Appreciation and Response

The third stage on The Institutes Developmental Profile is the *meaningful* stage. Up to this point the baby has been dealing with all incoming information at a *reflexive stage* or at a *vital stage.*

At the reflexive stage he reacts automatically without trying to figure out what is happening or why it is happening. At the vital stage he responds to strong and threatening stimulation instantly, again without weighing the possibilities.

Time is of the essence at these stages and Mother Nature has cleverly arranged for the baby to develop the reflexive and vital responses first. This gives the baby a better chance to survive and make it to the higher stages of function, where he begins to weigh and consider what he sees, hears, and feels.

He is now entering the stage of meaningful appreciation of the world around him. He no longer simply reacts to stimulation reflexively, or vitally, but begins to appreciate some of the *meaning* of his visual, auditory, and tactile environment.

When he arrives at this stage he has reached a much more interesting place. Rather than concerning himself with just survival and threats to life, he begins to really understand and enjoy life. That very serious newborn becomes a happy baby.

Now that he can see, hear, and feel more easily, he begins to appreciate *what* he is seeing, hearing, and feeling. As he does, we begin to get a glimpse of his personality for the first time. This is when mothers and fathers begin to notice the differences and similarities between this baby and his older brother or sister at the same age. At the reflexive and vital stages babies tend to react very similarly. But from this point on, each baby's likes and dislikes become gradually more apparent.

If you evaluated your baby at birth and began a program shortly thereafter, it is time for the third evaluation within two to three months after birth. As before, you re-evaluate Stage I and Stage II, which you evaluated one or two months ago. Again, you may be surprised to find that your baby's responses at Stages I and II are stronger and more consistent. Some areas that you may have marked "Functional" two months ago are now "Perfect."

Stage III of The Institutes Developmental Profile encompasses all the meaningful responses that are part of the development of the tiny baby. This stage is shown in yellow on the Profile.

It is still important to choose the best times in the day to evaluate your baby so that you can get a clear picture of what he can and cannot do. If you choose times when he is tired or out of sorts he may not appear to do well in some areas because you do not have his full attention and interest. There is a large and important difference between not being *able* to do something and not being *willing* to do something. If you choose the happiest moments in the day, you can avoid this dilemma.

VISUAL COMPETENCE: STAGE III

Appreciation of Detail Within a Configuration

At this stage parents need to evaluate the baby's ability to appreciate detail within the outline of a larger image.

For example, the details of mother's face within the configuration of the outline of her face or head are details that the baby has the opportunity to see frequently. At first he sees only the outline of mother's head. But as his opportunity to see mother grows, he begins to see some of the detail within that outline.

The first sure sign of this major change in his vision is when the baby begins to respond to mother's facial expressions. He not only begins to recognize that this is his mother's face and that it is different from all other faces, but when mother smiles at him he begins to smile back.

So the first and most natural evaluation of his ability to appreciate detail is his response when he sees mother. Again to evaluate this response it is important for mother to approach her baby without using her voice or touch, which might help him identify his mother.

Mother should place the baby in a comfortable position in which he can see clearly. She should be sure that her face is well-lighted so that the baby has the best chance to see the details of her face.

When mother approaches the baby it is important for her to place her face close to the baby's face. He will develop the ability to see detail near him much earlier than far away. Mother needs to place herself eight to twelve inches from his face at first.

Then mother should smile broadly at her baby and wait to see his response. Again, it is important to wait for a response. It does not always occur instantly, especially when the baby is just developing a new function, so be willing to wait a little bit.

When the baby smiles in response to your smile without any auditory or tactile clues of any kind, you can be sure that he is beginning to see detail.

This ability will not be consistent at first. You may do the same evaluation the next day and get little or no response, but each day this response will become more and more consistent.

When your baby consistently smiles when you smile, or instantly knows the difference between you and someone else within a distance of three feet, write "Perfect" in red ink on the appreciation of detail box of the Profile. Draw a red line across the top edge of this box (see Figure 15.1).

If the baby recognizes you or smiles in response to your smile inconsistently, write "Functional" on the appreciation of detail box on the Profile in red and draw a line across the top edge of this box (see Figure 15.2).

If the baby does not demonstrate any response to your smile, draw a red line on the top edge of the box marked at the last evaluation to show that he is still at the same stage in his vision (see Figure 15.3).

Appreciation of detail within a configuration

Perfect

Meaningful appreciation

Figure 15.1. Perfect appreciation of detail

Appreciation of detail within a configuration

Functional

Meaningful appreciation

Figure 15.2. Functional appreciation of detail

Appreciation of detail within a configuration

Meaningful appreciation

Figure 15.3. Zero appreciation of detail

AUDITORY COMPETENCE: STAGE III

Appreciation of Meaningful Sounds

Now you are ready to evaluate your baby's ability to differentiate meaningful sounds. The baby will begin to respond to the meaningful sounds that exist in his immediate environment and that he has been hearing for many weeks without being able to decipher what they mean. Now these sounds will begin to have more and more meaning for the baby.

Common meaningful sounds in the baby's environment are the sound of footsteps down the hallway and the normal sounds of activity in the kitchen when food is being prepared. He listens to the sound of water running in the bathtub or the vacuum cleaner, the blender, and other common household sounds. But the most important meaningful sound is the sound of mother's voice. Now the baby listens for mother's tone and meaning.

Now the baby begins to be able to tell when mother is happy or angry. He hears the tone of voice, the "music" if not the words, of what family members are communicating to one another.

It is not difficult for most mothers to evaluate this stage in their babies. When your baby consistently responds to your tone of voice, which is to say when he is upset and you are able to soothe him with your voice, it is clear that he has an appreciation of meaningful sounds.

When a family member uses an upset or angry tone of voice, the baby may cry. Again, this is a clear sign that the baby is appreciating the meaningful sound of anger or upset. Often the crying of another baby, or an older brother or sister crying, will cause the baby himself to cry, because what he hears upsets him.

When your baby shows any or all of these responses consistently, write "Perfect" in red on the appreciation of meaningful sound box on the Profile. Draw a red line across the top edge of this box (see Figure 15.4).

When your baby shows any or all of the above responses inconsistently, write "Functional" in red on the appreciation of meaningful sound box on the Profile and draw a red line across the top edge of this box (see Figure 15.5).

If a baby does not have any sign of appreciation of meaningful sounds, draw a red line across the top edge of the box that was marked in his previous evaluation to show that he is still at the same stage in his hearing (see Figure 15.6).

Appreciation of meaningful sounds

Perfect

Meaningful appreciation

Figure 15.4. Perfect appreciation of meaningful sounds

Appreciation of meaningful sounds

Functional

Meaningful appreciation

Figure 15.5. Functional appreciation of meaningful sounds

Appreciation of meaningful sounds

Meaningful appreciation

Figure 15.6. Zero appreciation of meaningful sounds

TACTILE COMPETENCE: STAGE III

Appreciation of Gnostic Sensation

Now we can evaluate the meaningful stage in tactility. We need to see how well the baby is able to feel gnostic sensation. "Gnostic" comes from the Greek root for knowledge, "gnosis." Gnostic sensation literally means knowing sensation or meaningful sensation. Gnostic sensation is less intense than vital sensation. Now the baby is learning the subtleties of warm and cool. These sensations are pleasant as opposed to the vital sensations of hot and cold. The baby begins to complain if he has a wet diaper, which is not painful but rather unpleasant and irritating. This requires a more sophisticated ability to differentiate sensations than merely having the vital perception of pain when he has been stuck with a diaper pin.

The baby now seeks those sensations that bring him pleasure and comfort. He will seek to be held, cuddled, stroked, and kissed because these sensations feel good to him. He will not tire of the fun of having someone pull up his shirt and blow on his tummy or back or face or arms. He will respond with pleasure to being tickled.

When your baby consistently responds to any or all of the pleasurable or annoying gnostic sensations listed above, write "Perfect" in red on the appreciation of gnostic sensation box on the Profile and draw a red line across the top edge of this box (see Figure 15.7).

If your baby responds inconsistently to any or all of these pleasurable or annoying gnostic sensations, write "Functional" in red on this box and draw a line across the top edge of this box (see Figure 15.8).

If your baby does not yet have any appreciation of gnostic sensation, draw a red line across the top edge of the box that was marked in his previous evaluation to show that he is still at the same stage in his tactile development (see Figure 15.9).

**Appreciation of
gnostic sensation**

Perfect

Meaningful appreciation

Figure 15.7. Perfect appreciation
of gnostic sensation

**Appreciation of
gnostic sensation**

Functional

Meaningful appreciation

Figure 15.8. Functional appreciation
of gnostic sensation

**Appreciation of
gnostic sensation**

Meaningful appreciation

Figure 15.9. Zero appreciation
of gnostic sensation

MOBILITY COMPETENCE: STAGE III

Creeping in Cross Pattern

At this stage of development parents need to observe their baby's ability to creep in cross pattern. A baby who has had the benefit of a very good floor environment right from birth and has built up a lot of distance crawling every day will creep much earlier than a baby who has been put on his back and bundled up since birth.

However, parents will find that the sensory side of the Profile is definitely much easier to climb than the motor side. As you evaluate your baby in the sensory areas at Stages I, II, and III, you may be very impressed with how well your baby is doing in respect to the time frame of the average baby.

For example, a baby who has had a good visual stimulation program since birth will be able to see detail consistently *much* earlier than seven months of age. As we have already said, the motor responses are more complex and more demanding. As a result, the baby will need more opportunity and experience to be able to crawl, creep, and walk than he would to move up the first few stages on the sensory side of the Profile.

Figure 15.10. Olivia creeps in a cross pattern.

Creeping is the ability to defy gravity and push up onto hands and knees in order to move forward. The baby will need to do a lot of crawling to be ready for this gigantic accomplishment.

At first he will simply experiment with pushing himself up. He will then see how long he can keep himself up on all fours. Then he will go right back to crawling for transportation.

Once the baby feels secure holding his position on hands and knees, he may experiment by

rocking back and forth a bit to test his balance. When he feels confident enough, he will move one hand forward. He may fall back on his belly or he may continue to try his luck at this new and exciting form of locomotion.

As he gets braver and more capable on his hands and knees, he will begin to use both his arms and his legs. At first there will be no pattern to his movement or he may sit back on his buttocks a bit and hop like a rabbit for awhile. He may move by putting his right arm and leg forward simultaneously and then putting the left leg and arm forward simultaneously. This is a homolateral pattern of movement. But as his experience grows, he will develop a definite cross-pattern movement.

This cross-pattern movement is the most sophisticated pattern and allows him to move quickly and safely. In cross-pattern creeping his right arm and left leg move forward together and then his left arm and right leg move forward together (see Figure 15.10).

Just as the sensory world is more meaningful at Stage III, his mobility becomes more meaningful also. At Stage II he crawled just for the sake of movement. He did not necessarily have a purpose or a destination.

But as he gets up to creep his movement will be goal-directed. When he takes off on his hands and knees, it is clear he is going somewhere. Perhaps there is an object he wants across the room, or there is some important destination that he has in mind.

When your baby can creep across the room consistently in cross-pattern, without falling over or going back to his belly from time to time to crawl, write "Perfect" in red on the creeping box on the Profile and draw a line in red across the top edge of this box (see Figure 15.11).

If your baby can creep across the room on hands and knees consistently using any pattern whatsoever, write "Functional" in red on the creeping box on the Profile and draw a red line across the top edge of this box (see Figure 15.12).

If your baby bunny hops or cannot yet move on hands and knees, draw a red line on top of the line of the previous evaluation to show that he has not yet reached Stage III (see Figure 15.13).

Creeping on hands and knees, culminating in cross-pattern creeping

Perfect

Meaningful response

Figure 15.11. Perfect creeping

Creeping on hands and knees, culminating in cross-pattern creeping

Functional

Meaningful response

Figure 15.12. Functional creeping

Creeping on hands and knees, culminating in cross-pattern creeping

Meaningful response

Figure 15.13. Zero creeping

LANGUAGE COMPETENCE: STAGE III

The Creation of Meaningful Sounds

There are few areas of a baby's function to which mother is more closely attuned than the area of language. Once she becomes attuned to her baby's attempts to communicate, this is a very easy area for mother to evaluate. She is literally evaluating her baby's sounds every waking hour of every day from the time the baby is born.

Parents now need to evaluate whether their baby creates meaningful sounds. When the baby reaches this stage in his development he begins to make sounds that are more mature than those he has previously used. Although he cannot yet speak, he is able to communicate many things to his mother based on the nuances of the different sounds that he makes.

The things that he wishes to communicate now go well beyond his basic necessities or the need to call her when he thinks that his life is threatened.

He has been hearing meaningful sounds now for many weeks and he has been decoding these sounds. As his auditory pathway develops to the meaningful stage, he begins to create meaningful sounds himself. For the first time he learns that he can use these sounds to get the things that he needs and wants.

Mothers become quite expert at decoding the sounds that their babies make at this stage. Now the baby can let mother know when he is a little unhappy, or a little cranky, or a little hungry. Mother becomes so good at understanding her baby that she knows when he is pretending to be very upset or frightened simply because he wants something done immediately, and he knows that if he sounds the alarm he stands a better chance of quick service.

This is a far cry from the little fellow who had only two or three different methods of crying two short months ago.

When your baby consistently uses meaningful sounds to communicate his needs, wants, and moods, write "Perfect" in red on the creation of meaningful sounds box on the Profile and draw a red line across the top edge of this box (see Figure 15.14).

If your baby inconsistently uses several meaningful sounds to communicate, write "Functional" in red on this

Creation of meaningful sounds
Perfect
Meaningful response

Figure 15.14. Perfect creation of meaningful sounds

Creation of meaningful sounds
Functional
Meaningful response

Figure 15.15. Functional creation of meaningful sounds

box and draw a line across the top edge of this box (see Figure 15.15).

If the baby does not yet have any meaningful sounds, draw a red line across the top of the box marked at his last evaluation to show that he is not yet reached Stage III in language (see Figure 15.16).

**Creation of
meaningful sounds**

Meaningful response

Figure 15.16. Zero creation
of meaningful sounds

MANUAL COMPETENCE: STAGE III

The Prehensile Grasp

When adults reach out to pick up an object we use our whole hand—the thumb and fingers wrap around the object. However, the prehensile grasp is just the beginning of this. The baby uses his four fingers pressed against the palm of his hand while the thumb is often not used at all. This is a prehensile grasp.

Parents have little difficulty knowing when their baby has mastered this ability, because once he has it he will use it almost constantly. More often than not, whatever he finds to pick up will go right into his mouth. Since these things are often hazardous to the baby, mother and father learn to be vigilant from the time the baby is able to use the prehensile grasp. At this stage he is not yet able to pick up small objects because he uses his entire hand in a crude but effective grasp.

The function of the prehensile grasp, like the other functions of Stage III, is goal-directed. He is now picking up things to visually inspect the object more closely—to look at it, or to see if it is edible, or has a smell, or makes a noise. Whatever the reason, he can now explore his environment by reaching out and picking up things.

When your baby is consistently able to pick up objects with either hand, write "Perfect" in red on the prehensile grasp box of the Profile and draw a line across the top edge of this box (see Figure 15.17).

If your child can consistently pick up an object with one hand but not with the other, or can inconsistently pick up objects with either hand, write "Functional" in red on the prehensile grasp box on the Profile and draw a line across the top edge of this box (see Figure 15.18).

Prehensile grasp

Perfect

Meaningful response

Figure 15.17. Perfect prehensile grasp

Prehensile grasp

Functional

Meaningful response

Figure 15.18. Functional prehensile grasp

Prehensile grasp

Meaningful response

Figure 15.19. Zero prehensile grasp

If the baby cannot yet pick up an object with either hand, draw a red line across the top edge of the stage he achieved at his previous evaluation to show that he has not yet achieved Stage III on the Profile (see Figure 15.19).

Summary

As the baby moves into Stage III and gains an appreciation of the meaning of sight, sound, and touch, mother and father will be able to get to know their baby better. The baby's unique personality will begin to emerge. As he gains the motor abilities to move toward something he wants, or to communicate his needs, or to pick up an interesting object, he becomes a real member of his family.

16

The Sensory Stimulation Program for Stage III

After you have completed your baby's third evaluation, you will have a clear idea of which of the lower areas of Stage I and II are now perfect and which areas remain functional.

Once again, before you put your attention on expanding your present program to include new and more sophisticated stimulation, it is best to strengthen the program that you are already doing. Based on your new evaluation, decide which parts of your present program can be decreased or even eliminated altogether.

If your baby is now perfect at Stage II in any area, you can stop the stimulation you were doing for that area. This will give you more time to devote to Stage III stimulation that your baby will need now.

In those lower areas where the baby is still functional, you will want to continue the stimulation for these functions. However, if the area is improved since the second evaluation, you may wish to decrease the frequency of that stimulation. If the areas that were functional at the second evaluation have not changed significantly, keep the frequency of stimulation at the same level.

THE SENSORY STIMULATION PROGRAM

At Stage II our objective was to create a black-and-white world for the baby, a world in which there are no shades of gray. That made it easy for the baby to see and hear and feel. At the meaningful stage he may still need the reinforcement of that black-and-white environment but we can quite literally add a bit of color and excitement to his life.

We will do this gradually so that we continue to give the baby the message that it is easy to see, easy to hear, and easy to feel. His central nervous system is still immature and he will still tune out or turn down his seeing, hearing, or feeling if too much effort is required.

THE VISUAL PROGRAM:

Detail Within a Configuration

At Stage III the baby needs opportunity to see detail within a configuration. In the evaluation of this stage we have already discussed the natural detail of mother's features within the outline of the larger shape of her face and head. The baby will naturally see this many, many times a day.

Mother should now make an extra effort to change the expression on her face so that the baby is attracted to the details of her face and becomes increasingly aware that those details vary and alter as mother's mood changes.

Mothers who naturally have very expressive faces will not need to put much attention on this, but mothers who know that they are not very expressive should work on this point.

Your face is the single most important visual image to your baby, and it will remain the most important image for a very long time to come. Make every effort to show your enthusiasm, excitement, tenderness, and admiration clearly on your face. If you do, it will not be long before your baby mirrors that same enthusiasm and excitement.

The following three visual programs are designed so that Parts I and II are a bridge between Stage II vision and the very beginning of Stage III. They are very easy for the baby to see and can be started as soon as you have completed the 21 outline Bit of Intelligence cards in the Stage II visual program. This should have taken no more than six weeks.

Part III vision of this next program should be started when you observe that the baby is beginning, at least occasionally, to see some detail.

Objective: To establish, improve, or reinforce the ability to appreciate detail within a configuration

Purpose: To stimulate appreciation of detail within a configuration

Part I—Simple Detail in a Contrasting Environment

Frequency: Every waking moment

Intensity: Large, brightly colored shapes on the checkerboard squares

Duration: Every waking moment

Environment: You will use the same well-lighted room that you have been using for the checkerboard environment. Take brightly colored construction paper or poster board and cut it into simple shapes (circle, star, square, etc.) Use those shapes that you have already introduced as outline Bit of Intelligence cards in your previous visual program, but now make each shape a different color. The shapes should be approximately six inches in diameter or larger. Place these colored shapes on the checkerboard squares. Continue to provide good lighting on the checkerboards (see Figure 16.1).

Materials Needed:
- black-and-white checkerboard
- 21 colored images

Technique: At first, place only two or three shapes, each one on a single square of the checkerboard. Make sure that you place them on squares that will contrast well with the color of the shape (i.e. red on white, yellow on black). Avoid fixing the shapes permanently on

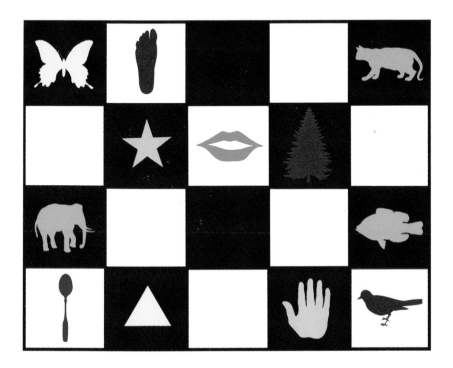

Figure 16.1. Checkerboard with randomly placed shapes.

the squares. This will enable you to move them and change the location and pattern daily. After a few days add another shape in a new color, then another. Keep changing the pattern. There does not have to be a shape in every square. It is important to keep changing the pattern. Your baby will be fascinated by the new colors and shapes. He will look forward to seeing his checkerboard. If the pattern changes he will keep looking to see his new environment each day. If the patterns stay the same he will quickly realize this and the checkerboard will become like old wallpaper: beloved but not very stimulating.

This checkerboard with the newly added colored shapes continues to travel with the baby wherever he goes, so that he has the opportunity to see these shapes often throughout the day (see Figure 16.2).

Please Note: At this point it will also help the baby if you add some color to his crawling track. It is particularly helpful to put a wide red stripe at the end of the track. As the baby's vision improves, he will look toward this red stripe and know that this is where he can literally crawl off the track. Again, the relationship between mobility and vision is very ancient and very important. These visual clues let the baby know that he is moving through space, which encourages him to move more. And the more the baby moves through space, the better his vision will become.

Figure 16.2.
Add simple detail to the checkerboard and crawling track to create an exciting and stimulating visual environment.

Part II—Simple Detail Bit of Intelligence Cards

Materials Needed:
- tempera paint
- small paintbrush
- 5 face "Bit" cards
- 10 black posterboard squares (11" x 11")
- 54 white label dots (1.5" to 2" in diameter)

Frequency: 10 times daily

Intensity: Brightly colored detail on black outline cards 11" by 11"

Duration: 5 to 10 seconds

Content: 3 cards

Environment: A well-lighted room with extra light shining on the Bit of Intelligence cards.

Technique: You already have at least 21 basic black-on-white outline Bit of Intelligence cards from your earlier visual program. Now you will get bright-colored tempera paint and paint some simple detail on each outline "Bit" card (see Figure 16.3).

It is also good to make several additional circle outline Bit of Intelligence cards. This allows you to make a set of "faces." You can paint a happy face, a surprised face, a sad face, a sleepy face, and an angry face on black circles (see Figure 16.4).

A third set of new cards will be simple quantity Dot Cards. To make these you will need ten pieces of 11" x 11" black poster board. Each of these cards will have a different quantity of white dots, each 1.5 to 2 inches in diameter. Make a set of cards from one to ten. The dots can be painted on the black poster board, or put on with self-

Figure 16.3. Simple outline Bit of Intelligence cards with simple detail on them

Figure 16.4.
Simple detail "Bit" cards: happy, sad, angry, sleepy, and surprised.

adhesive white dot labels. The dots on these cards should not be arranged in any pattern, and should not touch each other. There should be enough "breathing room" around each dot so that the baby can see the outline of the white dots against the black background (see Figure 16.5).

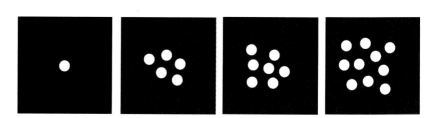

Figure 16.5.
White on black Dot Cards
with large dots—
1, 5, 7, 10 cards

Choose two simple detail outline Bit of Intelligence cards that look very different from one another, and one simple quantity Dot Card. Start with the card with one dot, since it's the easiest to see.

Now you have 21 outline Bit of Intelligence cards with simple detail added, *plus* five face cards and ten simple quantity Dot Cards: 36 cards in all.

Each day you will show two sets, and each set will be shown five times. Remember, one set contains: two outline Bit of Intelligence cards with simple detail (or faces) and one simple quantity Dot Card (see Figure 16.6).

Figure 16.6.
Each set has 2 simple
outline Bit of Intelligence
cards and one Dot Card.

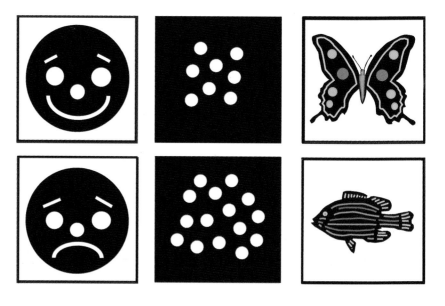

Each day choose six different cards. In six days you will have cycled through all 36 cards. Now cycle through these cards again for the next six days but reorganize the cards so that they are now in different groupings.

The two sets that you have chosen for each day can be kept with the baby's diaper bag. Every time the baby needs to be changed show one set of the cards. In this way you will find it very easy to show them five times in a day.

In order to show the cards, place your baby in the same comfortable position that you have been using to show the outline "Bits." Hold the cards up one at a time, about 12 to 18 inches from his face. Show him the card as you did before, and name it as you show it: "square," or "happy face," or "one."

Since his vision is considerably better than it used to be, you will not have to hold the card up for nearly as long. In fact, each day you will see that your baby locates the card, looks at it, and is ready to move on. His ability to respond more quickly and easily will be a pure product of how often he has received the appropriate stimulation.

You are growing his visual pathway, and as that pathway grows you will observe his reaction time getting faster. When that happens, your reaction time should speed up also.

The baby's ability to respond easily will be a product of how often he has received appropriate stimulation.

If you do not keep pace with your baby's accelerating reaction time, you will actually annoy and irritate him. You will bore him by holding up the image too long. There is no exact recipe, however, for the length of time you should hold a card up at this point.

Observe your baby carefully so you know when it is time to move a bit faster in showing the cards. This ability to observe and respond appropriately to the changes you see daily will become one of the most important elements in your teaching relationship with your child.

When you have completed cycling through the 36 simple detail outline Bit of Intelligence cards, your baby should be showing clear signs that he can see detail. This ability should be getting more and more consistent every day. If this has not happened by the end of the 12 days it took to show the 36 Bit of Intelligence cards, cycle through the cards one more time. As soon as you see that your child is seeing the detail of your face or the environment around him, even though he may still be rather inconsistent in his ability to do so, stop the simple outline Bit of Intelligence cards and go on to Part III, where you will be using all five sensory pathways to teach him more about visual detail within a configuration.

Part III—Using All Five Pathways

There are five pathways into the brain. We can see, hear, feel, taste, and smell. Up to this point we have emphasized seeing, hearing, and feeling because these are the three primary sensory pathways that are critical to human function. But in this next step of the program we will include taste and smell in order to enhance the growth of the primary sensory pathways.

Let's take a brief look at taste and smell. At birth a baby has the ability to taste and smell. In fact, these are his primary means of locating and identifying mother. These senses become less and less important as the three major pathways grow and become his primary means of relating to his environment.

However, they are very important to the baby in the first few months of life. We can, therefore, use the baby's sense of taste and smell to help develop his ability to see, hear, and feel.

Step One: Detail Bit of Intelligence Cards, and Words

Frequency:	10 times daily
Intensity:	Brightly colored image with detail, outlined in black, on white 11" by 11" poster board
Duration:	30 seconds
Content:	1 Bit of Intelligence card 1 taste, 1 smell, 1 tactile input, 5 auditory inputs
Environment:	A well-lighted room free from noise or commotion, with very good lighting on the Bit of Intelligence cards or objects as they are shown.

Materials Needed:

- 10 fruit "Bit" cards (11" x 11")
- 10 reading words (22" x 6")
- 10 fruit tastes
- 10 fruit smells
- 10 actual fruits
- 10 small jars
- cotton swabs

Technique: In this very important step all five pathways will be used, not just the visual pathway, to insure that a very simple and clear message arrives. This is a very easy step and a very important step for the baby.

For this mother needs items that are not only bright and attractive to look at but also have a taste and a smell and, hopefully, an interesting texture.

The best items for this step are fruits. Choose ten fruits. It is best to choose the brightest, tastiest, most perfumed fruits that are available in your area. Now make a detail Bit of Intelligence card of each fruit. This can be a very large, clear photograph or a very good illustration. Or, if you like, you can make a set of simple paintings yourself.

Each image that you choose or make should have a heavy black outline around the image. You can simply add this outline using a black marker. Again, this makes it easier for the baby to see the card. Make sure that any details within the configuration of the fruit are bold, using the black marker if necessary to make the details a little easier to see (see Figure 16.7).

Now make a very large and clear word card for each of the fruits that you have chosen. These should be made on white poster board cards that are 22 inches long and 6 inches wide. To print the cards use an extra-wide black marker (one-half-inch nib). This will make a very wide, bold line that will provide the correct intensity. The lettering should be 5 inches tall and 4 inches wide with one-half inch between each letter. The letters should be in lower case (see Figure 16.8).

Now mother will need a little jar with a lid in which to put a little bit of banana and some cotton swabs. These things will be used to give the baby a taste and a smell of the banana.

Finally mother needs a nice, fresh whole banana so that she can show the baby what the banana looks like in real life.

Now mother is prepared to teach the idea "banana" using the visual, auditory, tactile, gustatory, and olfactory pathways.

You may want to keep this set of materials in your diaper bag so that you can use them after you have diapered the baby. Place the baby in a comfortable position on his back or cradle him in your arms, whichever works best for you. With a cotton swab take a small amount of banana and place it on your baby's tongue.

Now say loudly and clearly "banana." Then wait a few seconds so that the baby has time to taste the banana. He may smile or make a face of some kind. For example, lemon, which we consider rather tart and strong, will often make the baby smile for a few seconds, then as he continues to savor the taste, he may wrinkle his nose, as we would do, to show that it is tart or sour. Mothers often comment that their babies continue to taste whatever fruit is used for 15 or 20 minutes afterward.

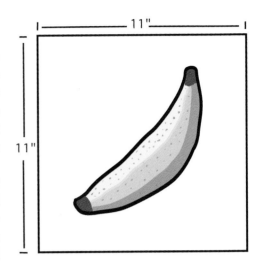

Figure 16.7.
A simple fruit Bit of Intelligence card—banana

Figure 16.8.
Reading card—banana

After he has tasted the banana, use the same cotton swab to hold a little dab of banana up to his nose. Again, say "banana." Give him a second to smell the banana. Now hold up the "Bit" card with the image of the banana. Say clearly "banana." Next hold up the card that says "banana" and show it to him, again saying clearly, "banana."

Now take the banana and hold it up where he can see it and tell him "banana." Finally let him feel the banana by running his fingers and hands over the banana. For the final time repeat "banana." Do this 10 times a day.

Mother has now used every possible means to teach her baby that there is a long, sweet, smooth, yellow fruit that we call a banana. The baby is able to use all five pathways to receive the same piece of information. The taste, smell, sensation, and sight of the banana are very concrete ideas.

However, the sound "banana" and the word written on the card are abstractions. Nevertheless, if the baby is shown this information in this way, clearly and consistently, he will understand those abstractions. He will not only learn very quickly that the long, smooth, sweet, pungent thing is what we arbitrarily call a banana, but he will also learn to recognize the written word "banana" without the slightest difficulty. That is reading.

In fact, to the baby the written word is no more difficult to perceive than the sound "banana." He will learn both easily when they are repeated in this clear presentation, which provides the correct intensity in terms of loudness for the sound and largeness for the word card.

This increased intensity is the key for the message to arrive in the rapidly developing brain of the tiny baby.

Each day choose a different fruit. It will take ten days to teach all ten fruits. However, at the end of those ten days the baby will have had 100 opportunities to use all five pathways to begin to see, hear, feel, taste, and smell the world around him. If all goes well he will have made a significant leap in his ability to appreciate not only detail within a configuration but also meaningful sound, words of speech, gnostic sensation, taste, and smell.

That is a lot to accomplish in 30 seconds, 10 times a day, for 10 days. This is 3,000 seconds in all, less than an hour altogether. It will be time very well spent in the life of a tiny baby who is growing and developing every minute of every day.

When you have completed this step you are ready to go on to sophisticated detail Bit of Intelligence cards.

Step Two: Sophisticated Detail Bit of Intelligence Cards, and Words

Frequency:　　3 times daily per set

Intensity:　　Large, brightly colored photographs, illustrations, or paintings that have clear, accurate detail, mounted on white 11" x 11" poster board

Duration:　　5 seconds per session (1 set shown)

Content:　　1 set of 10 Bit of Intelligence cards in a session (2 sets used in a day

Environment:　　A well-lighted room with special care that the Bit of Intelligence cards are in good light when they are shown.

Technique:　　Now you get to have some fun because the materials that you will use are things which we adults enjoy choosing and teaching. To some degree, you will have the opportunity to learn something new right alongside your tiny baby.

Now you want to find large, clear, and accurate photographs, drawings, or paintings of interesting information. Good categories to start with are flowers, birds, insects, and mammals. These items have interesting shapes and varying colors.

These should be high-quality photographs or excellent paintings. Your bookstore will generally have a wealth of last year's calendars or excellent full-color posters and books on sale that are old or damaged. These calendars, posters, and books make excellent sources for the photographs or illustrations that you want.

The images should be large, at least six inches in diameter. The photograph or illustration should have only one image, not a group of images (i.e. one banana, one orchid, one lion). At this stage it is important to keep the visual image simple. The challenge for the baby will be to see the detail within the configuration of the one image.

Each Bit of Intelligence card should be clearly labeled on the back with a specific name (example: "Two-spotted Ladybird Beetle," not "insect") (see Figure 16.9).

Before you begin, it is best to find at least 15 items or more in each category.

Choose two categories that contain ten Bit of Intelligence cards each. Teach each category three times daily for ten days. For example, teach ten insects and ten birds for ten days, then retire these two sets and introduce ten mammals and ten flowers.

Materials Needed:

- 20 images to create "Bit" cards (photos or drawings)
- 20 white poster board squares (11" x 11")
- black felt-tipped marker ($\frac{1}{2}$" nib)
- rubber cement

A *Bit of Intelligence* is:

- *Precise:* Having accurate scientific detail
- *Discrete:* One item only
- *Unambiguous:* Clearly labeled

Figure 16.9.
A clear, sophisticated detail Bit of Intelligence card—"Two-spotted Ladybird Beetle"

Baby's first set of "Bit" cards:

Insects

- Two-Spotted Ladybird Beetle
- Giant Walkingstick
- Green Darner Dragonfly
- Housefly
- Differential Grasshopper
- Little Black Ant
- Subterranean Termite
- Periodical Cicada
- Monarch Butterfly
- Golden Northern Bumblebee

Make sure you choose those times in the day when the baby is alert and awake to show these cards. The baby will be fascinated by the new world of color, detail, and unusual forms that you are introducing to him.

Hold up each card long enough for him to see it fully and to hear what it is, but not so long that he looks away, which he *will do* when he is finished looking. If you move on to a new card just an instant before he looks away, you will not run the risk of over-doing it.

By now your baby can see detail easily, and each day this ability gets better and better. Mothers are very good at knowing when their babies can see detail consistently without effort. (See Appendix C for materials available.)

Please Note: When your baby has reached this stage in his development he is well beyond needing to see simple outline and simple detail, so retire his checkerboard. It has done its job. Put it some place safe for his younger brother or sister to use when he or she arrives.

THE AUDITORY PROGRAM

To help their babies develop an appreciation of meaningful sounds, parents should use meaningful sounds all the time with the baby and around the baby.

Objective: To establish, improve, or reinforce the appreciation of meaningful sounds

Purpose: To provide abundant meaningful sounds in the environment

Part I—Conversation

Frequency: Every waking hour

Intensity: Loud and clear voice

Duration: Every waking hour

Content: Daily conversation

Environment: A relatively quiet room with unnecessary noises eliminated.

Technique: It is very easy for mother to put a lot of expression in her voice whenever she speaks to the baby. The baby will be listening very intently to hear "the music" or tone of voice that is being used. If mother is apt to speak in a monotone or with very little expression, or if she speaks very little to the baby, he will not have the opportunity he needs to develop an appreciation of meaningful sounds.

Please Note: In fact, everyone who lives with the baby should attempt to speak to him loudly, clearly, and using a voice full of expression and enthusiasm. This creates an atmosphere and environment where there is always something interesting to hear and pay attention to. Without these stimuli, the baby is likely to tune out because little of interest is happening.

It is also very important to eliminate household noises as much as possible when you are speaking to the baby. Some households have the radio or the television on constantly even though no one is watching or listening. These background noises create auditory chaos for the tiny baby. They make his job infinitely more difficult since he must try to sort out meaningful sounds and decode words heard over the blare of music, commercials, gunfire, car horns, bells, singing, laughing, crying, yelling, and all the other assorted cacophony that comes from television and radio.

We can make his life much easier by turning off the extraneous noise when he is awake. This will greatly reduce the auditory chaos.

Part II—Environmental Sounds

Frequency:	10 times daily
Intensity:	Loud, clear sounds
Duration:	5 seconds
Content:	A good variety of household sounds plus other interesting sounds: bells, cymbals, horns, a sound effects tape
Environment:	A quiet place

Materials Needed:
- pots
- pans
- bells
- cymbals
- xylophone
- triangle
- sound effects

Technique: Just as you have collected various tastes, smells, and detail Bit of Intelligence cards, now look for sounds to collect.

Household sounds occur naturally. Filling up the bathtub is a sound the baby hears daily. Make sure you always tell him, "That is the sound of water." When someone closes or bangs the door, do the same. When the car drives up the driveway or a truck makes the apartment or house shake, tell the baby "That was a truck." The vacuum cleaner, the blender, the lawn mower, the noisy toys of his older brother and sister, all of these sounds are naturally present in his everyday environment.

Now mother needs to identify each sound as it occurs, labeling it with a word, so that the baby begins to understand the sound.

At first the baby will hear the sounds, if they are loud enough, but he will have great difficulty locating them. This is disconcerting to the baby. Mother accelerates his ability to locate sound by consistently pointing out its origin as it occurs (example: "That was the dog barking *outside.*")

In addition to these sounds that occur naturally throughout the day, collect a group of interesting sounds. Again, it is helpful to keep these things wherever you usually change the baby. Each time you put a clean diaper on your baby you have one of the sounds handy.

Put the baby comfortably on his back so that he is looking up at you. Pick up the cymbals and say loudly and clearly "cymbals." Now bang the cymbals together. Repeat one more time and say "cymbals."

Use one sound ten times during the day. The following day replace that sound with a new one.

You will find that there are dozens of interesting sounds that you can make just with simple objects around the house.

Once you have exhausted the supply in the household, try a music store for simple musical instruments, such as a xylophone. Using the xylophone, you can introduce the baby to musical notes. Hit "A" and tell the baby "A." Each day you use the xylophone, teach the baby a new note.

You can also use a recording of sound effects. These recordings contain a wide variety of sounds, from the exciting sound of a locomotive to the wild sounds of exotic animals, and everything in between.

Continue to add new sounds for as long as you and your baby are enjoying yourselves.

Part III—Words

Whenever you do a proper visual stimulation program at Stage III, you will be using the auditory pathway as part of that program. All three parts of the visual program that are outlined in the beginning of this chapter involve using the auditory pathway to tell the baby what each image is. This is done loudly, clearly, and repeatedly. It is one of the most important parts of your auditory program. It enables your baby to gain a better appreciation of meaningful sounds.

Words are the most important meaningful sounds that your baby will ever hear. He hears words from the moment he is born. However, through the visual program described earlier he will hear the words associated with visual information. This helps him to decode the words: to understand what they mean.

So Part III of his auditory program is included in Parts II and III of the Visual Program.

THE TACTILE PROGRAM

One of the most pleasurable parts of being the parent of a newborn is the great fun of simply playing with the baby. A good deal of that fun consists of actions that provide an excellent opportunity for the baby to appreciate gnostic sensation.

Objective: To establish, improve, and reinforce the appreciation of gnostic sensation

Purpose: To provide ample stimulation of gnostic sensation

Part I—Tickling and Massage

Frequency: 5 times daily

Intensity: Varying degrees of light touch

Duration: 60 seconds

Content: Light fingertip touch, gentle rubbing touch, light fingernail touch

Environment: An environment warm enough for the baby to be naked or in a diaper only

Technique: Just after you have powdered the baby and before you put on his clean diaper, take a minute to give him a good tickling, rubbing, or massage all over.

One session may consist of lightly tickling him all over. As you do so tell him, "Now I am tickling your feet."

The next time you diaper him change the kind of gnostic sensation you are using. Take the flat part of your hand and give him a good gentle rubbing all over. The next session give him a gentle massage all over.

Other good gnostic sensations are the light touch of your fingernails or a good rub all over with a soft or a rough towel.

As you do this, you may find that some areas of his body are more sensitive to touch than others. If there are areas that seem "too sensitive" or "too dull" to you, concentrate on these. You will find that his "fine tuning" improves and his appreciation of gnostic sensation becomes more and more consistent.

When you feel that your baby's response to simple gnostic sensation is appropriate and consistent, begin Part II.

Please Note: These sessions are a perfect time to teach him all the parts of his body. When you begin say, "This is your arm" and "This is your leg" as you touch or massage it. After many weeks you can get more specific and more sophisticated saying, "This is your right arm," "This is your left leg," "This is your shoulder," etc.

Part II—Contrasting Gnostic Sensations

Frequency:	10 times daily
Intensity:	Rough and soft textures
Duration:	60 seconds
Content:	Many different pairs of contrasting textures
Environment:	A room warm enough for the baby to wear only a diaper

Materials Needed:

Contrasting Textures

- hard brush
- baby brush
- light sandpaper
- velvet cloth
- plastic non-abrasive pot scrubber
- silk cloth
- rough towel
- soft towel

Technique: Mother needs to find as many contrasting textures as she can. She wants to make contrasting pairs such as: a rough towel and a soft towel, a normal hair brush and a soft baby brush, a non-abrasive plastic pot scrubber and a piece of velvet, a plastic soap saver and a piece of foam rubber, a piece of burlap and a piece of satin.

These contrasting textures help the baby to differentiate two very different sensations. This contrast is easier to differentiate than if we used two very similar textures.

These pairs of contrasting textures are also kept in the diaper bag for convenience. Once again, after diapering the baby and before dressing him again, take the hair brush and lightly brush it over his arms and hands, legs and feet, abdomen and back, and shoulders and head. As you do this keep him in touch with what you are doing. Say, "Do you feel the hair brush on your hand?"

As you stimulate each part of his body tell him what you are doing. This should take approximately 30 seconds. Then take the contrasting texture, in this case the baby brush, and do the same thing with the baby brush.

Use this same pair of textures ten times in one day. Then retire these two textures and add a new pair of textures the following day. If you have ten texture pairs, you can cycle through them and begin again after ten days.

As you continue this program you will see your baby's appreciation of gnostic sensation change and mature before your eyes.

At first, he may be quite content to feel the normal hair brush. He may show little or no difference in his reaction to the hard brush and the soft baby brush. But as you continue to do this he will become more sensitive to these sensations. He will begin to appreciate the difference between the two brushes.

He may wrinkle his nose when he feels the hair brush. If so, use it even more lightly. This is not vital sensation you are doing, it is gnostic sensation, which is light touch. You will see him wriggle with pleasure when he feels the baby brush on his skin. He may actually start to complain or object to a harder texture like the hair brush. When he does, you can stop these harder textures altogether. He has the message and can differentiate instantly between the two contrasting textures. You have done your job.

Please Note: You should be careful to choose materials and textures that will not abrade the baby's skin. There are many hard textures and rough textures that are non-abrasive. These are what you want to use.

SUMMARY

Once again it will be helpful to make a daily checklist to follow. In the course of this sensory program this checklist will change and evolve as the baby gains new abilities and advances to more sophisticated stages in his abilities.

The daily checklists might look something like these:

THE SENSORY PROGRAM FOR PROFILE STAGE III
Initial Checklist

Visual Competence

Providing simple detail:
Checkerboard with colored shapes—All day ☐

Simple detail Bit of Intelligence cards
10x daily for 5 to 10 seconds

☐ ☐ ☐ ☐ ☐ ☐ ☐ ☐ ☐ ☐

Total time: 50 seconds to 1 minute 40 seconds

Auditory Competence

Providing meaningful sound:
Animated, vibrant and expressive conversation—All day ☐

Environmental Sounds
10x daily, for 5 seconds

☐ ☐ ☐ ☐ ☐ ☐ ☐ ☐ ☐ ☐

Eliminate auditory chaos _____

_____

Total time: 50 seconds

Tactile Competence

Creating gnostic sensation:
Tickling and massage
5x daily, for 60 seconds

☐ ☐ ☐ ☐ ☐

Total time: 5 minutes

Changes Noted Today: _____

_____

_____

Date: _____

THE SENSORY PROGRAM FOR PROFILE STAGE III

Intermediate Checklist

Using all five pathways: 10x daily for 30 seconds

Taste: ☐ ☐ ☐ ☐ ☐ ☐ ☐ ☐ ☐ ☐

Smell: ☐ ☐ ☐ ☐ ☐ ☐ ☐ ☐ ☐ ☐

Touch: ☐ ☐ ☐ ☐ ☐ ☐ ☐ ☐ ☐ ☐

Sight: ☐ ☐ ☐ ☐ ☐ ☐ ☐ ☐ ☐ ☐

Bit of Intelligence
card: ☐ ☐ ☐ ☐ ☐ ☐ ☐ ☐ ☐ ☐

Word card: ☐ ☐ ☐ ☐ ☐ ☐ ☐ ☐ ☐ ☐

Total time: 5 minutes

Auditory Competence

Loud, clear conversation _____

Eliminate auditory chaos _____

Environmental sounds:
10x daily, for 5 seconds

☐ ☐ ☐ ☐ ☐ ☐ ☐ ☐ ☐ ☐

Total time: 50 seconds

Tactile Competence

Tickling and massage:
5x daily, for 60 seconds

☐ ☐ ☐ ☐ ☐

Total time: 5 minutes

Changes Noted Today: _____

_____

_____

Date: _____

THE SENSORY PROGRAM FOR PROFILE STAGE III

Advanced Checklist

Visual Competence

Providing sophisticated detail:
Detailed Bit of Intelligence cards:
3x daily for 10 seconds (2 sets)

Set 1 ☐ ☐ ☐   Set 2 ☐ ☐ ☐

Total time: 1 minute

Auditory Competence

Providing meaningful sounds:

Conversation (loud, clear voice) _____

_____

Eliminate auditory chaos _____

_____

Environmental Sounds:
10x daily, for 5 seconds

☐ ☐ ☐ ☐ ☐ ☐ ☐ ☐ ☐ ☐

Total time: 50 seconds

Tactile Competence

Providing gnostic sensation:
Tickling and massage
5x daily, for 60 seconds

☐ ☐ ☐ ☐ ☐

Contrasting gnostic sensation:
10x daily for 60 seconds

☐ ☐ ☐ ☐ ☐ ☐ ☐ ☐ ☐ ☐

Total time: 10 minutes

Changes Noted Today: _____

_____

_____

Date: _____

Please Note: The above checklist should also include any re-maining parts of the sensory program for the reflexive and vital stages of the Profile.

In addition, the checklists you create as your program progress-es may be different than the ones shown because your baby may develop a bit faster in one sensory area than in another.

For example, you might begin the second part of your tactile pro-gram (contrasting gnostic sensations) when you are using the Inter-mediate Checklist, if your baby is ready for this.

Now you have all the tools needed to help your baby to gain a full appreciation of detail within a configuration, meaningful sound, and appreciation of gnostic sensation.

Along the way you will be using both taste and smell to help speed up this process. You will have begun a very strong program of introducing the baby to his primary language through the use of the visual, auditory, and tactile pathway.

What was a dark, chaotic, and difficult world for the baby only two or three two months ago has become a world of colorful detail, rich with sounds of happiness and excitement, full of wonderful sen-sations, and with new and exciting tastes and smells.

Now the baby will be ready to put these new found perceptions to the test and begin to use them to make his mark on the world.

Now he is ready to take that wonderful sensory information and put it to good use with his own mobility, language, and manual com-petence.

You have made it possible for him to know that there is a big, wonderful world to explore and he will not want to waste one moment. He will be chomping at the bit to get moving in every sense of the word.

17

The Motor Opportunity Program for Stage III

The baby is now beginning to have a better and better sense of the world around him. His ability to see detail, appreciate meaningful sounds and perceive gnostic sensation have become more mature and consistent. Now he has a much stronger reason to move, to make sounds, and to reach out and use his hands. Now he is prepared to extend dramatically his goals and objectives.

When he sees people he will move across the room to join them. He understands the sounds around him, and he can make his own sounds in response. His vision and his appreciation of light touch are so much better that he now wants to reach out and pick up things.

These motor abilities will develop much more rapidly when the baby is given an excellent sensory stimulation program to establish and enhance them, along with ample opportunity to move, make sounds, and use his hands to achieve his goals.

THE MOBILITY PROGRAM

The ability to push himself up on hands and knees, thus defying gravity for the first time, is one of the most remarkable physical feats that the tiny baby will ever accomplish. This ability will gradually develop into the ability to creep in a complete cross pattern.

The baby's skill in this advanced form of mobility will be almost totally dependent on the distance he has crawled and on his opportunity to develop his sense of balance. The long-range objective of the baby's mobility program up to now has been to crawl 150 feet in a day, but most infants will begin to get up on their hands and knees before they reach 100 feet of crawling daily. If the baby exceeds 100 feet of crawling daily and he is still not pushing himself up on to his hands and knees, mother should continue to provide the maximum floor time possible. She should also continue his daily balance activities so that the baby can achieve 150 feet of crawling in a day. If she continues to encourage him in this way, she will soon see him conquer gravity for the first time and pull himself up into the quadruped position.

Objective:	To establish, improve, or reinforce the ability to creep on hands and knees culminating in cross-pattern creeping
Purpose:	To provide the maximum opportunity to get up into the quadruped position and to move on hands and knees

Part I—Creeping

Frequency:	As many sessions as possible (approximately 20 to 30)
Intensity:	A few inches, increasing to feet and then to many yards
Duration:	Very brief sessions, which gradually lengthen as distance increases. A minimum of 4 hours daily on the floor.
Content:	The baby is placed in the ideal creeping environment and encouraged to push up. Once he is able to do this, he is encouraged to move forward.

Materials Needed:

• short-pile carpet

• open space

• protected stairways

Environment: In order to speed the baby's progress toward creeping it is important to begin to change the surface of the floor on which he is placed.

By evolution, begin to place the baby on an increasingly rougher surface. As he begins to be able to creep, remove objects or pieces of furniture that are unstable which the baby might pull over on himself if he grabs them. Now is the time to protect stairways so that the baby does not fall down.

Rooms with a minimum of furniture and a maximum amount of open space are best.

Technique: At first place the baby on a carpet with very short pile. He can crawl on this but the friction is greater than on a smooth surface. As a result, he will begin to put more weight on his arms and legs and less on his belly, which drags on the rough surface. When he can crawl easily on this surface, place him on a carpet that is a little bit thicker.

Once again, the baby will shift a little more weight to his arms and legs to make it easier to crawl on the thicker carpet. If at any point in this process the new surface is too heavy and the baby grows discouraged and stops moving, or moves much less, we have given him too rough a surface too quickly. Immediately go back to the surface where he was succeeding. Try a new surface again in a week or so.

Finally, place the baby on a thick shag carpet. By now the baby will begin to push himself up and rock back and forth or right and left.

Sometimes he will fall, but the thick carpet will cushion his fall. He will keep experimenting and each day he will be able to stay up longer and longer. A baby who has had maximum opportunity on the floor and an excellent balance program may actually be up on all fours getting ready to creep by 11 or 12 weeks of age.

Long-range goal:
• 400 yards daily

Once the baby begins to creep, he will very quickly make creeping his exclusive means of transportation. You can retire his infant crawling track. There is no going back now. Crawling will be a thing of the past as he finds this new form of mobility much more efficient and much more exciting.

His long-range goal is to creep a total of 400 yards in a day. This is actually a modest distance. Some floor babies have been known to creep four times that amount in a single day.

Please Note: Again it is important to keep simple records of the distances the baby creeps each day. This is not as difficult as it might seem. Once you measure the basic distances of the rooms and hallways that make up the baby's environment, you can keep a general account of how many times the baby went up the hall or across the room. By the end of the day you will have a good estimate of the distance that the baby crept.

Part II—Balance Activities

Frequency: 2 times daily for each activity

Intensity: Begin slowly and gradually increase the speed as baby adapts to it

Materials Needed:

• baby neck collar

Duration: 15 seconds for each activity; over 1 to 2 months increase to 60 seconds per activity

Content: 10 activities at each session

Environment: A safe space that is not cluttered with furniture. Floor areas cleared of toys or other objects. This program is best done on a good gymnastics mat, if possible.

The baby should be dressed in unrestrictive clothing and should wear a neck collar at all times. You can fold a soft towel and wrap it loosely around the baby's neck. This should fit like a thick collar on a turtleneck sweater and keep his neck in a stable position. You can also make a proper little neck collar to fit the baby (see Figure 17.1) . This is easy to do and it is easier to use than the towel. *There is a diagram of how to make a neck collar in the appendix of the book.*

Figure 17.1.
Maria wears a neck collar for all of the balance activities.

When you hold the baby for these activities, always hold him by the bare ankles or wrists, never over socks or other clothing that may slip and make you lose your grip on the baby.

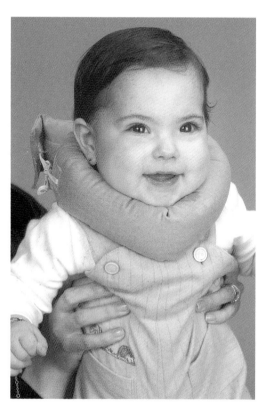

Technique: Do the following activities twice daily. Be careful to begin each activity very slowly and gently. This will help the baby to develop the balance areas of the brain. He needs slow movement now but will later need the greater intensity of slightly faster motion. As with everything that you do with the baby, stop before the baby wants to stop.

1. Horizontal spin in the prone position: Place the baby over your shoulder on his belly and spin around. Then stop and spin in the opposite direction. Be careful not to get dizzy enough to lose your balance (see Figure 17.2).

2. Horizontal spin on the left side: This is the same spin, but now place the baby on his left side on your right shoulder. Again spin in one direction and then in the other.

3. Horizontal rotation on the right side: Now put the baby on his right side on your left shoulder and spin in one direction and then the other.

Figure 17.2.
Maria does a horizontal spin in the prone position with her mother.

Figure 17.3.
Maria does a horizontal rotation in the prone position with her mother.

4. Rocking in the supine position: Hold the baby by his wrists with his face up while your spouse holds him by the ankles. Together, pick up the baby and gently rock him from side to side.

5. Horizontal rotation: Hold the baby's left wrist in your left hand and his left ankle in your right hand. The baby is facing you. Now gently lift the baby and spin him around clockwise. After he gently comes in for a landing, repeat this in a counterclockwise direction (see Figure 17.3).

6. Horizontal rotation in the supine position: Hold the baby's left wrist in your right hand and his left ankle in your left hand so that his belly is facing up. Gently spin in a clockwise direction. Then stop and do the same thing counterclockwise.

7. Horizontal rotation, head in, in the prone position: Hold the baby by his hands and wrists with the baby facing toward you. Gently spin the baby around with arms outstretched. Stop and do the same activity in the opposite direction (see Figure 17.4).

IMPORTANT NOTE: *Do not reverse this,* with baby's head outward! That would be dangerous.

8. Horizontal pitching: Place the baby on his back on the floor or mat. Take his right wrist and ankle while your spouse takes his left wrist and ankle. Together, gently swing the baby to a head up position, then back to a head down position, as a child on a playground swing (see Figure 17.5).

9. Acceleration (up and down): Facing the baby, grasp him underneath the armpits. Then gently throw the baby up in the air and catch him. Fathers invented this activity long ago. They love it and so do their babies (see Figure 17.6).

   Please Note: Parents should *gradually* increase the height of the upward throw. Babies adore this when it is done properly. This activity must be done very carefully. When the baby becomes heavier father may wish to take over this activity, as he usually has more upper body strength and will be more confident about doing it.

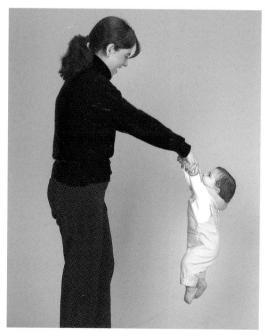

Figure 17.4. Maria is preparing to do a horizontal rotation, head in, in the prone position.

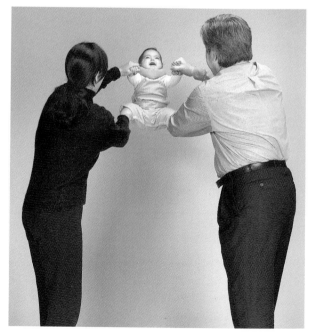

Figure 17.5. Maria enjoys pitching.

Figure 17.6. Maria's favorite—acceleration with her father.

Figure 17.7. Mother does vertical rocking, head down, with Maria.

10. Vertical rocking in the head down position: Place the baby on his back on the gymnastics mat or a thick comfortable carpet on the floor. Standing at the baby's head, bend down and pick the baby up by grasping his ankles firmly. The baby should be facing your legs. Now gently rock the baby from side to side, as if he were a pendulum (see Figure 17.7).

   IMPORTANT NOTE: When you are ready to put the baby down on the floor, be careful to place him on his back, not on his belly. This protects his neck from possible injury.

SUMMARY

This balance program begins with mother and father spending as little as 3 minutes twice a day. As the baby develops and matures, parents gradually increase these activities to 10 minutes twice a day.

Mother and father will be astonished to see what 20 minutes of opportunity to learn about balance and the effect of gravity can achieve in terms of the baby's ability to handle his own body.

Whereas before he was very shaky, constantly feeling some sense of danger, he now becomes more sure of himself and more confident every day.

THE MANUAL COMPETENCE PROGRAM

At this stage the baby can grasp an object and he can release that object when he wishes to do so. The next step is to be able to reach out and pick up the objects that he is beginning to see all around him. This program will help him to establish his ability to reach out and grasp an object using four fingers together and eventually his thumb.

We can help him to do this with a maximum of success and a minimum of frustration.

Objective:	To establish, improve, or reinforce the ability to reach out and pick up objects using a prehensile grasp
Purpose:	To provide the maximum opportunity to pick up objects using a prehensile grasp

Part I—Prehensile Grasp

Frequency:	10 times daily
Intensity:	Objects that are small enough to pick up easily
Duration:	60 seconds
Content:	1 to 3 objects per session
Environment:	The baby is placed in a prone position on the floor or sitting in his highchair

Materials Needed:
- small objects or
- small pieces of food

Technique: Begin to make a collection of many different objects. Find things that are brightly colored, the correct size for the baby's small hand, non-toxic, non-abrasive, and interesting to the baby. The object may have or it may make an interesting shape or an interesting sound.

Place one object at a time in front of your baby and give him the opportunity to reach out and pick it up. The baby will demonstrate tremendous determination and patience, even though at first the task may be difficult for him. Do your very best to find those objects with which he will succeed readily.

Once he has succeeded in picking up the first object, cheer and applaud him so that he knows his efforts have been appreciated. Make sure to use that same object for some time so that he can continue to get better and better. Once he has mastered picking it up but before he has grown tired of it, offer a second object and then a third.

As he becomes better able to pick up these rather large objects, offer him smaller and smaller objects. However, these small objects must be edible and nutritionally appropriate for him because from this point on everything is going to be put straight into his mouth. Small objects that are not edible should only be permitted in his territory when you are with him, supervising his manual program so that he does not eat these objects.

At some point, it will become very clear that it is no longer necessary to have formal sessions to encourage the baby to use his prehensile grasp. You will know to stop these sessions when you see that the baby is literally picking up everything in sight throughout the day.

An important point of etiquette: Once a baby has gone to the effort of picking up something, it is natural for him to want some time to observe it. Please do not snatch objects out of the hands of your baby. It is commonplace for adults to do this and babies and young children object to this strongly. Do everything in your power to persuade your baby to voluntarily release the object. Offer him a second object in exchange or simply ask, "Can you drop the ball into my hand?"

Please Note: You should now comb the environment very carefully for things that could be harmful to the baby and put them well out of his reach.

You should, however, place many interesting and completely safe objects well within his reach. Making the environment safe does not mean making the house a sterile wasteland devoid of anything from which the baby can learn.

Part II—Using the Bar

The purpose of teaching the baby to be able to hold onto a bar and eventually support his own weight is to prepare him to be able to brachiate.

Brachiation is the ability to swing from rung to rung on an overhead ladder. This activity is extremely easy for a very young child and extremely difficult for an adult. It is a very valuable ability

WARNING:

- Do not use food that might choke baby.

- Supervise baby diligently.

- Keep all small objects out of reach unless you are supervising baby.

because it helps the child to create a bigger, better chest and as a result he breathes more deeply, regularly, and maturely. Mature breathing gives him greater resistance to upper respiratory infection, and that resistance, in turn, makes him healthier and improves his overall fitness.

Brachiation also provides the baby with an excellent opportunity to develop better vision. This will be discussed at greater length in a later chapter.

Frequency: 15 times daily

Intensity: No weight-bearing to full weight-bearing

Duration: 20 to 30 seconds

Content: One opportunity to hold onto and hang from the bar

Materials Needed:

- ½" to ¾" bar hung in a doorway (place 6" above the height of baby with his hands extended overhead)

Environment: Place a bar between a doorway at a height that is six inches higher than the baby with his arms extended above his head. Make absolutely certain that the bar is secure and can bear the baby's weight. Make certain that the area directly under the bar is safe by putting a mat or thick carpeting there. Make sure the area around the bar has no pointed edges or corners that the baby might hit if he slipped from the bar.

Technique: Hold the baby firmly around his hips and lift him up to the bar so that he can grasp the bar easily. As he begins to grasp the bar, begin to lower his body a little bit until his arms are straight. Continue to hold him firmly. As the baby gets more confident doing this, begin to swing him back and forth a little bit. In this easy way he will become accustomed to the gentle motion of swinging taking place while brachiating.

Another way:

You can use a large wooden soup spoon for the baby to grasp. With the baby lying on his back, hold out the spoon so he can grasp it. Then gently pull him up so he can bear his weight.

Each day decrease the amount of weight that you are supporting and allow the baby to take a little bit more. Very gradually the baby will take more and more of his own weight until he can easily take all of his weight. He will be very proud of himself when he can do this. In fact, each session he will want to hang a little bit longer than before.

Sometimes you may have to pry his strong little hands off the bar when he has been on it long enough. It is always best to "underdo" the activity rather than overdo it.

Please Note: When the baby can consistently hang independently for 30 seconds, he is ready to graduate from the overhead bar to a real brachiation ladder, which you will learn about in the manual program for Stage IV.

SUMMARY

In order to stay organized and keep track of what is happening to the motor opportunity program, continue to make checklists that will make your life much easier. The following checklist summarizes the program that the baby will probably need at this point.

THE MOTOR PROGRAM FOR PROFILE STAGE III

Daily Checklist

Mobility

Opportunity to creep:
20x daily for 3 minutes

☐ ☐ ☐ ☐ ☐ ☐ ☐ ☐ ☐ ☐
☐ ☐ ☐ ☐ ☐ ☐ ☐ ☐ ☐ ☐

Total floor time daily: _____   Total distance daily: _____

Long-range goal: 400 yards daily

Changes Noted today: _____

_____

Manual Competence

Opportunity to use the prehensile grasp:

Picking up objects—10x daily for 60 seconds

☐ ☐ ☐ ☐ ☐ ☐ ☐ ☐ ☐ ☐

Total time: 10 minutes

Using the bar—15x daily for 20 to 30 seconds

☐ ☐ ☐ ☐ ☐ ☐ ☐ ☐ ☐ ☐
☐ ☐ ☐ ☐ ☐

Total time: 5 minutes to 7 minutes 30 seconds

Changes Noted today: _____

_____

_____

Date: _____

THE MOTOR PROGRAM FOR PROFILE STAGE III

Daily Checklist

Balance Activities

Opportunity to move through space dynamically.

Note: All 10 activities are done in one session

2 sessions daily, each activity done for 15 seconds increasing to 60 seconds

Total time: 2 minutes 30 seconds, increasing to 10 minutes

1. Horizontal spin prone	☐	☐
2. Horizontal spin left side	☐	☐
3. Horizontal spin right side	☐	☐
4. Rocking supine position	☐	☐
5. Horizontal rotation prone	☐	☐
6. Horizontal rotation supine	☐	☐
7. Horizontal rotation, head in	☐	☐
8. Horizontal pitching	☐	☐
9. Acceleration up and down	☐	☐
10. Vertical rocking, head down	☐	☐

Changes Noted Today: _____

_____

_____

Date: _____

Now the tiny baby has not only the sensory ability to appreciate and enjoy the world around him but he is firmly on the road to having the most important meaningful motor responses that he needs.

There are still many challenges ahead. He has just put his foot into the meaningful world, and he will be learning that there are a thousand layers of meaning in almost everything. This will be a life-long lesson, not simply a stage that he completes in the first few months of life.

The important thing, however, is that he now has the equipment he needs for the journey that will lead to all those wonderful discoveries. Of course, he will have to add experience, and from that experience gain wisdom, but he is now ready to plunge into the abilities that lead to being a fully qualified and capable human being.

18

The Fourth Evaluation

Perhaps the most important evaluations are those which mother is doing all day every day as she teaches her baby and cares for him. She becomes an expert on what he can do easily and consistently and on those things that are still a challenge for him.

He will be changing every minute of every day. Whenever he makes a major change mother should note that on her daily checklists or in a simple diary she keeps of his growth and development. Each stage on the Profile is a major stage, and once he achieves a new ability he will often need many months to strengthen and perfect it.

Sometimes parents expect that a baby will move up to a new stage on the Profile in all six areas simultaneously.

This is almost never the case.

First of all, most babies do not arrive at birth in absolutely perfect neurological condition. In fact, very few babies are neurologically perfect at birth or in the first 12 months of life.

Each baby has his areas of strength and weakness. Again, the very purpose of The Institutes Developmental Profile is to find out exactly which areas are strong so parents can reinforce them, and which areas need extra stimulation or opportunity so that these areas develop fully.

The formal evaluations that we have carefully outlined so far are important in this process, but just as important will be the daily observations of mother and father as they see how the baby responds to his program and the demands of everyday life.

With a clear understanding of the Developmental Profile, parents know exactly what to look for; that way they can assess the significance of events that might otherwise have gone unnoticed.

This is why a clear understanding of the Developmental Profile is so important. Once parents have this understanding, they are the keenest and best observers in the world, not to mention the very best teachers, coaches, and developmentalists for their children.

Stage IV on the sensory side of the Developmental Profile is the threshold for mature human understanding: for depth perception, for the ability to hear and decode human abstract language, and the tactile understanding of the third dimension.

On the motor side of the Developmental Profile resides the human expression of these abilities: standing upright and walking, the ability to use words to communicate, and the ability to oppose thumb and index finger in order to pick up small objects.

If you evaluated your baby at birth and began a program shortly thereafter, it is time for the fourth evaluation within five to six months. As in your previous evaluation, you may be surprised to find that your baby's responses at lower stages are stronger and more consistent. Some areas that you may have marked "Functional" two months ago are now perfect.

Stage IV of The Institutes Developmental Profile encompasses some of the most important landmarks in the growth and development of the tiny baby. This stage is shown in green on the Profile.

This is the first stage where all the new functions that the baby acquires are due to the development of the cortex.

The human cortex is unique in the animal kingdom. Each day that the baby grows and develops he will take advantage of this unique cortex to accomplish feats that no other creature on earth can do.

Mother should remember that each day her baby matures he becomes more sure of what he wants and what he does not want. She must therefore continue to choose the best times in the day to evaluate the baby so that she can get a clear picture of what he can and cannot do.

VISUAL COMPETENCE: STAGE IV

Convergence

Visual convergence is the ability to use two eyes together which results in simple depth perception. With careful observation, parents can observe the development of convergence in their baby.

When a baby is born he does not have any ability to use both eyes together. This can be quite disconcerting as mother and father hold the newborn baby and look into his eyes, because it will often be apparent that his eyes are going in different directions.

He cannot possibly develop the ability to converge his vision until he can see detail within a configuration. Once he can see detail without effort, he has the ability to target something and look at it. He starts by doing this exclusively at nearpoint, within a distance of two or three feet. As his ability to see detail improves, so does his range of vision. Soon he can see four feet away, then five feet, and so it goes until one day he can easily spot mother in a crowd thirty feet away.

In truth, from the moment that he begins to see detail, his need to converge is born. Furthermore, nature will make other demands that will require him to develop his convergence.

The primary demand for improved vision, most especially convergence, will come from his need to move. Visual development and mobility are inextricably linked. As he sees better, his desire to move will increase. As he moves through space faster, he will need to have much faster and more accurate vision. It is as simple as that.

From the time he begins to crawl he must, to some small degree, begin to converge his vision. He does not need much, and he doesn't have to use it except in brief bursts, but he must have at least a little. The reason for this is also simple. As he begins to move through space independently for the first time on his belly, he discovers, to his surprise, that there are things to bump into.

At first, he smashes into things regularly. This is because he is quite literally not looking where he is going. Remember, at this early stage he is moving for movement's sake. His movement is not goal-directed. When he bumps into things he gets the message "Look where you are going."

He begins to turn on his vision, and—what is more—to pull those two wandering eyes together to get at least a rough idea of how far away that object ahead might be. It is a very crude concept because he has just the earliest beginnings of what will become depth perception. But it is a beginning.

Each time he crawls he gets more opportunity to turn on his vision and use his two eyes together. If mother observes her baby when he is crawling across a room at full speed, she will see a look on his face that is quite different from any other time. The determined look on his face shows that his vision is turned on at these moments.

Later, when he is able to conquer gravity and push up on his hands and knees, he has an additional problem. He not only must calculate how far he is from the leg of the dining room chair, but he must also calculate the distance between his head and the floor since there is the very real possibility of smashing into it.

Observe the tiny baby who is just beginning to creep. He will often creep right into the floor. This is because he still does not have enough depth perception to tell the distance between his head and the floor. When he has a crash he no doubt wonders why the floor has come up and hit him in the face.

In any event, nature is a tough teacher at this point. When the baby fails to use his vision or miscalculates, he pays a small price by knocking into something and hitting his head.

Once he really begins to creep for transportation, he will have to use his rudimentary convergence more often. Now it becomes more apparent to mother and father when he is using both eyes together and when he is not.

Parents may notice at this point that one eye occasionally drifts out or in. This happens to almost all tiny babies at some point. Usually this occurs when they are very tired, or ill, and especially if the baby has a fever.

The reason is that the ability to converge is very sensitive to changes in the baby's neurological condition. The visual areas of the brain are very large, and as a result have very large oxygen demands.

When those demands are being met the baby's vision will be fine. Even mild suppression of the central nervous system, however, brought about by fatigue, or illness, will effect the baby's vision more readily than any other faculty.

This is when mother or father may observe that the baby has a moderate to mild "strabismus" in either eye. An eye going out away from the nose is called a "divergent strabismus" and an eye going toward the nose is called a "convergent strabismus." This phenomenon is very common in the tiny baby.

It is not a product of any problem with the eye. It is purely a product of the function of the brain.

Occasionally a baby will have one or both eyes constantly fixed in a convergent or divergent strabismus. This is a product of an injury to the brain. It cannot and should not be treated as if it is an injury to the eye. Surgery done on the eye or the muscles of the eye will not correct this situation. Often when such surgery is done, the eye goes back to its fixed position six months later and the same surgery may be repeated again and again.

This is quite tragic because the problem is not in the eye. The eye is merely the symptom. The problem will not be solved by operating on the symptom. The problem will be solved by treating the problem, which is in the brain.

When parents understand the process whereby the baby develops proper convergence, they can take effective measures to give the baby the correct stimulation and opportunity to solve these problems, and to prevent these problems in many cases.

The first and best means of evaluating the baby at Stage IV is to observe him in his daily life. Does he use both eyes together or appear to do so? Does he bump into furniture easily? When he comes to situations where there is a drop, such as the head of the stairs, does he stop and proceed with caution or does he not notice the first step at all. If you stand him on a table does he grab onto you the instant he realizes he is up high and therefore in danger, or would he happily jump off a cliff because he still has no notion how far he would fall?

How often does he notice little things on a page of a book or the writing or symbols imprinted on a toy? Parents are often amazed by the very tiny things that little babies notice. They have to have some convergence at near point to do this.

When you observe your baby's eyes do they look straight at you all the time or is one eye always a little bit turned in or out? Perhaps this situation varies and sometimes it is the right and sometimes the left. This is common.

Parents are used to looking at their own baby, so it is helpful to start looking at the eyes of other babies and adults to observe good and bad convergence. When adults are evaluated on The Profile, the most common weak point is the ability to converge perfectly. There are many people who do so poorly or inconsistently.

This not only affects their ability to have good depth perception but it can have a very profound affect on their ability to read and write easily and effectively.

Simple convergence is the basis for sophisticated

Convergence of vision resulting in simple depth perception

Perfect

Initial human understanding

Figure 18.1. Perfect convergence of vision

Convergence of vision resulting in simple depth perception
Functional
Initial human understanding

Figure 18.2. Functional convergence of vision

Convergence of vision resulting in simple depth perception
Initial human understanding

Figure 18.3. Zero convergence of vision

convergence. Sophisticated convergence is an absolute requirement if a child is going to be able to see the small print in any reading book or produce small print in his own writing.

This is a very, very important stage and we will return to it again in the discussion of mobility.

When you have observed that the baby consistently uses both eyes together, and has demonstrated in life that he has simple depth perception, write "Perfect" in red on the convergence box of the Profile and draw a red line across the top edge of this box (see Figure 18.1).

If the baby demonstrates that he has some depth perception but it is inconsistent or one or both eyes occasionally drift in or out, write "Functional" on the convergence box of the Profile in red and draw a red line across the top edge of this box (see Figure 18.2).

If the baby has a fixed convergent or divergent strabismus or demonstrates little or no depth perception consistently, draw a red line across the top edge of the box where he was at his last evaluation to show that he is still at the same stage in his vision (see Figure 18.3).

AUDITORY COMPETENCE: STAGE IV

Understanding Two Words of Speech

Parents have a great opportunity to make life much easier for their baby at Stage IV of the auditory column, which is the ability to understand two words of speech.

Remember that the time frame on the Developmental Profile shows the way things *are* for the average baby. The purpose of this book is to encourage parents to create a better world for the newborn baby so that in the first 12 months of life he has the opportunity to change that time frame and move it closer to what it *should* be.

If parents have been doing a good, consistent visual, auditory, and tactile program, the baby should long since have begun to understand two words of language.

Just consider what the baby has been taught: shapes, faces, simple quantity, fruits, animals, and flowers. In addition, there is the constant stimulation of mother's conversation with the baby.

"Are you hungry?" she asks him. "Are you wet?"/"Are you tired?"/ "Mommy loves you."/"You are a good boy."/"Where is daddy?"/ "Here is your red shirt."

It is highly likely that he understands a great many more than two words. What he lacks is the means to *demonstrate* what he understands. The baby will do his very best to show us what he understands. When mother asks, "Are you hungry?" sometimes he will move his lips in response. That's a clear demonstration that he understands the word "hungry."

Sometimes when mother asks the same question the baby will make a little short plaintive cry. This is not only a "Yes!" but a "Hurry up! I'm starving!" response. Sometimes when he is not hungry he will simply look contented. Again, this is an appropriate response to mother's question. He does understand her.

Making his thoughts and feelings clear is the challenge for the very tiny baby. He knows a great deal more than he can show us. As a result, most adults underestimate him tremendously.

If the only result of this book is to cause every mother and father who reads it to realize that their baby does understand a tremendous amount, it will have been worthwhile. The challenges facing the baby will lessen substantially. The world of tiny babies and the world of parents will be happier and more productive.

When mother knows that her baby does in fact understand at least two words of speech consistently, she should write "Perfect" in red on the understanding of two words of speech box of the Profile and draw a red line across the top edge of the box (see Figure 18.4).

This is one of those functions on the Profile where there is no "Functional." A baby either has this ability or he does not. If your baby still does not understand at least two words of speech, draw a red line across the top edge of the box where he was at his last evaluation to show that he is still at that stage in his auditory development (see Figure 18.5).

Understanding of two words of speech
Perfect
Initial human understanding

Figure 18.4. Perfect understanding of two words

Understanding of two words of speech
Initial human understanding

Figure 18.5. Zero understanding of two words

TACTILE COMPETENCE: STAGE IV

Understanding the Third Dimension in Objects Which Appear to Be Flat

Parents often think that Stage IV of tactility will be hard to evaluate. Here mother wants to see whether the baby has an understanding of the third dimension in objects which appear to be flat.

This is not as difficult as it may seem. The baby will begin at Stage III to reach out and pick things up. As he does, he will begin to reveal his understanding of the third dimension.

At first he will only notice and pick up those things that stick out in the environment, but as he conquers the most obvious objects, the more subtle objects will begin to attract him.

Occasionally, by accident, he will find something that he did not know was there because the object appeared to be flat.

This is a revelation.

Often a flat chain hanging around mother's neck will interest him but only when it dangles and moves and attracts his attention. Soon he will notice the chain even when it is lying flat on mother's blouse or sweater. At first his vision is doing all the work, but then he begins to use his tactility to find these hidden items that are flat but do have a third dimension.

He will feel coins that have fallen on the floor where he is creeping. He will grab paper that is lying flat on a table. These are all sure signs that he now has an understanding of the third dimension in objects which appear to be flat.

When mother observes that the baby consistently understands the third dimension in objects which appear to be flat, she writes "Perfect" in red on this box on the Profile and draws a line in red across the top edge of this box (see Figure 18.6).

This it yet another function where the baby either has it or he does not. There is no "Functional" at this stage. If the baby does not yet demonstrate any understanding of the third dimension in objects which appear to be flat, draw a red line across the top edge of the box where he was at his last evaluation to show that he is still at that stage in his tactile development (see Figure 18.7).

Tactile understanding of the third dimension in objects which appear to be flat
Perfect
Initial human understanding

Figure 18.6. Perfect tactile understanding

Tactile understanding of the third dimension in objects which appear to be flat
Initial human understanding

Figure 18.7. Zero tactile understanding

MOBILITY COMPETENCE: STAGE IV

Walking with Arms Used in a Primary Balance Role

There is probably no stage on the Developmental Profile on which parents place more importance than the incredible act of standing upright and walking with arms used in a primary balance role.

The baby has a love affair with standing upright. It is his supreme goal almost from the first moment he realizes that such a position exists. He will begin to experiment and play with this exhilarating posture even while he is still crawling. He will coach parents to stand him up on his feet. He will bounce and squeal in this position which, of course, has the effect of encouraging his parents to do this over and over again.

When he begins to creep he gains the ability to pull himself up. This is why it is so important to remove unstable objects from the creeping environment of the tiny baby, otherwise he will pull things over on himself.

The first and most difficult challenge he must conquer is not walking, but standing. In a sense, this is a great deal more difficult than walking.

No one knows this better than the baby. We adults like "to walk" the baby but the baby knows this is not real walking at all. This is an adult moving the baby through the motions of walking. This is because we adults are apt to underestimate the importance of standing. We tend to think that walking is primarily the ability to coordinate the movement of the legs and feet. Instead, walking is the result of the ability to balance well enough to stand still.

Any time mother or father are touching the baby when he is standing, he is not using his ability to balance. His parents are balancing him. It is the balancing mechanisms of the parents that are being used, not the baby's.

This may be legitimate for a two-month-old baby who is still crawling, but once a baby is creeping for transportation he should be permitted to make these experiments *independently* as much as possible.

Any evaluation of the baby's mobility at this stage must be made based upon what he is able to do *without being held or even touched*.

When the baby can stand upright and walk across

> **Walking with arms used in a primary balance role most frequently at or above shoulder height**
>
> **Perfect**
> *Initial human expression*

Figure 18.8. Perfect walking

Walking with arms used in a primary balance role most frequently at or above shoulder height
Initial human expression

Figure 18.9. Zero walking

the room with his arms used in a primary balance role (at or above shoulder height), write "Perfect" in red on this box on the Profile and draw a line in red across the top edge of the box (see Figure 18.8).

There is no "Functional" at this stage, so keep the baby at Stage II on the mobility column of the Profile until he can stand and walk across the room using his arms for balance (see Figure 18.9).

LANGUAGE COMPETENCE: STAGE IV

Using Two Words of Speech Spontaneously and Meaningfully

While fathers are most thrilled when the baby can take his first step, mothers are often most impressed by the first word. It would be hard to decide which is more important.

At this stage parents need only to decide when the baby has two words of speech that are used spontaneously and meaningfully.

These two words do not have to be perfect words that everyone understands. In fact, they surely will not be. Instead, the first words will be specific sounds that mother understands, that have a specific meaning, and that the baby uses consistently to communicate the same ideas.

If the baby consistently says "baba" and it always means "I want to nurse," then "baba" is functioning as the word "nurse" in the baby's language.

At first, mother and baby together work out their own means of communicating until the baby can make much more specific sounds that we adults call perfect words. The baby will not have this ability for many months.

When the baby has two specific sounds that he uses consistently and meaningfully, write "Perfect" in red on this box of the Profile and draw a line in red across the top edge of the box (see Figure 18.10).

There is no "Functional" at this stage. If the baby does not yet have two specific sounds that he uses consistently and meaningfully, draw a red line across the top edge of Stage III in language to show that the baby is still at this stage in his language development (see Figure 18.11).

Two words of speech used spontaneously and meaningfully
Perfect
Initial human expression

Figure 18.10. Perfect two words of speech

Two words of speech used spontaneously and meaningfully
Initial human expression

Figure 18.11. Zero two words of speech

MANUAL COMPETENCE: STAGE IV

Using Cortical Opposition in Either Hand

By the time parents are ready to evaluate the baby's ability to use cortical opposition in either hand, he usually has been doing so for some time. Cortical opposition refers to the ability to oppose the thumb to the forefinger in order to grasp something. It is called "cortical" for the simple reason that this is a function of the human cortex.

Once the baby becomes very good at picking up objects, he tends to try to pick up smaller and smaller ones.

At the same time his vision is getting better and better. He loves little things. He generally begins with the little crumbs left after he has eaten. He will often spot a tiny piece of fuzz on the carpet from ten feet away and zip over and grab it before mother can stop him.

At some point he tries to pick up something that simply cannot be picked up using a prehensile grasp. This baffles him but he does not give up. He will use every means he can think of to grasp this object.

By trial and error he will learn that if he stops trying to grab with his whole hand but instead uses just his thumb opposed to his forefinger he can succeed.

At this point most babies will develop this ability in one hand first. Only when they have mastered this ability in one hand will they work to achieve the same thing in the other hand.

In order to evaluate this ability it is best to place before the baby small, flat objects that he could not pick up easily using his prehensile grasp. These include beads or poker chips.

Be ready to applaud his efforts *but* make certain the beads and chips *do not end up in his mouth.*

When the baby can reach out with either hand and pick up an object consistently using his thumb opposed to his forefinger, write "Perfect" in red on this box on the Profile and draw a line in red across the top edge of this box (see Figure 18.12).

If the baby inconsistently uses his thumb opposed to his forefinger to pick up objects, write "Functional" in red on the cortical opposition box on the Profile and draw a red line across the top edge of this box (see Figure 18.13).

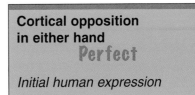

**Cortical opposition
in either hand**
    Perfect

Initial human expression

Figure 18.12. Perfect cortical opposition

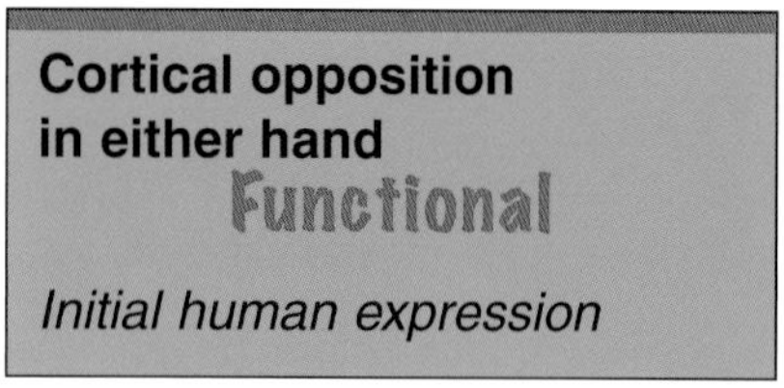

**Cortical opposition
in either hand**

Functional

Initial human expression

Figure 18.13. Functional cortical opposition

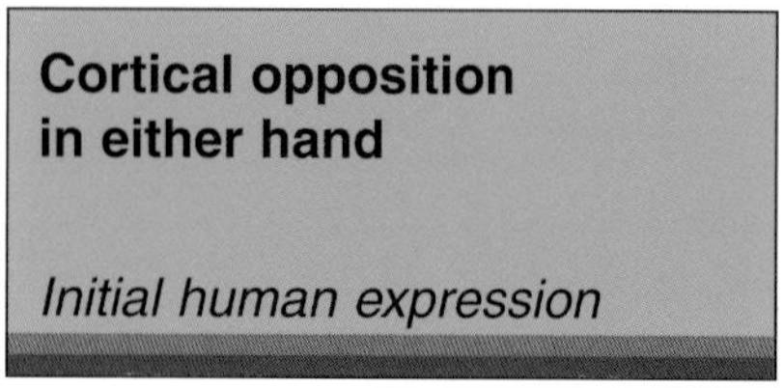

**Cortical opposition
in either hand**

Initial human expression

Figure 18.14. Zero cortical opposition

If the baby cannot yet pick up an object using cortical opposition, draw a line in red across the top edge of Stage II to show that this is still his present stage in manual competence (see Figure 18.14).

Now mother and father have a very clear idea of what to look for in the next stage of their baby's development. With a good understanding of how to evaluate Stage IV on the Developmental Profile, it is time to look at the best sensory stimulation to help the baby achieve Stage IV and the ideal environment to help the baby use that sensory information to walk, talk, and use his hands.

Now we are ready for the final program, which will help baby to achieve Stage IV.

19

The Sensory Stimulation Program for Stage IV

As the baby becomes more mature and capable, each area of function has greater influence upon the other functions. It will become very obvious to mother and father that as they improve one area on the Profile, they improve every area to some degree by providing stimulation and opportunity.

It now becomes impossible to discuss one column of the Profile in isolation from the others, because these different pathways do not develop alone. They are, in fact, completely interrelated at all times.

This is the beauty of the natural plan, which parents have the great privilege of observing every day in their tiny baby. The Developmental Profile allows mother and father to understand this creative process, and through a well-designed program to be actual participants rather than mere spectators in the growth and development of their baby.

THE SENSORY STIMULATION PROGRAM

Mother and father have already established a firm foundation for what is to come by doing an excellent sensory and motor program for Stages I, II, and III. Each new program becomes more exciting and each day is more dynamic than the one before as the baby becomes more capable and aware.

The visual and auditory programs will now consist of much more sophisticated information. The baby is ready and eager. Mother will only have to remember to be eager and enthusiastic as she teaches her baby. This is not school work—it is fun. For the baby, learning *is* play. He will approach the things mother is about to teach in a spirit of play. That natural joyousness that is native to every baby should be contagious. Mother must teach everything in that spirit of joyousness and fun. If it is not fun at that moment, don't do it. The morning time is the best time for this part of your program. Do as much as you and your baby enjoy and not one iota more.

VISUAL STIMULATION

The Visual Program at Stage IV will include parts that are primarily visual in nature, but it will also include the baby's mobility program, since mobility will have a profound effect on the baby's development of visual convergence and simple depth perception.

Parts I and II of the Stage IV visual program will emphasize the baby's ability to converge his vision at nearpoint. The mobility program for Stage IV will provide opportunity to converge at both nearpoint and farpoint.

Mother should also understand that this is her baby's very first intellectual program. This is where vision and mobility clearly start to feed into the baby's tremendously exciting and unique human potential.

The visual program provides frequent opportunity for the baby to converge his vision at nearpoint. As he uses his eyes in concert his convergence will become more established with each passing day. As this happens, the primary purpose of the program will shift to the development and expansion of baby's intellect.

Objective: To establish, improve, or reinforce the ability to converge vision resulting in simple depth perception

Purpose: To provide stimulation that will develop the baby's ability to converge his vision resulting in simple depth perception

Part I—Sophisticated Detail Bit of Intelligence Cards

Frequency: 3 times daily per set

Intensity: Large, brightly colored photographs, illustrations, or paintings with clear, accurate detail, mounted on white 11" x 11" poster board

Duration: 5 seconds per set

Content: 1 set of 5 cards per session, 5 sets of 5 cards in a day (25 cards total)

Environment: Good, normal lighting with a minimum of auditory noise or disruption

Technique: Since you began this program at Stage III and have been doing it consistently, you have already discovered that the biggest problem is keeping the baby supplied with new material. He has a voracious appetite for new information.

As his vision becomes better and better and his understanding improves, you can branch out to new categories.

Now you will change how you show the new information. Each day you will teach five sets (or categories) of five cards each (25 cards daily in all). After five days add one new card to each category and retire one old card. Continue to do this every day from that point onward. The baby will see five new cards. Each card will be seen three times daily for five days and then be retired.

When you add a new card, write the date in pencil on the back of it. This will let you know which cards to retire each day. File your retired cards because you are going to use them again in the future. When you exhaust one category, simply retire all five final cards at the same time and replace them with a brand new category.

Continue to find large, clear, and accurate photographs, drawings, or paintings of interesting information. Good categories to

Materials Needed:
• 5 sets of Bit of Intelligence cards

Figure 19.1.
Maria loves her Bit of Intelligence cards.

include are reproductions of great art masterpieces (Picasso and van Gogh are particular favorites of tiny babies), or a category of outstanding people, such as composers, inventors, or explorers. It is fine to continue to add to the categories of birds, insects, mammals, and flowers that you have already begun. These categories will continue to be of interest for a long time to come.

The images should still be large, at least six inches in diameter. The photograph or illustration should still have only one image, not a group of images.

Try to find at least 20 items or more for each category.

Since each session is very short, it should be easy to find a few seconds here and there throughout the day to show the cards. It is of the greatest importance that you only show the cards when you and the baby are in top form. Not all days are great for mother and baby. On good days it will be easy to find happy moments to show the cards. On a bad day do not show the cards at all.

Each and every session should stop *before the baby wants to stop,* regardless of whether all five Bit cards have been shown or not.

This is a good *beginning* program. Babies adore Bit of Intelligence cards. If you and your baby wish, you can expand to 10 categories, or even 20 a day, if you can do so in a joyous and relaxed way.

Now the baby has an excellent ability to see detail instantly, so it is vital that you show the cards very, very quickly. Adults almost always underestimate the speed at which babies learn. This applies not only to how quickly they introduce new material but also to the actual speed at which they teach the materials to the baby. The baby will learn at an astonishing rate. The baby is now ready for an expanded program of encyclopedic knowledge. If you wish to learn a great deal more about this program, we highly recommend the books *How To Multiply Your Baby's Intelligence, How To Give Your Baby Encyclopedic Knowledge,* and *How To Teach Your Baby Math.*

Please Note: Material preparation will definitely take a considerable amount of time. Some mothers prefer to make a few cards every day. In this way they gradually build up a library of Bit of Intelligence cards for the future. Other mothers set aside a block of time once a week and do all their organization and material preparation at that time. In some families father does all the material preparation. Sometimes this is the perfect responsibility for older brothers and sisters. After all, they deserve to be a part of the baby's program too.

Part II—Reading Words

Frequency: 3 times daily per set

Intensity: 5-inch-high red lettering on white poster board cards that are 22" long and 6" wide

Duration: 5 seconds per set

Content: 1 set of 5 words per session
5 sets daily

Environment: Good normal lighting with a minimum of auditory noise or disruption.

Materials Needed:

- 25 white posterboard strips (22" x 6")
- red felt-tipped marker (extra-wide)

Technique: The baby has already been introduced to single reading words through the program of seeing, hearing, tasting, and smelling fruit. Now make a list of all of the familiar words that you use constantly with the baby: the foods, the names of family members, and common household objects. These will comprise his first sets of reading words. His own name and "Mommy" and "Daddy" should be high on the list. Make a very large and clear word card for each of the familiar words that you choose. Write the words in bold, red, lower case letters, using capitals when needed for names (see Figure 19.2). Red is attractive and babies like it.

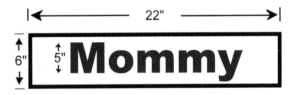

Figure 19.2.
Sample reading card with a large red word on the front.

Since you have already chosen words that are familiar to the baby, you no longer have to worry about showing the real object at the same time that you show the word, or rushing father into the room whenever you show the "Daddy" card. The baby will very quickly connect these ideas himself.

In order to be able to hold up the reading word cards and show each one easily, write the word in the upper left-hand corner in pencil on the back of each card. Also, write the date it was introduced in the upper right-hand corner (see Figure 19.3).

Figure 19.3.
Sample reading card with the card name and date on the back.

When you are going to show a set to the baby, take the card from the back of the set (which has "Mommy" written on the back), put it in the front of the set of cards, and say "Mommy." Then do the same with the next card at the back of the set.

Set 1	Set 2	Set 3	Set 4
Mommy	chair	toothbrush	juice
Daddy	table	tricycle	cereal
Olivia	bathtub	blanket	apple
Maria	refrigerator	shoes	carrot
Caleb	sofa	pajamas	bread

Set 5
elephant
whale
rhinoceros
giraffe
spider

Figure 19.4.
Reading card sets for family members, household objects, food, and animals.

In this way you do not have to try to look at the front of each card before showing it to the baby. This would be distracting and disruptive to the teaching session (see Figure 19.5).

Teach the five sets of five words for five days. On the sixth day retire one reading card from each set and place a new reading word in each set. Do this every day from this point onward. Again, she should put the date on the back of each new card as it is introduced so that you will know when it is time to retire it. Please note: The baby is now ready for a full reading program. In order to gain a complete understanding of the reading pathway, we strongly recommend the book *How To Teach Your Baby To Read*.

Figure 19.5.
Reading words are Maria's favorites at this point.

The initial Bit of Intelligence cards and the beginning reading program will provide excellent opportunity for the baby to converge his vision at nearpoint. You will also want to do those parts of the mobility program that will further develop the baby's ability to converge his vision and to develop depth perception.

The ability to converge at both nearpoint and farpoint develops into the ability to perceive depth—an ability that is extremely important throughout life.

AUDITORY PROGRAM

You have already begun the process that will give the baby the ability to understand two words of speech. Indeed, most mothers begin talking to the baby while he is in utero.

By the time baby is a few months old it is very natural for mother or father to carry him around the house, pointing out all sorts of things and telling baby what they are: "wall," "lamp," "thermostat," "refrigerator," "chair," etc. This is very good to do on walks in the outdoor environment as well.

This introduction to the environment in which the baby lives is very important. At this stage in his development the baby needs to know the name of everything. He will begin to point at things and you know that he wants to hear its name. The baby may point to the same object repeatedly—even after you have told him "radio." He does this not to annoy us or because he is unintelligent, but rather to hear the word "radio" enough so that this information will be stored permanently. When he does hear a word with enough frequency, his ability to *retrieve* that stored information will be assured.

You are also giving your baby an enriched vocabulary through his visual program of Bit of Intelligence cards and reading words. As these programs expand, so will his auditory understanding.

Baby also needs to understand time. We adults tend to believe that time is a wild abstraction and therefore very difficult for the baby to understand. In fact, if we are consistent in the way we talk about time, the baby will learn about it very quickly.

It is wise to use time frames in orienting your baby to what is going to be happening. It is good for mother to use "now" and "not now," "later," "before," and "after" in almost every reference she makes throughout the day.

At first the baby has no notion of what these words may mean,

Use time frames to orient the baby:

- "now"
- "not now"
- "before"
- "after"
- "later"

but as he hears them and as the actions that have been labeled "now" happen immediately, and the actions which have been labeled "not now" do not happen immediately the baby begins to put two and two together and to decode these two messages.

Even specific increments of time are not beyond the baby. For example, "I am going to change your diaper. It will take one minute."

The diaper change then takes one minute. The baby has been given a very concrete definition of one minute. Since this occurs with great frequency, baby eventually understands it.

After a while you will notice that when you start to diaper the baby he will be patient for one minute, but if you dawdle or get interrupted he will become impatient after the one minute is up. He has learned to accept having his busy schedule disrupted for one minute. That one minute is the deal we have struck with him, and when we violate it he protests.

At this point he already has the ability to understand the passage of time and the labels that we place on specific increments of time.

In addition to orienting the baby as to what you are doing and how you are doing it, be careful to tell the baby whenever you are leaving the house, and when you will return. This may sound foolish, but baby wants to know where you are at all times. He knows that his survival is closely linked to you, his mother.

When you must leave the baby with someone else, it is very important that you tell the baby that you are leaving and that you will be back, and how soon you will be back.

Always:

Tell your baby when you are leaving and when you will return.

Be careful to get the baby's full attention when you tell him you are leaving. Always deliver this message in the same way each time, so that baby realizes that this is the "leaving home ceremony." Pick the baby up in your arms and hold him so that you are face to face, then say, "Mommy is leaving the house. Mommy will be back in two hours. Daddy will be here with you. Be a good boy for Daddy."

Then go out, and make certain that you do return in two hours.

Of course, the baby has no idea at first how long two hours will be. But as both parents do this consistently, always being honest and accurate with the baby, he will learn.

Many parents over the years have told us how easily their babies learned to listen to them, understand them, and, what is most important of all, believe them, because they always kept the baby informed of what was going on.

Or, that if mother forgot to tell the baby that she is leaving he may be very upset and fussy the entire time she is gone. Sometimes he may cry when mother returns, to express his annoyance at her unannounced departure.

Sometimes a mother will intentionally leave the house without telling her baby that she is leaving. Mothers do this to avoid the screams and upset caused by simply saying "Bye-Bye" to the baby.

When the baby realizes that mother is out of sight, he will scream and cry in a futile attempt to call mother back to him. It will be hard, if not impossible, to comfort him.

This is not fair to the baby. As is so often the case with children, whenever we adults think we have a short cut it turns out to be a long detour. There are no short cuts in honest conduct and good communication with a child. This process begins right from birth, not when a child is thirteen years old. Babies learn very early in life that they can trust their parents, or that they cannot trust their parents.

The baby needs to know what is happening, when it is happening, and who will be with him.

Parents should use the very best language and vocabulary in talking to the baby. Each day his understanding grows by leaps and bounds. "Baby talk" is essentially disrespectful of the intellectual ability of the tiny baby. He has every right to hear his native language spoken properly, not in a degraded fashion that he will have to *unlearn* later. Parents should give the baby proper words of speech.

Use real words— never "baby talk."

If your baby sees and shows interest in a dog, say, "That is a dog." Better yet, say "That dog is a Saint Bernard." Never offer the baby the patronizing: "See the bow wow!" Not only can the baby handle a clear specific description, but he will prefer it.

Once you have given baby the names for everything in his world, you can begin to enrich that world with more descriptive words. For example, once he knows that the vegetables he is eating are called peas, you can tell him that they are "green peas." Then say, "These are delicious green peas." In this way you make a point of gradually escalating the sophistication of the language that you use with the baby.

This is the most important auditory program that parents will ever do for the baby. The language that they use will be the language that he uses.

It will be his calling card for life.

Whether we like it or not, there is nothing in life by which we human beings so quickly judge each other than by the language we use.

TACTILE COMPETENCE

The baby is his own best programmer when it comes to tactile stimulation because he simply cannot keep his hands off of anything. The question here is not so much how to give him enough stimulation but how to make sure he is safe and does not swallow the tiny objects in the household.

At this stage you want to provide a wide variety of objects to touch and to pick up, especially those objects that will develop the baby's ability to understand objects that appear to be flat but have a third dimension.

RULES FOR EFFECTIVE TEACHING

1. Teach your baby because you think it is a great idea and a privilege for you and for your baby.

2. Talk clearly, loudly, and with great enthusiasm.

3. Relax and enjoy yourself.

4. Trust your baby in your attitude, manner, and actions.

5. Provide new information constantly.

6. Don't bore your baby with old materials over and over again.

7. Be organized and purposeful in your teaching.

8. Make everything easy to see.

9. Eliminate visual, auditory, and tactile distractions when you teach.

10. Teach your baby only at times when he is happy, rested, and well-fed.

11. Always stop before your baby wants to stop.

12. Trust that your baby knows the things you have taught him.

13. Be on your baby's side—bet on him.

14. Be willing to change your approach. Make each day new and exciting.

15. Don't test your baby.

THE SENSORY PROGRAM FOR PROFILE STAGE IV

Daily Checklist

Visual Competence

Providing sophisticated detail:

Detailed Bit of Intelligence cards
5 sets: Each 3x daily for 5 seconds

☐ ☐ ☐   ☐ ☐ ☐

☐ ☐ ☐   ☐ ☐ ☐

☐ ☐ ☐

Reading Words

5 sets: Each 3x daily for 5 seconds

☐ ☐ ☐   ☐ ☐ ☐

☐ ☐ ☐   ☐ ☐ ☐

☐ ☐ ☐

Total teaching time needed: 2 minutes 30 seconds

Changes Noted today: _____

_____

_____

Date: _____

SUMMARY

The Sensory Stimulation Program now becomes easier in the sense that there is technically less to do. By now you will find that those things at Stages I, II, and III that were functional are now becoming perfect.

Now you can focus on creating an intellectually stimulating environment through the Bit of Intelligence cards and the reading program. The following checklist summarizes what your baby's program may be at this moment.

As the need for basic sensory stimulation decreases the baby needs a large amount of time to develop his mobility, his language, and his manual competence. You will now offer less time for sensory pursuits and provide a great deal more time for motor opportunity.

The baby will lead the way in this. Given the chance, he will spend many hours developing, reinforcing, and expanding his motor abilities.

An important question arises at this point: Will we be encouraging him or doing our best to stop him? It is a lot easier to help him than to try and defeat his rage to learn. So now we will take a close look at how mother, father, and baby together can become one of the best learning teams on earth.

20

The Motor Opportunity Program for Stage IV

When a baby reaches the stage where he is clearly ready to walk and talk, and he can just about crack a safe with his bare hands, parents may wonder why they need to encourage their baby to do any of these things. He is clearly bound and determined to do all three without any special attention from us.

A well baby develops so quickly that it would seem that parents who have created a sound neurological foundation for the baby at Stages I, II, and III could sit back and relax.

Mother Nature, however, has other plans.

Once the baby is consistent and capable at Stage III, and is therefore ready to move on to the abilities of Stage IV, he has reached only "the end of the beginning" of his mobility, language, and manual development.

He needs mother and father as much as ever, but now in a very different way. He needs to have great opportunities, but they must be within a controlled environment where he is completely safe at all times.

Very few babies get this kind of opportunity these days. Once babies reach this stage they are generally restricted, not only in their mobility but also in their use of language and in the development of manual competence.

They spend hours and hours every day in pens that we call "play" pens, or strictly confined in "walkers" in which they cannot walk, and "strollers" in which they cannot stroll, or in backpacks, or confined in car seats.

Please Note: Car seats are essential for the safety of the baby. It is the amount of time spent *confined* in the car seat rather than the protective nature of the seat that is cause for concern here. These environments severely limit the baby's mobility; that's what they are designed to do. At the same time they also limit the baby's language opportunity and ability to explore the world manually.

All these restrictions are based upon the modern notion that the baby should adapt to the needs of the adult world. He should, in a sense, go along for the ride because it is convenient for our schedule.

But the baby cannot and should not adapt to our world.

Ours is a world that says, "Ride, don't walk." He is desperate to walk.

Ours is a world that says, "Be quiet—you are interrupting." He is desperate to talk.

Ours is a world that says, "Don't touch, you will break it." He must touch it to learn about it.

In short, he has a very, very busy agenda. Before the sun sets each day he has a mobility imperative that says, "I must walk a mile today and roll off the sofa 400 times." He has a language imperative that says, "I must learn a word for everything I see today." He has a sensory and manual imperative that says, "I must touch, taste, smell, and pick up everything in the world at least once."

This imperative is greatly at odds with a world that to a very large degree has no time for babies.

The more time mother and father invest in the baby at this critical stage in his development the happier he will be, and the faster and better he will learn and develop.

After more than a half-century of watching our babies grow up, we are convinced that what the baby will be like as an adult in terms of physical and neurological ability is determined more strongly in the first year of life than in any other period. It is as simple as that.

To fulfill his needs, he must have the supervision and participation of his parents. He needs mother and father to be on the "rage to learn team" not part of the "lock him up and don't let him get at anything mob."

This is the exact moment when parents start to divide into two very distinct groups. The first group of parents become better and better at helping the baby to learn every moment of every day because these parents see their role in their baby's life as crucial.

The second group begins to distance themselves from the baby because he is disruptive to the adult household.

They are in shock that the baby is "acting like a baby." They spend less and less time with the baby. The baby spends more and more time with babysitters or in day care. When they are with the baby they are generally trying to stop him from doing whatever it is he wants or needs to do.

The result for these parents and their little babies is that parents end up complaining endlessly about everything the baby does. This then sets the stage for what will become their relationship for the next 10 or 20 years, if not longer.

What a tragic end to a love affair that was meant to last a lifetime but never really got started!

The Developmental Profile can do many things, but it cannot do the most important thing: it cannot make parents love and respect their baby.

A good understanding of how the baby develops and grows, however, and why he does the things he does, will greatly increase the parent's respect for the baby, and when respect increases very often love also grows. This understanding eliminates the view that baby is some sort of alien bent on destroying the house.

There is a reason for each and every thing the baby does. He does not waste his time. He is not interested in leisure, or even entertainment.

He is interested in survival, and in developing his potential, and he believes that learning is a survival skill.

He is right. Learning *is* a survival skill.

Since he makes learning look easy, we are apt to devalue the process that we are watching.

He believes that learning is *fun.*

He is right. Learning *is* fun. But it has been so long since most adults have experienced the sheer joy of discovery and creativity that we have forgotten what it feels like. A baby experiences this joy every minute of the day.

Give the baby a rattle and he will look at it. That is why toys are made in bright colors. He will bang it to find out whether it makes noises. That is why rattles rattle. He will feel it. That is why toys do not have sharp edges. He will taste it. That is why toys are made of non-toxic materials. He even smells it. We haven't yet figured out how toys ought to smell, which is why they don't have any smell at all.

This entire process takes about 30 seconds. Now that he knows everything that there is to know about the rattle he abandons it and will give the same amount of intense attention and interest to the box in which it came.

In fact, the baby will frequently pay more attention to the box in which the toy came because he will be permitted to break the box and, as a result, he may discover how the box is made. He will not have this opportunity with the toy because we have made it unbreakable.

With each and every object in his environment he uses the same five laboratory tests. He looks at it, listens to it, feels it, tastes it, and smells it. Then, having learned everything there is to learn about it, he throws it away.

This brilliant demonstration of the scientific method is then used against the baby, as evidence that he has a short attention span.

Question: *How long should a baby play with a rattle?*

Answer: As long as there is something to *learn* from it—and not one second longer.

The only decision we have to make at this point is: Do we join him or get in his way?

If we join him we enter a world that is exciting and dynamic. Nothing stays the same in this world of the tiny child. He changes every day and this means we have to change too. Sometimes it is hard work for us to change, especially *every day!*

The prize, however, is a happy, respected, productive, and highly capable child who loves and respects his parents and values the good teaching, wisdom, and experience of the adults around him.

The truth is that this process begins right now: not when he is six or ten or fifteen, but right now.

This is the moment.

If we are going to bring children into this world, we need, as a society, to ask ourselves this question: Should we not be prepared to provide for their needs and adapt to those needs during that vital first year of life?

After all, we are the adults. We have the choice; the baby does not.

We must not restrict the baby simply for our convenience at the very moment when freedom is so precious to him.

MOBILITY PROGRAM

Now you need to give the baby unlimited opportunity to stand upright and to walk. It is of the greatest importance that the baby be permitted to stand and walk independently.

Every time you permit the baby to balance himself, he learns about gravity and the dynamics of his own body when he moves his body, both with and against the force of gravity.

Every time you help the baby by holding him or taking his hand as he stands or walks, the baby learns much less. When this occurs, it is not the baby's brain but *your* brain that is learning about gravity and balance.

Goal: To establish, improve, or reinforce the ability to stand and walk

Purpose: To provide the maximum opportunity to stand up and to walk with arms used in a primary balance role at or above shoulder height

Part I—Walking

Target: 40 feet nonstop walking—200 yards of walking daily

Frequency: 20 to 30 opportunities daily

Intensity: 1 step, gradually building up to more

Duration: Sessions are a few seconds at first. At least 2 hours of opportunity daily

Content: The baby is placed in the ideal walking environment and encouraged to take one or two steps, followed by hugs and kisses all around.

Environment: The ideal surface for walking is a wooden floor that is not slippery, or a very short pile carpet. The room should contain low, stable furniture that will allow the baby to pull himself up into the standing position independently and then move from one piece of furniture to another. Examine the furniture in the room to make sure there are no sharp edges for the baby to fall into and hurt himself.

The baby should begin with bare feet until he is reasonably sure-footed, and wear clothing that does not restrict his movement. Long pants help to minimize the effects of falls.

Technique: Place some of the furniture so that it is only a baby's step away from another piece. This encourages the baby to try taking a step between the two. Gradually (step by step) separate the furniture. Each day it will be a little farther for the baby to walk between

Materials Needed:
- non-slip wooden floor or short-pile carpet
- low, stable furniture without sharp edges

the chairs, or between the sofa and the table. What took one small step now takes two steps. Step by step the baby gets better and better at maintaining his balance.

This can also be done using you and your spouse as the furniture. Baby pulls himself up on mother's leg and gets himself balanced and then takes a step and falls into father's arms. Then the process begins again. Each day you stand a little bit farther apart.

When he can get up onto his feet without pulling himself up on furniture, or climbing up your leg, and when he can take several steps easily, give the baby opportunity to walk in a room with little or no furniture. Give him the largest uncluttered area available.

When the baby has reached the point where he can walk across a room, encourage him to walk longer and longer distances each day so that he can build up his stamina and respiration through nonstop walking.

Please Note: At this stage in his development the baby is going to fall down from time to time. This is part of the learning process. Since you have been careful to make the environment safe and are vigilant to protect him, the vast majority of his falls will be harmless.

When a baby does fall, do not immediately and automatically cry out or scoop him up and soothe him. This may not be what he needs or wants. When he falls be quiet, and help him up only if he needs it. If he is hurt, find out what is wrong and take care of him. If he is all right, set him on his feet and keep going.

Usually when adults do not startle or cry out, the baby will pick himself up and continue on happily. If you automatically assume all falls are a disaster, and if you cry out or startle the baby, he will get the idea that any fall is bad. He will then learn to cry even though he is not hurt.

What a difference this simple piece of advice will make!

Part II—Balance Activities

Continue with the same passive balance activities that you began at Stage III (Chapter 17).

Frequency:	2 times daily for each activity
Intensity:	Gradually increase the speed as the baby adapts to it
Duration:	60 seconds per activity
Content:	10 activities at each session

Environment: A safe space, not cluttered with furniture. Floor areas cleared of toys or other objects. The baby should be dressed in nonrestrictive clothing and *should continue to wear a neck collar during these activities.*

Materials Needed:
- baby neck collar

Techniques:

1. Horizontal spin in the prone position
2. Horizontal spin on the left side
3. Horizontal rotation on the right side
4. Rocking in the supine position
5. Horizontal rotation in the prone position
6. Horizontal rotation in the supine position
7. Horizontal rotation in the prone position (with the head in)
8. Horizontal pitching
9. Acceleration (up and down)
10. Vertical rocking in the head-down position

MANUAL PROGRAM

The same opportunities that mother is providing as part of the tactile program for Stage IV will help the baby to develop cortical opposition in either hand.

Objective: To establish, improve, or reinforce the ability to use cortical opposition in either hand

Purpose: To provide the maximum opportunity to pick up objects using cortical opposition

Part I—Cortical Opposition

Frequency: 10 times daily

Intensity: Gradually decrease the size of objects

Duration: 30 to 60 seconds to experiment with each object

Content: 1 object per session

Environment: Place the baby in a comfortable position sitting on the floor or in his highchair, or lying prone nose-to-nose with you. *Supervise these opportunities closely so*

that the baby does not put these objects in his mouth or swallow them.

Materials Needed:

• small objects or pieces of food

Techniques: Choose objects that will be difficult for the baby to pick up using his whole hand in a prehensile grasp. These can include: small pieces of food, such as cooked carrots, banana, or cereal. At first the baby will not be able to pick up these objects, but as the baby is given uninterrupted time to experiment he will master one object. Then he will want to improve his technique before he tackles a new object. Do not retire an object until you think the baby has learned everything possible for now. When this occurs, introduce another object.

Please Note: From this time on, you must completely baby-proof the house. Each day the baby will gain new abilities. Sometimes he will master the ability to get into a low cupboard or reach a shelf before you realize it.

If there are poisonous or dangerous substances or objects anywhere that the baby might get into, move these things to much higher ground and lock them up.

Never underestimate the skill of the baby. When the baby's determination and problem-solving abilities meet unsupervised opportunity, the results can be truly astonishing. Sometimes the results are riotously funny, but sometimes they are tragic.

Part II—Brachiation

The baby is about to embark on a mobility adventure that will result in his ability to move hand over hand on an overhead ladder.

Children have been doing this for as long as there have been overhead ladders, or the jungle canopies that inspired them. Sadly, most children do not master this ability until they are nine or ten years old, if at all. This is a shame, because the ability to brachiate is quite easy for the tiny child to master, and it has tremendous benefits for him. It helps him develop respiratory maturity, and establish and improve his ability to converge his vision—and he has a great time doing it!

A. Using the Bar

Materials Needed:

• ³/₄" bar in doorway

Frequency: 5 times daily

Intensity: Full weight-bearing

Duration: 30 seconds

Content: 1 opportunity to hold onto the bar

Environment: $^3/_4$" bar securely hung in a doorway (used for Stage III)

Technique: Hold the baby up and encourage him to grab on to the bar. Then allow him to take his own weight for 30 seconds while you spot him to make sure he is safe. At the end of each session, hug and kiss the baby and tell him he is the best baby in the world–because he is! When the baby can hang completely independently for 30 seconds, he is ready to begin on the brachiation ladder. (See Appendix C for building instructions.)

B. Brachiation

Goal: The baby enjoys brachiating with mother supporting some of his weight.

Frequency: 10 times daily

Intensity: Starting with the baby bearing no weight, to almost full weight-bearing.

Duration: 20 to 30 seconds

Content: Beginning with 2 to 3 rungs, evolving to a trip down the length of the brachiation ladder

Environment: A brachiation ladder made to the correct specifications as described in the appendix. The ladder should be set at your height so that you can comfortably and safely support the baby by standing under it. It should be located in a place in the house where it can be used often.

Materials Needed:
• brachiation ladder

The baby should be in comfortable clothing that will not restrict the swinging motion needed in brachiation. The baby must have bare hands to hold on to the rungs properly.

Technique: You have already begun learning how to "spot" the baby while he is holding on to the overhead bar. Now you need to perfect your technique. This will keep the baby safe at all times by preventing a fall but will also coach him to learn the graceful swinging motion that is critical in brachiation.

To brachiate the baby must swing forward and backward. This backward swing gives him the momentum to move forward.

It is very difficult to brachiate without swinging and it is not

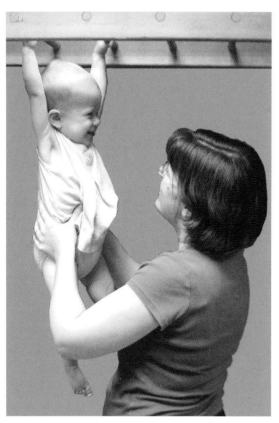

Figure 20.1. Olivia enjoys learning to brachiate with her mother's help.

much fun. It is the sensation of swinging freely from rung to rung that the young child finds so delightful when he has mastered it.

You need to pattern this swing into his motion as he moves from rung to rung down the ladder. Do this by holding him at the hips and giving him a gentle swing, as you support him and help to propel him forward (see Figure 20.1).

In the beginning mother and father should be together while doing this with the baby. Mother can stand behind the baby to hold him and spot him while father stands in front and helps him to move his hands from rung to rung. Father co-ordinates the movement of the baby's hands with the swinging movements created by mother.

In this way the baby gets the feel of brachiation right from his very first day.

At this point you are taking all of the baby's weight. The baby will quickly get the idea of how to move his hands by himself so a second person will not be needed after the first few days.

Now each day begin to let him take a little bit more of his own weight, just as you did when he was learning to grasp your fingers or hold the bar.

Please Note: Each and every time the baby brachiates with mother or father there should be a lot of cheering and noisy celebration. The baby needs to know that he is doing a great job. Brachiation can be fun for everyone in the family, and before the baby begins, it is a good idea to have him watch a sibling or parents brachiate. The more the baby sees other family members on the ladder, the more he will want his chance.

A brachiation ladder in the home will very soon become the hottest item in the neighborhood. The problem you will soon face is not how to get the children to use it but rather how to get the entire neighborhood off of it.

This is a nice problem to have.

Now you will want to make a new set of daily checklists to reflect your baby's new program. These lists may look like this:

THE MOTOR PROGRAM FOR PROFILE STAGE IV

Daily Checklist

Mobility Opportunity

Maximum opportunity to stand up and walk

Create ideal walking environment

Goal: 40 feet nonstop walking, 200 yards walking each day

20x daily for a few seconds increasing to 2 hours total opportunity

☐ ☐ ☐ ☐ ☐ ☐ ☐ ☐ ☐ ☐
☐ ☐ ☐ ☐ ☐ ☐ ☐ ☐ ☐ ☐

Average distance per session: _____

Total distance today: _____

Changes Noted Today: _____

_____

_____

Date: _____

THE MOTOR PROGRAM FOR PROFILE STAGE IV

Daily Checklist

Manual Competence

Picking up objects

Providing opportunity to pick up objects using cortical opposition:
10x daily for 30 to 60 seconds

☐ ☐ ☐ ☐ ☐ ☐ ☐ ☐ ☐ ☐

Total time: 5 to 10 minutes

Using the Bar

Goal: To be able to hold onto the bar independently for 30 seconds consistently.
     5x daily for 30 seconds

☐ ☐ ☐ ☐ ☐ ☐ ☐ ☐ ☐ ☐

Total time: 2.5 minutes

Brachiation

Goal: To enjoy brachiation with Mother supporting some of baby's weight.
     10x daily for 20 to 30 seconds

☐ ☐ ☐ ☐ ☐ ☐ ☐ ☐ ☐ ☐

Total time: 3 to 5 minutes daily

Percentage of weight bearing: _____

Total # of trips: _____

Changes Noted Today: _____

_____

_____

Date: _____

THE MOTOR PROGRAM FOR PROFILE STAGE IV

Daily Checklist

Balance Activities

Opportunity to move through space dynamically

Note: All 10 activities are done in one session

Two sessions daily, each activity done for 60 seconds

Total time: 20 minutes

1. Horizontal spin prone ☐ ☐

2. Horizontal rotation left side ☐ ☐

3. Horizontal rotation right side ☐ ☐

4. Rocking supine position ☐ ☐

5. Horizontal rotation prone ☐ ☐

6. Horizontal rotation supine ☐ ☐

7. Horizontal rotation, head in ☐ ☐

8. Horizontal pitching ☐ ☐

9. Acceleration up and down ☐ ☐

10. Vertical rocking, head down ☐ ☐

Changes Noted Today: _____

_____

_____

Date: _____

SUMMARY

Now the baby is walking confidently and without needing to keep his arms up for balance all the time. In using his cortical opposition, he is practicing with one hand and beginning to try it with the other hand. He is also beginning to get the idea of how to brachiate, and as each day passes he will become more and more able to swing and to take his own weight.

For a little while longer we will call him a baby, but in truth when he has conquered Stage IV he is not a baby anymore. He is a little boy.

Maria and her mother enjoy every moment together.

He has made a heroic journey, and although we have helped him as much as we could he has had to make most of his journey alone.

He has crawled many miles; no one could do that for him.

He has taken the risk of defying gravity so that he could get up on his hands and knees for the first time. No matter how loved he may have been, no one could do that for him.

Now he is a walker, but his mobility imperative urges him on. He will not rest until he has made every experiment needed to increase his walking speed, until one day he can take both feet off the ground at once and run.

But that is another chapter of another book. For the moment we have reached the end of the beginning for our baby.

He has done a fabulous job. He has shown courage and determination. He has been tough and tenacious. He has almost never accepted defeat no matter how daunting the task at hand. When all is said and done, he is a most admirable little fellow.

And if we are very wise we will have told him that many, many times.

21

What To Do and
What Not To Do

The purpose of this book has been to provide mothers and fathers with an understanding of how the newborn baby grows and develops in the first 12 months of life. It is our hope to teach parents about the process of growth and development so that they understand why the first 12 months of life are so important—and so they know how they can *use* this precious period to the enormous benefit of their babies.

To this end we have provided detailed instruction as to how to evaluate a tiny baby at the first four stages of the Developmental Profile, which encompasses the first 12 months of life. In addition, we have outlined a sensory program for each stage, which will help parents to establish each stage at the earliest possible moment. We have also explained how parents can create improved opportunities and a favorable environment for the full development of mobility, language, and manual competence.

There now remain a few final practical points that will help mother use her time wisely, so that she and the baby can get the most out of each moment they spend together.

BE A PROFESSIONAL MOTHER

Professional mothers are fulltime mothers who approach their work with the same passion and dedication that other top-flight professionals devote to being engineers, doctors, lawyers, etc. If you are a fulltime mother, you are a member of the oldest and most honorable profession in the world. If you are not able to be home fulltime, it is even more important to adopt the same discipline of a fulltime pro-

The oldest and most honorable profession in the world is mothering.

fessional mother. When you are with your baby put out a "Mother At Work—Do Not Disturb" sign. In other words, plan to be only with your baby and don't answer your phone. You have the most important job in the world—protect it.

BE CONSISTENT

The most frequent advice we hear from mothers who have done a wonderful program with their babies is to *be consistent*. This is excellent advice.

Do your program every day.

Whatever you decide to do with your baby, do it *every* day.

Your baby will need and want stimulation every day. His need for stimulation and opportunity does not go away on Saturday or Sunday or on holidays. Babies do best on a regular routine. It is good for baby to know what is expected of him, and he will learn this far more easily if he is following a routine. You will also benefit from a predictable schedule. This cuts down on a lot of wasted stopping and starting. When you and your baby have a predictable schedule, the two of you will work well as a team.

BE FLEXIBLE

As soon as you make a schedule, real life will intervene and turn your schedule upside down. Be prepared for this by having alternative plans for when your ideal schedule is put aside by a pressing problem or unexpected change. But make sure that the problem or disruption is legitimate. Don't let anything frivolous change your priority to give your baby stimulation and opportunity.

BE ORGANIZED

It is very helpful to keep all the materials needed for your baby's program in one place. Since you and your baby may need to move from room to room throughout the day, it is wise to keep the materials in a box or a bag that travels easily from place to place.

Once a session is over, quickly arrange the materials so that they are organized for the next session. Then when you see that the baby is set for another session, everything is ready to go and you are not wasting time trying to get organized.

Once a week, set aside time to reorganize for the week ahead and to plan for the month ahead. This will help you to figure out and obtain what new items you may need. This is a great time for father and older brothers and sisters to be with the baby so that you can devote your full attention to organization and materials preparation.

PUT HOUSEWORK ON HOLD

We all know the old expression "A mother's work is never done." It's not only old, but it's true. The house is a big part of this work; it is always screaming for attention. Our mothers are very tough on this point. They do not listen to the household when it screams at them. They find that once the new baby arrives they cannot have as perfect a household as they did before the baby. The baby is simply more important than a perfect house. Our mothers strongly recommend that dishes, beds, and cleaning take a back seat to the baby.

> The baby is more important than a perfect house.

Baby's naptime should be reserved first for you to catch up on your own lost sleep. Otherwise naptime is used for food preparation. The household should be left for last and whenever possible divided among mother, father, and older siblings. Our fathers are superb—they are among that growing percentage of fathers who regularly help around the house. This is a huge help to you and your baby.

STAY HOME

In the first eight weeks of the newborn's life, try to stay home as much as possible. First of all, it will be very hard to maintain the daily routine if you have to do a lot of coming and going.

Every time the baby is taken out of his home, he must work very hard to orient himself to the new environment. The result is that he will easily become exhausted and he will sleep a great deal. Of course the baby should sleep if he is tired, but babies who are constantly taken out of their home environment will simply end up sleeping more than babies who are home.

Travel is also quite tiring for you. At this stage it is better to batten down the hatches and make sure that you have what you need at home. During these early weeks it is best for father, grandparents, or friends to do the errands that need to be done.

MAKE THE MORNING SACRED

Morning time is precious—it is the golden time of the day for little children. This becomes more true each day as the baby matures. In

> Morning is the golden time for your baby.

the first few weeks the baby's life is eating and sleeping, with only a little time in between for stimulation and opportunity. But this changes very rapidly as the baby matures.

Always protect the morning and keep it sacred for you and your baby. Some mothers work outside the home in the morning and are at home in the afternoon. If this is the case, do everything in your power to reverse it. Stay home with the baby in the morning and work outside the home in the afternoon. You will find that you can accomplish a huge amount with your baby between 7 A.M. and noon. Then the afternoon is available for other things that need to be done.

FATHER'S DAY

Let father be "mother"—
he will surprise you.

At The Institutes for the Achievement of Human Potential we have a tradition of our mothers and fathers switching places at some point after the baby arrives. In most cases, our staff mothers choose to be fulltime mothers. However, some of our fathers trade places one day a week and become fulltime fathers, and some trade for a few months at a time once the baby is no longer nursing.

On these days, mother hands off her program checklist and instructions to father and he has the challenge of trying to accomplish one day a week what mother does every day. He almost never completes his daily checklist but he always has a great time trying, and so does the baby. At first the day is filled with lots of phone calls to mother, but as father gains confidence he becomes a very good "mother."

Fathers do things differently. Sometimes they do things that mothers never do, and that is wonderful. Fathers are superb teachers too. One of the best-kept secrets in our society is how much fun fathers and babies have when they are given the chance to be alone together.

BROTHERS AND SISTERS

If we could advise couples who are contemplating having a second child, we would recommend strongly not to have that child too soon after the first one. Many mothers have been advised to have children back-to-back. "Get through the diaper years as fast as possible," they are told.

This may rank as one of the worst pieces of advice for mothers and babies that has ever been given. An 18- to 30-month-old child wants fulltime attention from his mother. He not only wants her undivided attention, but he really *needs* it. He is not fully independent in anything except getting into trouble.

We strongly recommend that the first baby be given the time and attention he needs to gain independence. Usually between the ages of three and four he is able to take care of himself—and what is equally important, *help mother.* It is very important for the first child to be able to contribute to the new baby from the start. If older brother or sister is simply too immature to be helpful, he or she will compete with the baby for time and attention.

As soon as you become pregnant with your second baby, we propose that your first child begin to learn all the things he can do to help you and the new baby once he arrives. Create a checklist for each responsibility, and for the next nine months lovingly coach your child through these checklists.

> It makes a huge difference to give your first baby the chance to mature *before* the second baby arrives.

Your young child knows he or she is in training now to be the "older brother" or "older sister." It is the first real job he or she has ever had. It is an important job, and your child knows it. When the baby does arrive, older brother is ready and he can begin to help you. Each day he gets better and better at his responsibilities. He does not see the baby as a competitor. Far from it, he views the baby exactly as you do—as his little sister or brother who needs his help and who adores him. What a difference it makes to give your first baby the chance to get on his feet and be able to help *before* the second baby arrives.

Our mothers say that the older brothers and sisters are a vital part of the teaching team from the moment the baby arrives. This is the start of a wonderful relationship between brothers and sisters that will last a lifetime.

MATERIAL PREPARATION—STAY AHEAD

Material preparation is part of being a professional mother or father. While it does take time and effort, it should be fun. You have the chance to make materials that are custom-designed to meet the needs and interests of your own baby. Materials should be made in a high-quality way so that they will hold up to the wear and tear of daily use, and so that they can be put away and saved for the next baby.

Often fathers do the material preparation or mother and father do this together in the evening. It is important to make materials well in advance. Babies move through materials more rapidly each day. If you have not created a large stockpile, you may find yourself using the same materials over and over again. This is lethal for the baby. He will tolerate a lot from us, but he will not tolerate seeing old material when he is ready for something new. When you need to restock, it is best to get more than is needed. We have never, ever met a mother who found that she had too many new teaching materials for her baby.

Babies will not tolerate old materials over and over.

KEEP RECORDS

We have suggested the intervals at which you should evaluate your baby. Each time you evaluate the baby you should make a new Profile and date it.

We have also proposed a daily diary in which you note the days when the baby gains a new function. This simple diary will be a very precious record of your baby's development, along with his Developmental Profiles.

It is important to keep records, especially in mobility, so that you can see how the baby is doing on a daily basis with respect to his long-range goals.

The daily checklists can be made in whatever way is best for you. We have found that these checklists help to simplify what may seem a bit overwhelming. It is really not that difficult when each activity is listed and checked off as it is done.

These checklists have also proved to be valuable for fathers, since they do not usually do the baby's program as often as mothers do. The checklists give fathers the structure and confidence to jump into the program and learn how to do it.

KNOW WHEN NOT TO DO IT

One of the benefits of doing a good, consistent program is that the baby will have a greater resistance to illness and be less likely to be ill. If he is ill, however, you should stop the program and do whatever is necessary to get him healthy and fit again.

Another problem for a baby is teething. This can be a big problem for some babies. Each mother learns the best ways to comfort her baby and get him through this painful experience. Sometimes continuing with his program helps him to forget about his teething for a bit. At other times this may not be the case, and it is better to stop for a while.

EAT PROPERLY

Mothers are usually very careful about what they eat while they are pregnant but they can be quite careless of their own nutrition once the baby is born. Mother needs fewer calories now, but a nursing mother's nutritional needs are tremendous.

Regardless of whether you are nursing or not, it is very important that you eat fresh, wholesome foods at regular intervals. This will help you to maintain excellent health and have the energy you need to keep up with the baby.

GET ENOUGH SLEEP

Mothers never get enough sleep. In fact, mothers of tiny babies live in a state of exhaustion. After a while mother is so numbed by her chronic fatigue that she is no longer even aware of it.

Father usually recognizes mother's chronic fatigue well before she does. He needs to jump in to make sure mother gets more sleep.

As the mother of a newborn, there are steps you can take to avoid exhaustion. Nap whenever the baby naps. At night when the baby wakes up to be fed, feed the baby and immediately put him back down to sleep.

Under no circumstances should you show the baby animal cards at 2 A.M. If you allow yourself to be seduced by the baby's alert and eager little face and show him cards or even chat with him in the middle of the night, you can be sure that at exactly 2 A.M. the next night you are going to have a wake-up call. This time it won't just be food he is after—he will want those animal cards too.

Try to be as boring as possible at night. Do not turn on the lights, and do not even talk to the baby. Simply nurse the baby and put him back to sleep. In this way the baby learns that there is nothing happening in the house and he goes back to sleep.

You need your sleep very badly, and you need to be ruthless about getting it. When both you and your baby are well rested, there is no end to the magic you can make together.

Sleep deprivation is an occupational hazard for *all* mothers.

IF YOU HAVE A PROBLEM, TAKE ACTION

Most mothers experience a significant change of energy or mood after the birth of the baby.

The change that takes place in the body after delivery is dramatic. Hormones are powerful. It is a rare mother who does not experience a significant alteration of energy or mood, or both, after the birth of the baby. You may feel a heightened sense of exhilaration and energy at one end of the spectrum to a full depression at the other end.

Oddly, this entirely understandable and predictable change is a well-kept secret. New mothers often have no idea of what to expect or to expect anything at all. When mother finds herself feeling strange and out of sorts at just the moment when she needs to be at her best, she is doubly distressed. After all, she is supposed to be overjoyed to have her baby. She now has a huge new responsibility and there is a lot to do. All of a sudden she is frightened and overwhelmed, whereas a few days earlier she was in top form. If mother does not know to expect this change, she may be too upset to talk to anyone about it. This change may last a few days, or a few weeks, or a few months.

If you are not feeling well after the birth of the baby, *don't wait it out.* Talk to your mother, your aunt, or your best friend who already has three children. Talk to the person you respect and trust most in the world, but communicate immediately what is going on. Then find effective help from the source that you trust and respect most. You need to be fully in command of yourself and feeling great again as soon as possible.

IF YOUR CHILD HAS A PROBLEM, TAKE ACTION

The Institutes Developmental Profile clearly shows the progress of your child. It is a neurological road map. If your child is progressing nicely, it will be clear. If your child is not progressing, it will also be clear. If you are concerned about your child's development, act upon that concern.

The Institutes clinical archive is the largest archive on earth with carefully documented developmental histories on more than 15,000 brain-injured children. Those children range from profoundly injured (blind, deaf, and paralyzed) to mildly injured (developmentally delayed), and every kind of brain-injured child in between those two extremes.

The careful developmental histories done on those 15,000 children show that in almost every case it was mother who recognized that the child had a problem. Those histories show that mothers saw a problem months or years before health care professionals finally agreed that the child was in trouble.

Mothers are the best observers. If you are concerned about your baby, we strongly recommend that you learn more and get the answers to your questions.

LEARN MORE

- Children have a greater potential intelligence than Leonardo da Vinci ever used in his lifetime.

There is a lot more to learn about your baby!

- It is easy to teach a baby to read and it is important to teach a baby to read.

- It is easy to teach a baby math and it is important to teach a baby math.

- Babies can learn absolutely anything that we can teach in an honest, factual, and joyous way.

- Babies should be physically excellent, and when they are it has a profound effect on their intellectual and social development.

- Tiny children can be socially excellent. Social growth is largely a product of intellectual and physical growth.

- Brain-injured children are not hopeless. All brain-injured children deserve a fighting chance to be well.

- There are many different labels for brain-injured children (such as brain-damaged, mentally retarded, mentally deficient, cerebral-palsied, epileptic, autistic, athetoid, hyperactive, attention deficit disordered, developmentally delayed, and Down syndrome).

All of the above statements are true. They are the product of a half-century of search and discovery at The Institutes for the Achievement of Human Potential. But they are not the subject of this book. They are the subject of what is next for babies who are graduates of this book.

Recommended Reading

How To Teach Your Baby To Read, Glenn and Janet Doman. Square One Publishers, Garden City Park, NY.

How To Teach Your Baby To Be Physically Superb, Glenn and Douglas Doman, Bruce Hagy. Square One Publishers, Garden City Park, NY.

How To Teach Your Baby Math, Glenn and Janet Doman. Square One Publishers, Garden City Park, NY.

How To Multiply Your Baby's Intelligence, Glenn and Janet Doman. Square One Publishers, Garden City Park, NY.

How To Give Your Baby Encyclopedic Knowledge, Glenn and Janet Doman, Susan Aisen. Square One Publishers, Garden City Park, NY.

What To Do About Your Brain-Injured Child, Glenn Doman. Square One Publishers, Garden City Park, NY.

22

The Gentle Revolution

A pregnant mother would have to live on a desert island, a thousand miles from land, to go through nine months of pregnancy without receiving advice about what to do or not do with her new baby.

If she is brave, she goes to the library or to a bookstore, where she finds dozens of books by adamant professionals. Many of them tell her not to do much of anything with her new baby except feed him. Some warn her that if she does not do as they say something awful will happen.

This is not one of those books.

After almost half a century of nose-to-nose experience with mothers, we have learned that parents should never do anything with their babies that they do not understand and agree with one hundred percent.

Parents should decide what is best for their children.

If parents do something with a child that they do not understand fully, it could actually be dangerous for the child.

If parents do something with their child that they do not agree with completely, they will not do it well.

If someone must decide what is best for children, thank heaven it is parents who have that right. Parents, and only parents, should decide what is best for their children.

They make the best decisions.

If, after reading this book, mother does nothing more than look at her baby with new respect, that will be wonderful. For surely that new respect will profoundly effect the way in which she raises her child.

If mother decides that this program is not for her, she should not do one iota of it. In such a case no one will support her decision more than we will.

Never in history have mothers been subjected to such a cacophony of absolute, utter balderdash on the subject of child rearing as they are today.

It is enough to discourage women from having children altogether.

Mothers should not be bullied out of exercising their intelligence, intuition, and maternal instincts in making their own decisions about what is best for their children.

For five decades, we have had a secret weapon—mothers. We not only ask mothers questions, we *listen* to the answers.

Almost no one else does.

What a shame that professionals (usually bachelors who have never diapered a baby or spent 10 minutes alone dealing with one) do not listen to mothers. If they did, they would learn about a whole new world of child development that they do not even know exists.

We believe that mothers make the best mothers and fathers make the best fathers.

If mother decides that she wishes to teach her baby for 10 minutes a day, then she should do so and not have to explain herself to anyone.

If she decides she wants to use 30 minutes a day teaching her baby, then she should teach her baby 30 minutes a day and she surely does not need to justify that to anyone.

If she decides to teach her baby and finds along the way that she derives honest pleasure in so doing, and therefore wishes to do more, then she should do whatever it is she wishes to do.

Parents should do exactly and precisely what they think is best and not one jot more or less.

It has been our experience that the vast majority of parents in the world want what is best for their children. Mothers and fathers know their babies better than anyone else does. Parents love their children more than anyone else can.

Parents make the best parents.

Many parents believe that the environment that they create at home, and the example they set, will affect the course of their children's lives more strongly than any other environment or relationship.

All the evidence we have gathered, in 50 years of search and discovery in brain development, supports this view.

Mothers make the best mothers and fathers make the best fathers.

When parents take honest pleasure in the company of their children they become the best teachers their children will ever have.

It is our hope that this little book will lead every parent who reads it to look at their baby with new eyes.

It is our hope that those new eyes will see the tremendous potential and ability of the tiny baby.

This is the story of the beginning of a revolution, a gentle revolution. A revolution to bring about the most splendid of changes, but a revolution in which there is no bloodshed, no hatred, no death, and no destruction.

In this gentlest of revolutions there are only two enemies. The first is Ancient Myths, and the second is the Status Quo. It is not necessary that the ancient traditions be smashed to the ground, but only that ancient falsehoods should wither away unmourned. It is not necessary that what is presently good be burned to the ground, but only that so much in the world that is presently terrible rust slowly away as a product of disuse.

The Gentle Revolution simply proposes that tiny children have within them the capacity to learn virtually anything while they are very young. We propose that what children learn without any conscious effort between birth and six can only be learned with great effort in later life, or may not be learned at all. We propose that what adults learn painfully, tiny children learn joyfully. We propose that what adults learn at a snail's pace, tiny children learn speedily. We propose that adults sometimes shy away from learning, while tiny children would rather learn than eat.

Parents are not the problem, they are the answer.

Is it a revolutionary idea that parents and children belong together?

Children don't think so. If every baby had his way, he would have mother or father by his side every minute of every day.

He's right.

The means to accomplish this gentle revolution are simple, straightforward, and clear.

Parents.

Parents are not the problem in the world of kids, they are the answer.

Is it difficult to imagine that the world would be a saner, safer, richer place if all babies had the stimulation and opportunity in the first year of life that they need?

Is it difficult to imagine what the world would be like if tiny children had their burning rage to learn fed and fanned?

For in truth, the baby has an infinite appetite to learn all that he does not know.

We have reached the end of this book, but for every parent and every newborn baby it is just the beginning—the beginning of the Gentle Revolution.

Afterword

The working title of a book in progress rarely survives to become the real title. It may surprise the reader to learn that often it is not the author who decides the final title, but rather the publisher. Such was the case with this book, which was actually written a number of years before it finally went to press.

Authors naturally want the title to reflect what the book is actually about. However, publishers want the title to inspire the purchase of the book. While these two viewpoints do not have to be mutually exclusive, they often are. We pointed out to our publisher that our book never posed the question "How smart is your baby?" or what's more ever answered it! It is not of the slightest interest to us how smart your baby is compared with the baby next door (and we hope it is of little interest to you too). This book was never meant to be about some infantile competition. Rather this book is entirely about how smart your baby is compared with the conventional adult view that babies are not smart at all.

If the question is "How smart is your baby?" then the answer must be "VERY."

Enjoy trying to stay a step ahead of your baby. If you find you cannot, join the rest of us. We couldn't either.

About Our Babies

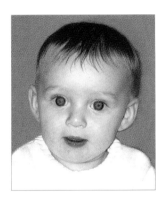

Caleb Canepa is the third child of Jennifer and Polo Canepa. Jennifer has been a staff member at The Institutes since 1999. Caleb has enjoyed a wonderful program since birth and has the advantage of having an older sister, Anais, and an older brother, Benjamin, who also began at birth and who are delighted to have someone to teach everything they have already learned.

Maria Diaque is the daughter of Beatriz and Juan-Pablo Diaque. Her grandmother is Beatriz Carrancedo, who was Glenn Doman's translator when he first visited Mexico to lecture about his book *How To Teach Your Baby To Read*. When Beatriz was about to have her first baby, she visited The Institutes to learn more. As a result, Maria's mother, Beatriz Martin-Moreno, began on The Institutes Early Development Program right from birth, as did her little brother, Enrique. Today Maria has a very experienced mother and father, grandmother, and uncle who are having a great time teaching her at home.

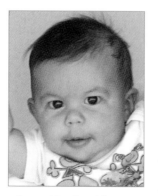

Isolda Maauad is the daughter of Federica and José Maauad. José was an exchange student at The International School of The Evan Thomas Institute from age 13 to 14. After he married, his wife, Federica, came to The Institutes to join the staff as a volunteer and to attend the *How To Multiply Your Baby's Intelligence* Course to prepare for the birth of their first child. Isolda has had the great benefit of the experience and knowledge of both of her parents.

Olivia Rumpf, our cover girl, is the daughter of Colleen and Mike Rumpf. Colleen is the oldest of four children, all of whom were on The Institutes Early Development Program as little children. Colleen's parents, Kathy and John Brown, attended the *How To Multiply Your Baby's Intelligence* Course when Colleen was four years old. They then began a full home program with their four children. Colleen is now enjoying teaching Olivia many of the same things she learned at a very young age.

About The Institutes

The Institutes for the Achievement of Human Potential is a non-profit educational organization that serves brain-injured children and well children. The Institutes introduces parents to the field of child brain development. Parents learn how the brain grows and how to speed that growth in their brain-injured child or enhance that growth in their well child.

The goal of The Institutes is to raise significantly the intellectual, physical, and social abilities of all children.

The Institutes believes that every brain-injured child deserves a fighting chance to be well. It is the mission of The Institutes to give parents the knowledge they need so that their brain-injured children may have that fighting chance.

Further, The Institutes proposes that every child born has a right to be intellectually, physically, and socially excellent. The goal for well children is to achieve excellence in all three areas.

The Institutes recognizes that when parents know how the brain grows and why it grows the way it does, they are the very best teachers their children will ever have.

About the Authors

Glenn Doman is the founder of The Institutes for the Achievement of Human Potential. He received his degree at the University of Pennsylvania in 1940. He then began studying with Temple Fay, the famous neurosurgeon at Temple University Hospital. His work with Fay inspired him and he began pioneering the field of child brain development. In 1955, he founded The Institutes for the Achievement of Human Potential in Philadelphia. By the early sixties the world-renowned work of The Institutes with brain-injured children had led to vital discoveries about the growth and development of well children. Since then The Institutes have been demonstrating that babies are far more capable of learning than we ever imagined. The Brazilian government knighted Glenn Doman for his outstanding work on behalf of the children of the world.

Janet Doman is the director of The Institutes for the Achievement of Human Potential. She literally grew up on the campus of The Institutes. After completing studies in zoology at the University of Hull in England and physical anthropology at the University of Pennsylvania, she devoted herself to the work with brain-injured children. She spent two years in Japan where she created programs for mothers and babies at The Early Development Association in Tokyo. In 1975 she became the director of The Evan Thomas Institute in Philadelphia, a school for mothers and babies. In 1980 she was made the director of The Institutes for the Achievement of Human Potential.

The authors have lived with, studied, and worked with children from more than 100 nations, ranging from the most civilized to the most primitive. They are the authors of the best-selling Gentle Revolution Series: *How To Teach Your Baby To Read, How To Teach Your Baby Math, How To Multiply Your Baby's Intelligence, How To Give Your Baby Encyclopedic Knowledge,* and *How Smart Is Your Baby?* Glenn Doman also wrote *How To Teach Your Baby To Be Physically Superb* and *What To Do About Your Brain-Injured Child,* a landmark work for the parents of brain-injured children.

Appendix A

Resources

QUESTIONS?

Write to:
Smart Baby
The Institutes for the Achievement
   of Human Potential
8801 Stenton Avenue
Wyndmoor, PA 19038
Email: smartbaby@iahp.org
Website: www.iahp.org

Courses for Parents

HOW TO MULITIPLY YOUR BABY'S INTELLIGENCE COURSE

WHAT TO DO ABOUT YOUR BRAIN-INJURED CHILD COURSE

For information regarding these courses, please contact:

The Institutes for the Achievement
   of Human Potential
8801 Stenton Avenue
Wyndmoor, PA 19038 USA
www.iahp.org
Phone: 215-233-2050
Fax: 215-233-9646
E-Mail: institutes@iahp.org

Books for Parents

HOW TO TEACH YOUR BABY TO READ
Glenn Doman and Janet Doman

How To Teach Your Baby To Read provides your child with the enjoyment of reading. It shows you just how easy and pleasurable it is to teach a young child to read. It explains how to begin and expand the reading program, how to make and organize your materials, and how to more fully develop your child's potential.

Also available:
How To Teach Your Baby To Read Video or DVD
How To Teach Your Baby To Read Kits

HOW TO TEACH YOUR BABY MATH
Glenn Doman and Janet Doman

How To Teach Your Baby Math instructs you in successfully developing your child's ability to think and reason. It shows you just how easy and pleasurable it is to teach a young child math. It explains how to begin and expand the math program, how to make and organize your materials, and how to more fully develop your child's potential.

Also available:
How To Teach Your Baby Math Video or DVD
How To Teach Your Baby Math Kits

HOW TO GIVE YOUR BABY
ENCYCLOPEDIC KNOWLEDGE

Glenn Doman, Janet Doman, and Susan Aisen

How To Give Your Baby Encyclopedic Knowledge provides a program of visually stimulating information designed to help your child take advantage of his or her natural potential to learn anything. It shows you just how easy and pleasurable it is to teach a young child about the arts, science, and nature. Your child will recognize the insects in the garden, know the countries of the world, discover the beauty of a painting by van Gogh, and more. It explains how to begin and expand your program, how to make and organize your materials, and how to more fully develop your child's potential.

Also available:

How To Give Your Baby Encyclopedic Knowledge Video

How To Give Your Baby Encyclopedic Knowledge Kits

HOW TO MULTIPLY YOUR BABY'S
INTELLIGENCE

Glenn Doman and Janet Doman

How To Multiply Your Baby's Intelligence provides a comprehensive program that will enable your child to read, to do mathematics, and to learn about anything and everything. It shows you just how easy and pleasurable it is to teach your young child, and to help your child become more capable and confident. It explains how to begin and expand this remarkable program, how to make and organize your materials, and how to more fully develop your child's potential.

Also available:

How To Multiply Your Baby's Intelligence Kits

HOW TO TEACH YOUR BABY
TO BE PHYSICALLY SUPERB

Glenn Doman, Douglas Doman, and Bruce Hagy

How To Teach Your Baby To Be Physically Superb explains the basic principles, philosophy, and stages of mobility in easy-to-understand language. This inspiring book describes just how easy and pleasurable it is to teach a young child to be physically superb. It clearly shows you how to create an environment for each stage of mobility that will help your baby advance and develop more easily. It shows that the team of mother, father, and baby is the most important athletic team your child will ever know. It explains how to begin, how to make your materials, and how to expand your program. This complete guide also includes full-color charts, photographs, illustrations, and detailed instructions to help you create your own program.

Also available:

How To Teach Your Baby To Be Physically Superb Video or DVD

WHAT TO DO ABOUT YOUR
BRAIN-INJURED CHILD

Glenn Doman

In this breakthrough book, Glenn Doman—pioneer in the treatment of the brain-injured—brings real hope to thousands of children, many of whom are inoperable, and many of whom have been given up for lost and sentenced to a life of institutional confinement. Based upon the decades of successful work performed at The Institutes for the Achievement of Human Potential, the book explains why old theories and techniques fail, and why The Institutes philosophy and revolutionary treatment succeed.

THE PATHWAY TO WELLNESS

How To Help Your Brain-Injured Child or Your Brain-damaged, Mentally Retarded, Mentally Deficient, Cerebral Palsied, Epileptic, Autistic, Athetoid, Hyperactive, Attention Deficit Disordered, Developmentally Delayed, Down's Child

Glenn Doman and the Staff of The Institutes

This important book is written for parents whose children may have been given any of these labels and may have problems with movement, sensation, vision, hearing, language, learning, behavior, or a combination of these things. In addition, they may have problems with allergies, digestion, elimination, seizures, and general health and well-being, or may be in a coma. All of these are symptoms of brain injury. If your child has any of these symptoms or has been given any of these labels, this book is for you. It contains in simple terms what you need to know, what you should do, and what you should not do with your brain-injured child.

Books for Children

Very young readers have special needs. These are not met by conventional children's literature, which is designed to be read by adults to little children, not by them. The careful choice of vocabulary, sentence structure, print size, and formatting is needed by very young readers. The design of these children's books is based upon a half-century of search and discovery of what works best for very young readers.

ENOUGH, INIGO, ENOUGH (AGES 1 TO 6)

written by Janet Doman
illustrated by Michael Armentrout

NOSE IS NOT TOES (AGES 1 TO 3)

written by Glenn Doman
illustrated by Janet Doman

For information about these books and teaching materials, please contact:

The Gentle Revolution Press
8801 Stenton Avenue
Wyndmoor, PA 19038 USA
Phone: 215-233-2050, Ext. 2525
Fax: 215-233-3852
Toll-Free: 866-250-BABY
E-Mail: info@gentlerevolution.com
www.gentlerevolution.com

ASICS Infant Crawling Track

The ASICS crawling track is constructed of yellow and green polyethylene foam and folds in half for portability and storage: 19" (49 cm) wide / 6.7" (17 cm) high / 46.5" (109 cm) long when opened.

To purchase, call: 215-233-2050, ext. 2525
                    or toll-free 866-BABY-2229

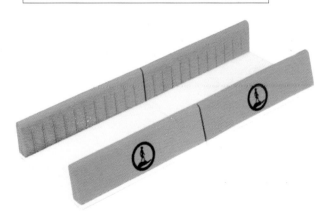

Bit of Intelligence Cards

Anatomy
Organs of the Body

Natural History

Amphibians Set I	Insects Set II
Birds	Leaves
Birds of Prey	Mammals Set I
Butterflies and Moths	Mammals Set II
Dinosaurs	Primates Set I
Flowers Set I	Reptiles
Insects Set I	Sea Creatures

People
Composers
Explorers
Great Inventors
Presidents of the United States Set I
World Leaders

Mathematics
Regular Polygons

Music
Musical Instruments

Vehicles
Air Vehicles

Works of Art
Great Art Masterpieces
Self-Portraits of Great Artists
Masterpieces by da Vinci
Masterpieces by Picasso
Masterpieces by van Gogh

CD-ROMS

THE PICTURE DICTIONARY

The Gentle Revolution Series includes ten volumes of the Picture Dictionary CD-ROMs.

The Picture Dictionary Program is designed to give parents a very easy-to-use method of introducing a program of encyclopedic knowledge in five different languages. A child may concentrate on a favorite language or gain ability in all five languages.

Each CD-ROM contains fifteen categories of Bit of Intelligence images, with ten images in each category. That is a total of 150 different images that can be viewed in English, Spanish, Japanese, Italian, and French on each CD-ROM.

For each image there is a large reading word provided. The child may choose to view the image and the reading word, the image alone, or the reading word alone. This program is so easy to navigate that children as young as three years old have been able to use it independently.

Appendix B

A Reassessment of the SIDS Back to Sleep Campaign

Ralph Pelligra (Corresponding author), *Ames Research Center, National Aeronautics and Space Administration (NASA), Moffett Field, CA 94035, Ralph.Pelligra-1@nasa.gov.*

Glenn Doman, *The Institutes for the Achievement of Human Potential, Wyndmoor, PA 19038.*

Gerry Leisman, *Carrick Institute for Clinical Ergonomics, Rehabilitation and Applied Neuroscience, School of Engineering Technologies, State University of New York, College at Farmingdale, Lupton Hall, 2350 Broadhollow Road, Farmingdale, NY 11735.*

The Back to Sleep Campaign was initiated in 1994 to implement the American Academy of Pediatrics' (AAP) recommendation that infants be placed in the nonprone sleeping position to reduce the risk of the Sudden Infant Death Syndrome (SIDS). This paper offers a challenge to the Back to Sleep Campaign (BTSC) from two perspectives: (1) the questionable validity of SIDS mortality and risk statistics, and (2) the BTSC as human experimentation rather than as confirmed preventive therapy.

The principal argument that initiated the BTSC and that continues to justify its existence is the observed parallel declines in the number of infants placed in the prone sleeping position and the number of reported SIDS deaths. We are compelled to challenge both the implied causal relationship between these observations and the SIDS mortality statistics themselves.

KEYWORDS: SIDS, public health, medical research, epidemiology, public health, child health, infancy, United States

INTRODUCTION

Medical advice that stems from epidemiological research can have a profound effect on public health because of the many individuals affected. This applies to false as well as correct advice. It is for this reason that we should attempt continually to identify the benefits or the harm of preventive measures and to question the premises on which they are based. Few would argue with this. In practice, however, there is often resistance to change and a reluctance to believe data that contradict previously held beliefs[1].

Received June 1, 2005; Revised June 30, 2005; Accepted June 30, 2005; Published July 21, 2005
Review *TheScientificWorldJOURNAL* (2005) 5, 550–557 ISSN 1537-744X; DOI 10.1100/tsw.2005.71
Pelligra, R., Doman, G., and Leisman, G. (2005) A reassessment of the SIDS Back to Sleep Campaign. *TheScientificWorldJOURNAL* 5, 550–557.
Handling Editor: Joav Merrick, Principal Editor for *Child Health and Human Development*—a domain of *TheScientificWorldJOURNAL*.
The opinions expressed are solely those of the authors.   © 2005 with author.   Reprinted with permission.

The *S*cientificWorld
www.thescientificworld.com

The "Back to Sleep Campaign" (BTSC) was initiated in 1994 to implement the American Academy of Pediatrics' (AAP) recommendation that infants be placed in the nonprone sleeping position to reduce the risk of the Sudden Infant Death Syndrome(SIDS)[2]. This paper offers a challenge to the BTSC from two perspectives: (1) the questionable validity of SIDS mortality and risk statistics, and (2) the BTSC as human experimentation rather than as confirmed preventive therapy.

The Questionable Validity of SIDS Mortality and Risk Statistics

The principal argument that initiated the BTSC and that continues to justify its existence is the observed parallel declines in the number of infants placed in the prone sleeping position and the number of reported SIDS deaths[3,4]. We are compelled to challenge both the implied causal relationship between these observations and the SIDS mortality statistics themselves.

SIDS mortality data derive exclusively from epidemiological studies and both the AAP recommendation and the BTSC were launched primarily on the basis of such reports from various countries outside the U.S. However, while it is axiomatic that the validity of any epidemiological study is critically dependent on diagnostic accuracy, there exists today no global consensus on a definition of SIDS. For example, Sawaguchi et al.[5] acknowledge that "a SIDS diagnosis is not uniform throughout Japan and such a diagnosis is not made based on any internationally recognized definition." Official views concerning a SIDS diagnosis in Japan differ among pediatricians, legal scholars of forensic medicine, and pathologists. In the same reference, they note that in Scotland in the 1980s, many cases of sudden unexpected infant death (SUD) were reported as

"SIDS", whereas in the 1990s there was a trend reversal and the majority of similar cases were classified as "unknown".

In 1999, 5 years after the start of the BTSC, Cote et al.[6], in a study of 623 cases of SUD in infancy, found that the percentage of non-SIDS diagnoses was much higher for autopsies performed in a center with expertise in pediatric pathology than in a general hospital or medico-legal institute. Non-SIDS diagnoses were also much higher at age ranges atypical (12–18 months) as compared with typical (1–6 months) for SIDS.

It is reasonable, in light of the above, to question the validity of SIDS prevalence rates that emerge from diverse clinics in diverse countries with varying degrees of expertise in pediatric pathology and with inconsistent diagnostic criteria. One might ask to what extent can the decreasing SIDS rate of the past decade be attributable to increased awareness and improved methodologies and procedures for distinguishing SIDS and non-SIDS deaths and changing diagnostic criteria[7,8]? To what extent does the propensity to assign a diagnosis of SIDS to infants who die during the known vulnerable period between 1 and 6 months, or who are found in the prone position, weaken epidemiological analysis?

Paris et al.[9] attempted to address the concern that decrease in SIDS may be a reflection of changes in diagnostic criteria. They reported that alternative diagnostic criteria did not increase over the period studied (1985–1995, excluding 1991). However, they reviewed only deaths attributed to aspiration, suffocation, or positional asphyxia and make no mention of the number of diagnoses, if any, that were documented by death scene investigations. Changes in alternative diagnoses such as infection, cardiovascular abnormalities, or metabolic disease, which may not show serious symptoms prior to death[6], were not considered. In support of the notion that alternative diagnoses may have increased is the observation that while the reported cases of SIDS decreased from 1999–2001, the overall postneonatal mortality remained stable[10].

There is another important variable that must be taken into account when attempting to establish the validity of SIDS mortality statistics. In 1991, an expert panel convened by the U.S. National Institute of Child Health and Human Development (NICHD)[11] expanded the criteria for establishing a SIDS diagnosis to include a thorough coroner's investigation of the death scene and a review of the infant's clinical history in addition to the performance of a complete autopsy. This was a critical change, because cases of suffocation due to unsafe sleeping environments or to infanticide could not be distinguished from SIDS by autopsy alone. Prior to the NICHD recommendation in 1991, the annual rate of SIDS in the U.S. was stable at 1.3–1.4 per 1,000 live births.

Fig. 1 shows that the number of reported SIDS deaths was already in decline prior to the issuance, in June 1992, of the AAP recommendation to place infants in the supine sleeping position. By the time the BTSC was begun in 1994, the prevalence rate that year had already dropped to 1.03 SIDS deaths per 1,000 live births from the 1991 rate of 1.3 SIDS deaths per 1,000 live births. It is not currently known to what extent the decline in reported deaths is due to the adoption in 1991 of the new, more stringent, NICHD diagnostic criteria for SIDS. Nor is it known to what extent a decade of educating parents about modifiable risk factors such as smoking, co-sleeping, and unsafe sleeping environments has contributed to the actual decline in SIDS deaths[12]. It cannot be

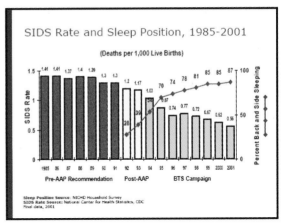

FIGURE 1. The reported rate for SIDS was already in decline prior to the issuance, in June 1992, of the AAP recommendation to place infants in the supine sleeping position and dropped 26% between 1989 and the start of the BTSC in 1994.

known, therefore, to what extent altered sleep position is responsible for the reported decline in SIDS deaths.

In the U.S., evidence of an association between infant sleeping position and SIDS risk remains limited[13,14,15,16,17]. Only one study has been conducted completely after the BTSC was initiated[18]. However, this population-based, case-control study was limited by a low participation rate of 50% among eligible cases and 41% among eligible controls and a small sample size of 185 SIDS cases. Epidemiological analysis is also weakened by its reliance on retrospective questionnaires, which are subject to recall bias, and on interviews that often illicit responses intended only to please the interrogator. Furthermore, it is not possible to determine the relative importance or the combined effects of the many risk factors, in addition to sleeping position, that are thought to contribute to SIDS[19,20].

Clearly, the epidemiology of SIDS is confounded by cases where death may be due to other causes. Until the cause or causes of SIDS are found or a specific diagnostic test is developed, it cannot be known with certainty which infants succumb to "true" SIDS. Haas et al.[20] caution that the many overlapping epidemiological features of SIDS and non-SIDS infants illustrates the fallacy of assigning biological import only because of statistically significant differences. If a study sample is large enough, a small effect may be statistically significant even if the association is spurious because of a confounding variable[21]. Even risk factors with very large effects may not be important to individual cases if the disease is rare[21]. SIDS is a rare disease.

The BTSC as Human Experimentation Rather than Confirmed Preventive Therapy

Neither the cause of SIDS nor a causal mechanism linking SIDS to the prone position have been documented despite more than a decade of intensive research. Multiple and unsubstantiated etiological theories abound. More than 49 causal mechanisms for SIDS have been recorded[22] and more than 38 epidemiological and biological risk factors proposed[19]. Various authors have disputed the major hypotheses (and their variants) that presume that a SIDS event results from abnormal cardiopulmonary regulation[23], arousal deficit[24,25], and asphyxia in general[26]. Until the etiology for SIDS has been validated and a causal relationship to the prone position has been established, scientific rigor requires that the BTSC be viewed as a large-scale human experiment rather than as a documented preventive therapy program.

It can be argued, of course, that a preventive program such as smoking cessation can be effective even though a causal mechanism has not yet been identified between smoking and lung cancer. However, the alternative to smok-

ing, that is, not smoking, is not associated with harmful side effects. Such may not be the case with infant supine sleeping. Accordingly, it is appropriate to define and quantify clearly the relative risks and benefits of the BTSC and sleeping position intervention.

Risks vs. Benefits of Infant Sleeping Position

In 2003, Hunt et al.[27] reported various health outcomes associated with infant sleep position and found that no identified symptoms such as cough, stuffy nose, spitting, vomiting, diarrhea, fever, or respiratory problems were significantly increased among nonprone sleepers. However, their data were retrieved from a 1995–1998 cohort study and were not examined for the risks of positional facial and head deformities (posterior *plagiocephaly*) and early developmental delay.

Plagiocephaly

SIDS is a rare disease that claims the lives of approximately 0.5–3.0 infants per 1,000 births yearly in the developed countries of the world. By contrast, the incidence of positional facial and head deformities due to the supine position has increased dramatically since the BTSC and now affects 1 in every 60 live births[28]. Plagiocephaly sometimes requires physical therapy or head orthosis (helmet) and, if misdiagnosed as *craniosynostosis*, can result in unnecessary surgery. Plagiocephaly should not be dismissed lightly as merely "cosmetic".

Delayed Early Development

There are indications of a rapidly growing population of infants who show developmental abnormalities as a result of prolonged exposure to the supine position[29,30]. These infants do not have the opportunity to lift their heads when waking up or to explore the immediate environment around them. Poor development of antigravity extensor muscles leads to overall motor delays and difficulty acquiring key milestones such as rolling over, unsupported sitting, and crawling[29]. Although it is claimed that these developmental abnormalities are transient and tend to normalize in about 18 months[31], the evidence to support this viewpoint is scant and no long-term randomized clinical studies have been conducted.

Sleeping Behavior

In the health outcomes study referred to above[27], it was also reported that sleep problems were not more frequent in infants sleeping supine compared to those sleeping prone. However, these observations conflict with an earlier report by this group that used the same 1995–1998 database[32]. In the earlier study, prone sleeping increased from 18% at 1 month to 29% at 3 months. The major reason given for changing the infants sleeping from supine at 1 month to prone at 3 months was that the infant "slept better or seemed to prefer that position". One possible explanation for the discrepancy is that the later study[27] excluded infants whose sleeping position may have changed after the first month due to sleeping problems or other adverse consequences of supine sleeping.

It is likely that prone is the normal sleeping position for infants[33] and offers the deepest, most restful sleep[34,35,36,37]. Because infants spend more time in sleep than children or adults, it is logical to assume that sleep is even more important for their rapidly developing nervous systems and for preserving the integrity of their sleep cycles[38].

What is the Presumed Benefit of the Supine Sleeping Position?

Reference to Fig. 1 shows that the incidence of SIDS in the U.S. declined from 1.03 deaths per 1,000 live births in 1994, at the start of the BTSC, to 0.56 deaths per 1,000 live births in the year 2001. Proponents of the BTSC attribute these declining mortality statistics to altered sleeping position, and choose to characterize this effect as a dramatic 47% drop in the incidence of SIDS. However, these same data can also be presented as evidence that one infant death in 2,127 live births was prevented since the start of the BTSC if, in fact, placing infants in the supine rather than the prone position to sleep was the sole contributing factor.

These comments are not meant to diminish the importance or desirability of preventing even one SIDS event. Rather, they are intended to show the very low probability of a SIDS event occurring and the lower probability of it being prevented by placing an infant in the supine sleeping position.

However, the risks associated with the supine sleeping position, i.e., positional head deformities, delayed motor development, and disturbed sleep patterns, are substantive and relatively common. Finally, supine sleeping is not a guarantee against SIDS since some infants succumb in the supine position as well.

CONCLUSION

In our enthusiasm to eradicate SIDS in the 0.2% of infants who are potential victims, we have tended to overlook other relative risks and benefits of the supine vs. the prone position in the 99.8% of infants who will not succumb to SIDS. An intuitive first reaction might be that the prevention of a SIDS event justifies virtually any intervention risk, since the unexpected death of an apparently healthy infant is one of the most devastating human tragedies in medicine. Indeed, if some 2,000 infant deaths are being prevented yearly by the BTSC, the campaign has made a substantial contribution to human welfare. However, this paper proposes that there are sound reasons for questioning these data and a sound basis for concern about the incompletely identified short- and long-term risks to child development of infant sleeping position intervention.

The hazards to public health that can result from failure to quantify a risk-benefit ratio accurately can be seen in the current controversy regarding hormonal replacement therapy in women[39]. The preponderance of epidemiological studies that strongly supported the protective effects of postmenopausal estrogen replacement against coronary heart disease[40], and the growing need for an effective means to treat and prevent heart disease in women, led to a nearly unshakable belief in the benefits of hormone therapy. As a consequence, many thousands of menopausal women may have received ineffectual treatment or possibly been exposed to an increased risk of heart disease.

Herrington[39] has proposed that while observational (epidemiological) studies may have important value for generating hypotheses, they should not be used to justify medical interventions for widespread use. Although the BTSC purports to recommend, rather than dictate, a preferred infant sleeping position, it has, in fact, set a standard of care that many pediatricians are reluctant to disregard[41]. Similarly, many parents are conflicted by their instinctive rejection of the supine infant sleeping position and their fear of charges of negligence in the event a SIDS death should occur.

The evidence in support of the premise of this paper, while compelling, is admittedly indirect and inconclusive. It is not the intention of the authors to discredit the BTSC. Rather, it is a plea to the pediatric research community to validate the nonprone infant sleeping position scientifically before it becomes inexorably imbedded in medical practice.

Until causal mechanisms are documented and risk/benefit ratios are identified, it may be more appropriate to regard the BTSC as investigational rather than as confirmed preventive therapy. In that context, the decision to place a child in the supine or prone position to sleep should be a personal and ethical choice that rests with the properly informed parent and not with the health care provider.

ACKNOWLEDGMENTS

The authors are indebted to Drs. Coralee Thompson, Leland Green, Philip Bond and David Bergner for their critical reviews of the manuscript and insightful comments.

REFERENCES

1. Bailer, J. (2003) Hormone-replacement therapy and cardiovascular disease. *N. Engl. J. Med.* **349(6)**, 521–522.

2. American Academy of Pediatrics (1992) Task force on infant positioning and SIDS. *Pediatrics* **89**, 1120–1126.

3. Willinger, M., Hoffman, H., and Harford, R.B. (1994) Infant sleep position and risk for sudden infant death syndrome: report of meeting held January 13 and 14, 1994, National Institutes of Health, Bethesda, MD. *Pediatrics* **93**, 814–819.

4. Dwyer, T., Couper, D., and Walter, S.D. (2001) Sources of heterogeneity in the meta-analysis of observational studies. The example of SIDS and sleeping position. *J. Clin. Epidemiol.* **54**, 440–447.

5. Sawaguchi, T., Sawaguchi, A., and Matoba, R. (2002) Comparative evaluation of diagnostic guidelines for

sudden infant death syndrome (SIDS) in Japan. *Forensic Sci. Int.* **130S**, S65–70.

6. Cote, A., Russo, P., and Michaud, J. (1999) Sudden unexpected deaths in infancy: what are the causes? *J. Pediatr.* **135**, 437–443.

7. Iyasu, S., Hanzlick, R., Rowley, D., and Willinger, M. (1994) Proceedings of "Workshop on Guidelines for Scene Investigation of Sudden Unexplained Infant Deaths", July 12–13, 1993. *J. Forensic Sci.* **39**,1126–1136.

8. Peterson, D.R., van Belle, G., and Chinn, N.M. (1979) Epidemiologic comparisons of the sudden infant death syndrome with other major components of infant mortality. *Am. J. Epidemiol.* **110**, 699–707.

9. Paris, C.A., Remler, R., and Daling, J.R. (2001) Risk factors for sudden infant death syndrome: changes associated with sleep position recommendations. *J. Pediatr.* **139**, 771–777.

10. CDC Wonder. Compressed Mortality File: Underlying Cause of Death: Mortality for 1979–1998 with ICD 9 codes and Mortality for 1999–2001 with ICD 10 codes. (Accessed 2004, at http://wonder.Cdc.gov/mortSQL.html.)

11. Willinger, M., James, L.S., and Catz, C. (1991) Defining the sudden infant death syndrome (SIDS): deliberations of an expert panel convened by the National Institutes of Health and Human Development. *Pediatr. Pathol.* **11**, 677–684.

12. Pollack, H.A. and Frohna, J.G. (2001) A competing risk model of sudden infant death syndrome incidence in two US birth cohorts. *J. Pediatr.* **138**, 661–667.

13. Hoffman, H.J., Damus, K., Hillman, L., and Krongrad, E. (1998) Risk factors for SIDS: results of the National Institute of Child Health and Human Development SIDS Cooperative Epidemiological Study. *Ann. N. Y. Acad. Sci.* **533**, 13–30.

14. Taylor, J.A., Krieger, J.W., Reay, D.T., Davis, R.L., Harruff, R., and Cheney, L.K. (1996) Prone sleep position and the sudden infant death syndrome in King County, Washington: a case-control study. *J. Pediatr.* **128**, 626–630.

15. Klonoff-Cohen, H.S. and Edelstein, S.L. (1995) Case-control study of routine and death scene sleep position and sudden infant death in Southern California. *JAMA* **273**, 790–794.

16. Hauk, F.R. and Hunt, C.E. (2000). Sudden infant death syndrome in 2000. *Curr. Probl. Pediatr.* **30**, 237–261.

17. Sullivan, F.M. and Barlow, S.M. (2001) Review of risk factors for sudden infant death syndrome. *Paediatr. Perinat. Epidemiol.* **15**, 144–200.

18. Li, D.K., Petitti, D.B., Willinger, M., McMahon, R., Odouli, R., Vu, H., and Hoffman, H.J. (2003) Infant sleeping position and the risk of sudden infant death syndrome in California, 1997–2000. *Am. J. Epidemiol.* **157**, 446–455.

19. Hunt, C.E. (2000) Sudden infant death syndrome. In *Nelson Textbook of Pediatrics.* 16th ed. Behrman, R.E., Kliegman, R.M., and Jenson, H.B., Eds. W.B. Saunders, Philadelphia. pp. 2139–2145.

20. Haas, J.E., Taylor, J.A., Bergman, A.B., van Belle, G., Felgenhauer, J.L., Siebert, J.R., and Benjamin, D.R. (1993) Relationship between epidemiologic risk factors and clinicopathologic findings in the Sudden Infant Death Syndrome. *Pediatrics* **91(1)**, 106–112.

21. Angell, M. (1990) The interpretation of epidemiological studies. *N. Engl. J. Med.* **323**, 823–825.

22. Byard, R.W. (1994) Sudden infant death syndrome. In *Sudden Death in Infancy, Childhood, and Adolescence.* Byard, R.W. and Cohle, S.D., Eds. Cambridge University Press. pp. 417–497.

23. Jobe, A.H. (2001) What do home monitors contribute to the SIDS problem? *JAMA* **285(17)**, 2244–2245.

24. Patel, A., Paluszynska, D., and Thach, B.T. (2001) Desaturations associated with motor arousals in rebreathing infants. *Pediatr. Res.* **49**, 460A.

25. Galland, B., Bolton, D., Taylor, B., Sayers, R., and Williams, S. (2000)) Ventilatory sensitivity to mild asphyxia: prone versus supine sleep position. *Arch. Dis. Child.* **83**, 423–428.

26. Goldwater, P.N. (2001) SIDS: more facts and controversies. *Med. J. Aust.* **174(6)**, 302–304.

27. Hunt, C.E., Lesko, S.M., Vezina, R.M., McCoy, R., Corwin, M.J., Mandell, F., Willinger, M., Hoffman, H.J., and Mitchell, A.A. (2003) Infant sleep position and associated health outcomes. *Arch. Pediatr. Adolesc. Med.* **157**, 469–474.

28. Biggs, W.S. (2000) Diagnosis and management of positional head deformity. *Am. Fam. Physician* **67(9)**, 1953–1956.

29. Majnemer, A. and Barr, R.G. (2005) The influence of supine sleep positioning on early motor milestone acquisition. *Dev. Med. Child Neurol.,* in press.

30. Schindler, A.M. and Hausman, C. (2001) Do we need to reassess normal gross motor milestones? *Arch. Pediatr. Adolesc. Med.* **155**, 96.

31. Task Force on Infant Positioning and SIDS, 1998–1999 (2000) Changing concepts of sudden infant death syndrome: implications for infant sleeping environment and sleep position. *Pediatrics* **105(3)**, 650–656.

32. Lesko, S.M., Corwin, M.J., Vezina, R.M., Hunt, C.E., Mandell, F., McClain, M., Heeren, T., and Mitchell, A.A. (1988) Changes in sleep position during infancy. *JAMA* **280**, 336–340.

33. Togari, H., Kato, I., Saito, N., and Yamaguchi, N. (2000) The healthy human infant tends to sleep in the prone rather than the supine position. *Early Hum. Dev.* **59(3)**, 151–158.

34. Kahn, A., Grosswasser, J., Sottiaux, M., Rebuffat, E., Franco, E., and Dramaix, M. (1993) Prone or supine position and sleep characteristics in infants. *Pediatrics* **6**, 1112–1115.

35. Ottolini, M.C., Davis, B.E., Patel, K., Sachs, H.C., Gershon, N.B., and Moon, R.Y. (1999) Prone infant sleeping despite the "Back to Sleep" campaign. *Arch. Pediatr. Adolesc. Med.* **153**, 512–517.

36. Skadberg, B.T. and Markestad, T. (1997) Behavior and physiological responses during prone and supine sleep in early infancy. *Arch. Dis. Child.* **76**, 320–324.

37. Douthitt, T.C. and Brackbill, Y. (1972) Differences in sleep, waking and motor activity as a function of prone or supine resting position in the human neonate. *Psychophysiology* **9**, 99–100.

38. Thach, B.T. (2001) Sleep, sleep position, and the sudden infant death syndrome: To sleep or not to sleep? That is the question. *J. Pediatr.* **138(6)**, 793–795.

39. Herrington, D.M. (2003) From presumed benefit to potential harm - hormone therapy and heart disease. *N. Engl. J. Med.* **349(6)**, 519–521.

40. Stampfer, M.J. and Colditz, G.A. (1991) Estrogen replacement therapy and coronary heart disease: a quantitative assessment of the epidemiologic evidence. *Prev. Med.* **20**, 47–63.

41. Carolan, P.C., Moore, J.R., and Luxenberg, M.G. (1995) Infant sleep position and the sudden infant death syndrome, *Clin. Pediatr.* **34(8)**, 402–409.

Biosketches

Ralph Pelligra, M.D. is currently chief medical officer and Chair of the Institutional Review Board at NASA Ames Research Center. He has been instrumental in applying aerospace technology to a wide range of medical conditions, including clinical shock states and respiratory problems in brain injured children. He has published scientific and medical articles on diverse topics in *The J. of Aerospace Medicine, JAMA, the Journal of Applied Physiology, Neuropediatrics, Emergency Medicine,* and others. In 1996, Dr. Pelligra was inducted into the Space Technology Hall of Fame, sponsored by NASA and the U.S. Space Foundation. E-mail: ralph.pelligra-1@nasa.gov

Glenn Doman, DSc, is the founder of The Institutes for the Achievement of Human Potential. He and The Institutes are famous for their pioneering work with brain-injured children and for their work in early development for well children. In addition to dealing intimately with more than 20,000 families over the last 50 years, he has strongly influenced millions of families through the book *What to Do About Your Brain-Injured Child* and the creation of the groundbreaking Gentle Revolution Series of books and materials that teach parents how to teach their babies at home. Glenn Doman has lived with, studied, or worked with children in more than 100 nations, ranging from the most civilized to the most primitive. E-mail: vicedirector@iahp.org

Gerry Leisman, MD, PhD, is the Dr. Ted Carrick Professor of Human Factors at the Institute for Clinical Ergonomics, Rehabilitation, and Applied Neuroscience in the School of Engineering Technologies at the State University of New York, College at Farmingdale and Affiliate Professor at the University of Haifa in Israel. He was elected Fellow of the American Psychological Society in 1990 and Life Fellow of the American College of Forensic Examination-International in 1994. He is the author of numerous studies, textbooks, and patents in rehabilitation sciences, mathematical modeling of the nervous system, human memory, development of motor and cognitive function, and in cognitive neuroscience. E-mail: leismag@farmingdale.edu

Appendix C

Equipment You Can Build and Make for Your Baby

THE CRAWLING TRACK

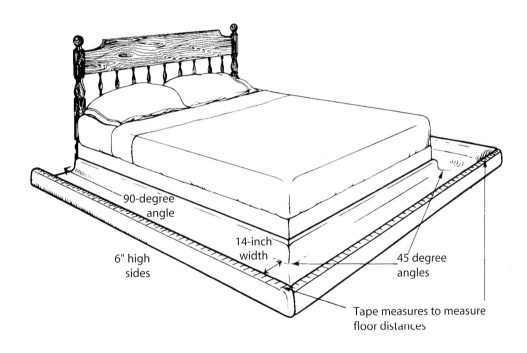

90-degree angle

14-inch width

6" high sides

45 degree angles

Tape measures to measure floor distances

Track is constructed from ³⁄₄" plywood covered with 1" thick foam rubber, and then covered with smooth, ungrained naugahyde. Three-section track is entirely detachable.

How to Build a Crawling Track

Each of the three sections shown is completely detachable.

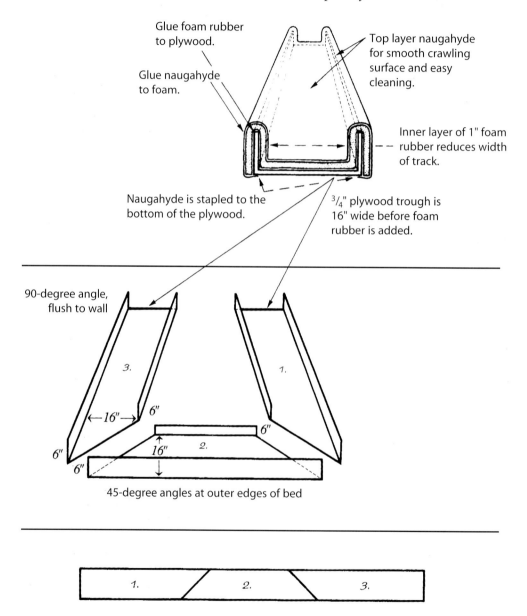

Glue foam rubber to plywood.

Glue naugahyde to foam.

Top layer naugahyde for smooth crawling surface and easy cleaning.

Inner layer of 1" foam rubber reduces width of track.

Naugahyde is stapled to the bottom of the plywood.

$^3/_4$" plywood trough is 16" wide before foam rubber is added.

90-degree angle, flush to wall

3.

1.

←16"→

6"

6"

6"

16"   2.

6"

6"

45-degree angles at outer edges of bed

1.   2.   3.

The bottom drawing shows all three pieces placed end to end to make one long crawling track for distance; this gives the total bird's eye view of the tracks put together.

How to Make a Neck Collar for Your Baby

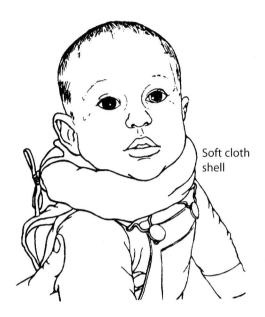

Soft cloth shell

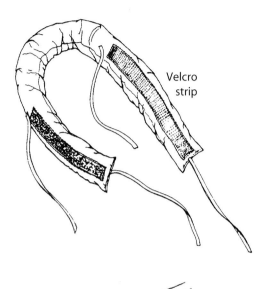

Velcro strip

In all the activities we recommend you do with your baby, your baby's safety is our prime concern. It's important to be particularly careful of babies' necks, so neck collars are definitely in order, especially for every single one of the passive balance activities at Stage III.

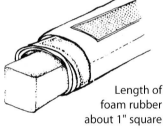

Length of foam rubber about 1" square

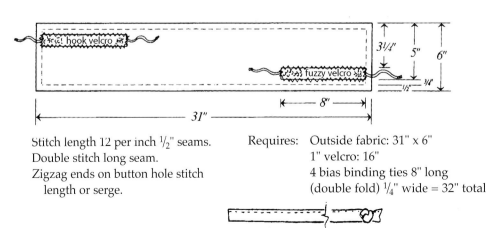

Stitch length 12 per inch ½" seams.
Double stitch long seam.
Zigzag ends on button hole stitch
   length or serge.

Requires: Outside fabric: 31" x 6"
1" velcro: 16"
4 bias binding ties 8" long
(double fold) ¼" wide = 32" total

Tie: 8" total before knotting.

The Dowel Traversing a Doorway

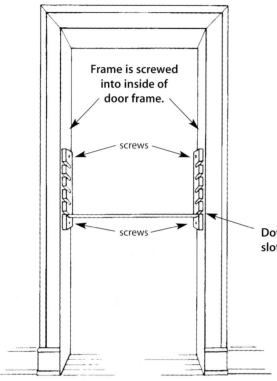

Frame is screwed into inside of door frame.

← screws →

← screws →

Dowel is seated in slots or notches.

The height of the first notch is determined by measuring from the child's toes to the tips of his fingers (with arms held straight above his head) and adding 2 inches. From this notch upward, the notches are slanted downward and are $\frac{1}{8}$" larger than the diameter of the dowel.

The bar across the doorway should serve you well. You will use it until your child becomes an independent brachiator. Even after he brachiates, he will enjoy playing on it.

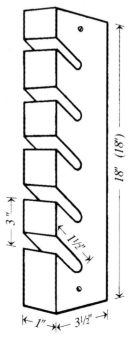

Building a Brachiation Ladder

The brachiation ladder is constructed by first making its major parts, then assembling the whole for a sturdy ladder that can be used by either babies or adults.

Oak is recommended for the rungs, because of its strength. For the rest of the brachiation ladder, fir is recommended, because of the absence of knots.

The first parts to build are the two vertical post assemblies.

The third part is the ladder itself.

The final step is to assemble the parts.

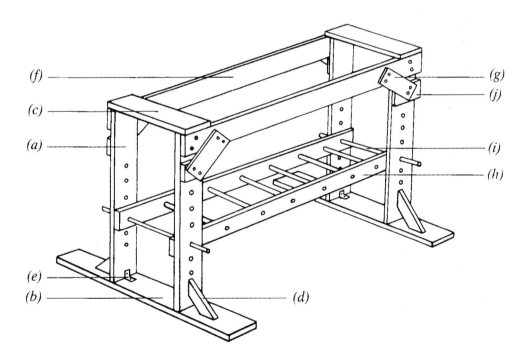

Brachiation Ladder: Vertical Post Assemblies (two required)

Materials: Four 2" x 6" x 7½' sides (a)
Two 2" x 6" x 5' bottom plate (b)
Two 2" x 6" x 21" top plate (c)
Four 2" x 4" x 29" braces (d)
Eight ¼" x 3" lag bolts
Eight 1" wide 4" leg, angle irons with clearance holes (e)
Thirty-two No. 12 ½" screws for angle irons

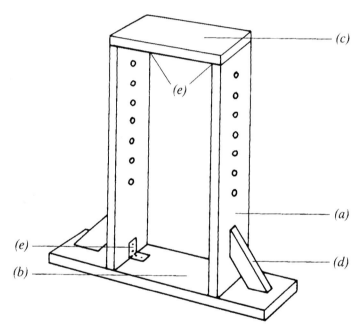

Assembly Instructions

1. Drill ¾" clearance holes in sides (a), starting 28 inches from floor, and spaced every 2 inches up sides (29 holes).

2. Nail sides (a) to bottom plate (b), maintaining 18 inches between sides (inside dimension).

3. Nail top plate (c) to sides.

4. Set braces (d) in place (after cutting to proper angle) and nail to both side pieces and bottom plate.

5. Drill ¼" clearance holes through side pieces and bottom plate for screwing lag bolts through sides and bottom plate into braces. Countersink holes to make bolt heads flush with surfaces.

6. Insert lag bolts. Mount angle irons as shown, with two screws per leg.

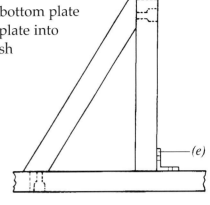

(e)

Brachiation Ladder: Horizontal Top Rail Assembly (two required)

Materials: Two 2" x 6" x 10' rails (f)
Four 2" x 6" x 22" braces (g)
Eight ¼" x 4" round-head bolts
Eight 4" nuts
Eight washers

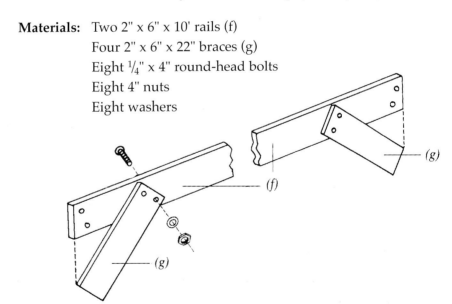

To Assemble

1. Drill ¼" clearance holes at each end of the rail for bolts, as shown in the diagram.

2. Hole locations should be clear of angle irons mounted from top plate (c) to sides (a).

3. Loosely mount braces to rail with bolts and nuts with washers. Head of bolts should be towards inside of ladder; washers and nuts on outside. Tightening will take place at final assembly stage.

Brachiation Ladder: Ladder Assembly (one required)

Materials: Two 2" x 4" x 10' sides (h)
Nineteen 1" diameter hardwood rungs*, 18" long (i)
Thirty-eight finishing nails

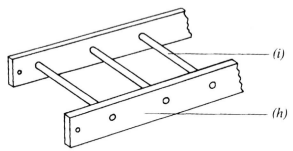

(i)

(h)

To Assemble

1. Drill ³⁄₄" clearance holes, 3 inches from both ends of each side.

2. Drill 1" clearance holes, same diameter as rungs, 6 inches from ends and then every 3 to 12 inches thereafter, according to child's size.

3. Put rungs in holes and secure with finishing nails and wood glue, if desired.

Brachiation Ladder: Final Assembly

Materials: Two vertical post assemblies
Two horizontal top rail assemblies
One ladder assembly
Eight ¹⁄₄" round-head bolts, 4" long
Eight ¹⁄₄" round-head bolts, 6" long
Sixteen ¹⁄₄" nuts
Sixteen washers
Two 2" x 6" x 6" spacers (j)
Two ³⁄₄" diameter dowels, 30" long (k)

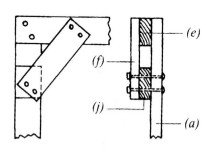

(e)

(f)

(j)

(a)

NOTE: Diameter of rungs and spacing between them depend on child's size. Suggest:

6–18 months	18–36 months	36 months and older
¹⁄₂" rungs, 4" spacing	³⁄₄" rungs, 6" spacing	1" rungs, 12" spacing

Brachiation Ladder: Construction

1. Place vertical post assemblies 10 feet apart.

2. Place horizontal rails at top and mark hole locations for drilling corresponding holes in vertical sides.

3. Drill $\frac{1}{4}$" clearance holes in side.

4. Mount rails to vertical post assemblies with 4" bolts, nuts, and washers.

5. Clamp 2" x 6" x 6" spacers in position.

6. Drill $\frac{1}{4}$" clearance holes through vertical sides, rail brace, and spacer.

7. Bolt rail braces to sides with 6" bolts, nuts, and washers, with head of bolt towards inside of ladder.

8. Tighten all hardware securely.

9. In mounting of rails and braces to vertical sides, if any holes in the vertical sides are covered, drill through so the dowel can be put in place.

10. Place ladder at desired height and hold in place with dowels at both ends.

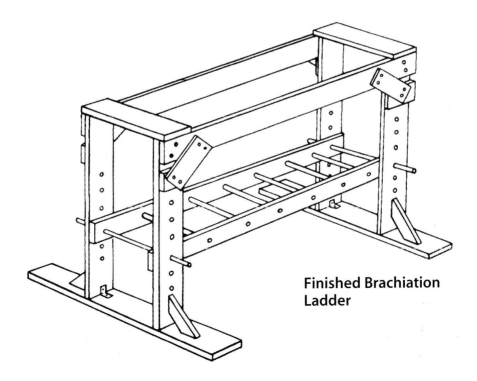

Finished Brachiation Ladder

DIMENSIONS AND ADJUSTMENTS FOR CHILDREN OF DIFFERENT AGES

	6–18 Months	18–36 Months	36 Months and up
Dowel size	$1/2$ inch	$3/4$ inch	1 inch
Ladder width	18 inches	18 inches	18 inches
Ladder length	10 feet	10–15 feet	15–18 feet
Space between rungs (center to center)	4 inches	6 inches	12 inches
Ladder height	Walking height of baby *or* mother's height	Mother's height	Add an extra 4 inches to the measurement of the brachiating child (from hands to toes)

Index